"There are few books on teaching academic skills and even fewer on the field of Learning Development, but this is the only one with practical guidance deeply embedded in the unique context of this new profession. Just what new LDers have long needed".

Dr Helen Webster, *University of Oxford, UK*

Doing Learning Development in Higher Education

Doing Learning Development in Higher Education is an essential introductory companion for those new to working in this emerging and exciting field. Filled with actionable tips, real-world advice, and illuminating anecdotes, this book will help readers navigate the challenges and opportunities of helping students unlock their full academic potential, whilst highlighting the important role that Learning Developers have.

Covering the fundamental aspects of Learning Development practice, it explores everything from conducting effective workshops, collaborating with colleagues and students, leading tutorials, creating impactful learning resources, and much more. Readers will gain valuable insights into building productive relationships with students and colleagues, understanding the wider institutional context, and charting their own professional development journey. Each chapter blends theoretical foundations with practical applications, providing the tools to make an immediate impact.

This practical guide will be helpful for new and early career Learning Developers working with undergraduate and postgraduate students across higher education institutions. It is equally valuable for early career academics and university staff in student-facing roles who wish to enhance their practice.

Joy Igiebor is Learning Development Tutor for Birkbeck Law School and the School of Creative Arts, Culture and Communication at Birkbeck, University of London, UK. She is Advance HE Fellow, Fellow of the Association for Learning Development in Higher Education, and a qualified teacher.

Doing Learning Development in Higher Education

A Practical Guide for New and Early Career Learning Developers

Joy Igiebor

Routledge
Taylor & Francis Group
LONDON AND NEW YORK

Cover image: Ratana21 via Getty Images

First published 2026
by Routledge
4 Park Square, Milton Park, Abingdon, Oxon OX14 4RN

and by Routledge
605 Third Avenue, New York, NY 10158

Routledge is an imprint of the Taylor & Francis Group, an informa business

© 2026 Joy Igiebor

The right of Joy Igiebor to be identified as author of this work has been asserted in accordance with sections 77 and 78 of the Copyright, Designs and Patents Act 1988.

All rights reserved. No part of this book may be reprinted or reproduced or utilised in any form or by any electronic, mechanical, or other means, now known or hereafter invented, including photocopying and recording, or in any information storage or retrieval system, without permission in writing from the publishers.

For Product Safety Concerns and Information please contact our EU representative GPSR@taylorandfrancis.com. Taylor & Francis Verlag GmbH, Kaufingerstraße 24, 80331 München, Germany.

Trademark notice: Product or corporate names may be trademarks or registered trademarks, and are used only for identification and explanation without intent to infringe.

British Library Cataloguing-in-Publication Data
A catalogue record for this book is available from the British Library

ISBN: 978-1-032-99459-8 (hbk)
ISBN: 978-1-032-99172-6 (pbk)
ISBN: 978-1-003-60426-6 (ebk)

DOI: 10.4324/9781003604266

Typeset in Galliard
by Apex CoVantage, LLC

For my parents.

Contents

Foreword — *x*
Preface — *xiii*
Acknowledgements — *xv*
List of acronyms and abbreviations — *xvii*
List of illustrations — *xx*

1 Introduction — 1

2 What does it mean to 'do' Learning Development? — 12

3 New to Learning Development in Higher Education — 28

4 Teaching tutorials — 44

5 Teaching and delivering workshops — 73

6 Embedding Learning Development — 104

7 Developing teaching and learning materials — 124

8 Working with students and colleagues — 150

9 Professional development — 175

10 Final thoughts and further inspiration — 197

Appendices — *205*
Index — *219*

Foreword

Sandra Sinfield

In early 2023, we published a #Take5 blog (the CPD blog of ALDinHE, the Association of Learning Development in Higher Education) from someone new to Learning Development (LD) who had much to say about both being new – and about the rather strange and nebulous LD profession itself. Her name was Joy Igiebor, and her first blog for us was #Take5 #84 What the Learning Developer needs to know (viz. https://lmutake5.wordpress.com/2023/04/20/take5–84-what-the-learning-developer-needs-to-know/). Joy captured our attention immediately with her fresh voice and her insight:

> I guess in those initial years I was really searching for 'a step-by-step manual' on how to do the job. I had so many questions at a time when I was just trying to find my feet e.g., How do I run effective tutorials? What is a workshop and what should students be doing in a workshop? What if a student asks me a question that I don't know the answer to? What *exactly is* a learning development tutor? Imposter syndrome was real and, darn-it, I just couldn't find that step-by-step manual.

Joy's blog started to answer those questions – and it became one of the most talked about #Take5s ever. In 2024, we got back to Joy to see what she had to say now – and so came #Take5 #106 (viz. https://aldinhe.ac.uk/the-importance-for-learning-developers-to-understand-and-engage-with-identity-to-develop-their-professional-footing/). Joy continued her story, building on the early exploration of the needs of the 'newbie' LD to unpack the complexity of the role and the relationships we have to build – with ourselves, with the field, with our students, and with our wider community – to more fully inhabit that troublesome LD space.

And now I have the joyful honour of writing the Foreword to this wonderful book, for Joy has written herself the very one that she was searching for all those years ago – elegantly, accessibly, and beautifully.

The book unpacked

Chapter 1, 'Introduction', sets the scene for the book as a whole helping the new LDers orientate themselves to the book itself – and the journey they are about to undertake together, companions exploring the field and the relationships that have to be navigated. Each chapter speaks directly to the reader, setting the scene, offering thoughtful provocations and activities – and space for the reader as a reflective practitioner to make the learning conscious – and their own. As Joy says – there is not a one-size-fits-all manual – but there are successful approaches and a range of good liberatory practices that the reader can explore and then adapt to their own contexts, wants, and needs.

Chapter 2, 'What does it mean to do Learning Development?' explores the multiplicity of routes in LD – and the values and successful practices that underpin the role.

Chapter 3, 'New to Learning Development in Higher Education', helpfully unpacks HE itself – exploring regulatory bodies and the topical issues impacting the HE sector – and thus impacting how LD is positioned, framed, and enabled to 'be'.

Chapter 4, 'Teaching tutorials', deconstructs the infamous 'one-to-one' tutorial from what they are, how long they should last and how to prepare for them – to tackling challenging ones.

Chapter 5, 'Teaching and delivering workshops', unpacks the workshop, face to face and online – from preparation and planning to all the sorts of multimodal resources you might harness for better impact and effect.

Chapter 6, 'Embedding Learning Development', explores embedding and integrating LD within the curriculum – and how to get buy-in for this powerful practice from staff and students alike.

Chapter 7, 'Developing teaching and learning materials', beautifully explores making your own teaching and learning materials – including when to draw on generative artificial intelligence for support and creating your own toolbox for the essentials: From essay and assignment writing skills to referencing, citing, and avoiding plagiarism.

Chapter 8, 'Working with students and colleagues', unpacks that more relational side of the job: Working with students and staff – especially initially when feeling so much the imposter!

In *Chapter 9*, 'Professional development', and *Chapter 10*, 'Final thoughts and further inspiration', Joy situates our ongoing CPD as central to our professional identities and overarching professionalism. Great advice on the power of keeping a journal or diary, and of networking – including through participating in webinars and talks, observations and co-teaching, and writing.

Finally

This is essential reading not just for those new to Learning Development but for everybody who is a Learning Developer – and all those who want to develop their students' learning.

- Table 3.1 UK degrees by level and the powers to award them (QAA, 2018). Reproduced with permission *from The Right to Award UK Degrees*. Quality Assurance Agency for Higher Education, 2.
- Syska, A. and Buckley, C. (eds) (2024) *How to Be a Learning Developer in Higher Education: Critical Perspectives, Community and Practice*. Abingdon: Routledge, 248. Quote used by permission of Routledge, Taylor and Francis Group.
- Webster, H. M. (2024) 'The five Ps of LD in practice: Student partnership approaches in one-to-one, workshops and online work', *Journal of Learning Development in Higher Education*, 32. https://doi.org/10.47408/jldhe.vi32.1457. This material was originally published in the *Journal of Learning Development in Higher Education* by Helen Webster and is licensed under CC-BY 4.0.

This book would not have been possible without the feedback and guidance of my editors at Routledge: Maddie Gray, Sarah Hyde, and Sophie Ganesh. Writing a book whilst working full-time has been a huge learning curve and you made the process a very enjoyable one. Thank you for believing in the idea and for getting it through to a finished product.

A special thank you to Sandra Sinfield, Associate Teaching Professor at London Metropolitan University, Dr Katharine Jewitt, Associate Lecturer at the Open University, and Dr Ian Johnson, Teaching Fellow in Learning Development at the University of Portsmouth, for their insights and written contributions to this book. Thank you also to Ursula Canton, Zara Hooley, Claire Olson, Robert Ping-Nan Chang, Barry Poulter, and Tim Worth for granting permission to include their ALDinHE collective diary entries to illustrate a day in the life of a LDer. To the LD community, thank you for your comments, reviews, and input into this work. It is a privilege to be part of such a dedicated community of professionals.

On a personal note, my thanks to Sophia Krasny, a great writer and friend, for reading over an early draft of the introductory chapter and providing such helpful edits and feedback. To Mr Barry, and his team, without you it would not have been possible to write this book. Thank you for the marvellous job you do. I cannot name you all personally but my thanks to the teachers, mentors, and lecturers from my school days to university who inspired my love of learning: I have come a long way since setting off the school fire alarm. To my parents, Benedict and Roseline, and my siblings, Amadin and Michael, who know what it has taken to get to this point, thank you. Finally, a big thank you to the students I have had the pleasure to meet and teach throughout my career, who strive every day regardless of personal challenge, and who remind me through their determination to never give up.

Acknowledgements

I am grateful to the following organisations for granting permission to use third-party material in this book:

- ALDinHE (2024a) *About ALDinHE*. Available at: https://aldinhe.ac.uk/about-aldinhe/ (Accessed: 9 April 2024). Quote used by permission of the Association for Learning Development in Higher Education.
- Blaisdell, B. (ed) (2013) *Essays on Teaching*. Mineola, New York: Dover Publications, Inc., iii. Quote used by permission of Dover Publications, Inc.
- Buckley, C. and Frith, L. (2024) 'The development of expertise and identity within a community of practice: A networking model', in A. Syska and C. Buckley (eds) *How to be a Learning Developer in Higher Education: Critical Perspectives, Community and Practice*. Abingdon: Routledge, 34–42. Figure and adapted summary used by permission of Routledge, Taylor and Francis Group.
- Hilsdon, J. (2011) 'What is learning development?', in P. Hartley, J. Hilsdon, C. Keenan, S. Sinfield and M. Verity (eds) *Learning Development in Higher Education*. Basingstoke: Palgrave Macmillan (Red Globe Press), 13–27. Quote used by permission of Bloomsbury Publishing Inc.
- Johnson, I. and Bishopp-Martin, S. (2024) 'Conceptual foundations in learning development', in A. Syska and C. Buckley (eds) *How to Be a Learning Developer in Higher Education: Critical Perspectives, Community and Practice*. Abingdon: Routledge, 15–24. Quote used by permission of Routledge, Taylor and Francis Group.
- Mentimeter screenshots used by permission of Mentimeter.com.
- Office for Students (OfS) (2025b) *Registration with the OfS*. Available at: https://www.officeforstudents.org.uk/for-providers/registering-with-the-ofs/registration-with-the-ofs-a-guide/conditions-of-registration/ (Accessed: 20 February 2025). Contains public sector information licensed under the Open Government Licence v3.0. Used under the terms of the Open Government Licence: https://www.officeforstudents.org.uk/copyright/ and https://www.nationalarchives.gov.uk/doc/open-government-licence/version/3/

librarians with a teaching remit, writing tutors, and subject lecturers involved in teaching academic skills or those wanting to transition to LD will also find it a helpful resource. Experienced LDers may also find the book a useful supplementary resource.

Chapters 1–3 are more abstract in nature as they situate the practice of LD within the higher education context: what it is, how it evolved as a profession, and its values. The remaining chapters are pragmatic and include tasks, exemplars, and questions to increase your understanding of how to go about the day-to-day aspects of doing LD. Whilst the book recognises the need for a scholarly approach, it does not focus on theoretical or critical perspectives on LD as this has been done extensively in the recently published, *How to Be a Learning Developer in Higher Education* (Syska and Buckley, 2024) and its predecessor, *Learning Development in Higher Education* (Hartley et al., 2011). Instead, the aim is to provide practical guidance and ideas – from first-hand experience – for doing the job, whilst highlighting how LD values might emanate in your everyday practice in order that you can confidently navigate the role.

The book considers the practicalities of doing LD as an important 'third space' role (Whitchurch, 2008) where the intention is to 'work in partnership with students and staff to make sense and get the most of higher education' (ALDinHE, 2024). Due to its concise nature, it does not cover all facets of LD in depth. Rather, it focuses on the key aspects of the job, including conducting effective tutorials, workshops, and embedded teaching, how to develop teaching and learning materials, and ideas for continuing professional development. Given discussion and debate in the field about the professionalisation and status of LD, it is hoped that this book will serve as a means for you to gain a clearer sense of what LD is, why it matters, and how you might do it. I hope you find it helpful.

References

ALDinHE (2024) *About ALDinHE*. Available at: https://aldinhe.ac.uk/about-aldinhe/ (Accessed: 9 April 2024).

Hartley, P., Hilsdon, J., Keenan, C., Sinfield, S. and Verity, M. (eds) (2011) *Learning Development in Higher Education*. Basingstoke: Palgrave Macmillan.

Syska, A. and Buckley, C. (eds) (2024) *How to Be a Learning Developer in Higher Education: Critical Perspectives, Community and Practice*. Abingdon: Routledge.

Whitchurch, C. (2008) 'Shifting identities and blurring boundaries: The emergence of third space professionals in UK higher education', *Higher Education Quarterly*, 62(4), 377–396. https://doi.org/10.1111/j.1468-2273.2008.00387.x

Preface

Seven years ago, as a new Learning Developer (LDer) at a University of London institution, I found myself routinely searching for resources and advice about effective Learning Development (LD) practice. Although there were existing materials on the Association for Learning Development in Higher Education (ALDinHE) website, at the time, there was little in the way of a road map for specific aspects of the job such as how to conduct tutorials and workshops or how to work effectively with students. In my former life as a teacher, there had been an abundance of advice, even mandates, about effective pedagogy. Feeling somewhat lost and wanting to do the job well, I began searching for a guide aimed at those new to the role that would provide suggestions to adapt and use within my own teaching context. I could not find it, so I started noting down ideas about what worked well in my own practice; first, for my own professional development, and then later to share in an ALDinHE #Take5 blog. Had it not been for the encouragement and feedback from Sandra Sinfield, Tom Burns, and Dr Katharine Jewitt to submit that blog post, I would not have believed that anyone would have been interested in what I had to say about LD. Sometimes, all you need is a little bit of inspiration and kindness from others. Thank you for all you do, and did, for the LD community.

This book was borne out of those initial scribblings and the realisation that other new LDers might find such a guide useful. Since then, ALDinHE have begun work on a continuing professional development (CPD) programme aimed specifically at new LDers covering many facets of the role including exploring its values and conceptual foundations, offering ideas for teaching tutorials and workshops, and examining the scholarship of LD. This CPD programme will be a much-needed addition for those new to the role. The book you hold in your hands should also serve as a useful aid in your growing understanding of LD.

Doing Learning Development in Higher Education is an introductory-level, practical, guide for new and early career LDers and will be of most use to those within the first five years of their role. The focus is on LD practice; however, those working in related roles such as academic advisers, academic

Acronyms and abbreviations

AALL	Association for Academic Language and Learning
ACDAP	Advisory Committee on Degree Awarding Powers
AD	Academic Development
AFHEA	Associate Fellowship of the Higher Education Academy (Now Advance HE)
AI	Artificial Intelligence
ALDinHE	Association for Learning Development in Higher Education
APA	American Psychological Association
ATLAANZ	Association of Tertiary Learning Advisors of Aotearoa New Zealand
BALEAP	British Association of Lecturers in English for Academic Purposes
BAME	Black, Asian and Minority Ethnic
CAST	Centre for Applied Special Technology
CC	Creative Commons
CeP	Certified Practitioner
CeLP	Certified Leading Practitioner
CHE	Council on Higher Education
CoP	Community of Practice
CPD	Continuing Professional Development
DfE	Department for Education
DfE NI	Department for the Economy, Northern Ireland
EATAW	The European Association for the Teaching of Academic Writing
ED	Educational Development
EDer	Educational Developer
EDI	Equality, Diversity, and Inclusion
FAQ	Frequently asked question
F-ALDinHE	Fellow of the Association for Learning Development in Higher Education
FE	Further Education

FHEA	Fellowship of the Higher Education Academy (Now Advance HE)
GenAI	Generative Artificial Intelligence
GDPR	General Data Protection Regulation
HE	Higher Education
HEI	Higher Education Institution
HEFCW	Higher Education Funding Council for Wales
HESA	Higher Education Statistics Agency
HERA	Higher Education and Research Act 2017
HR	Human Resources
ICALLD	International Consortium of Academic Language and Learning Developers
JLDHE	*Journal of Learning Development in Higher Education*
KWL	What I know, What I want to know, What I have learned
LD	Learning Development
LDer(s)	Learning Developer(s)
LDHEN	Learning Development in Higher Education Network
LGBTQAI+	Lesbian, Gay, Bisexual, Transgender, Queer or Questioning, Intersex, and Asexual/Aromantic+
LMS	Learning Management System
LSAC	Learning Specialists Association of Canada
NSS	National Student Survey
OSCOLA	Oxford Standard for the Citation of Legal Authorities
OED	Oxford English Dictionary
OfS	Office for Students
PFHEA	Principal Fellowship of the Higher Education Academy (Now Advance HE)
PGCAP	Postgraduate Certificate in Academic Practice
PGCHE	Postgraduate Certificate in Higher Education
PSF	Professional Standards Framework
QAA	The Quality Assurance Agency for Higher Education
Q&A	Question and answer
REF	Research Excellence Framework
SAAALP	South African Association for Academic Literacy Practitioners
SF-ALDinHE	Senior Fellow of the Association for Learning Development in Higher Education
SAQA	South African Qualifications Authority
SEDA	Staff and Educational Development Association
ScotHELD	Scottish Higher Education Learner Developers' network
SFC	Scottish Funding Council
SFHEA	Senior Fellowship of the Higher Education Academy (Now Advance HE)

SMART	Specific, Measurable, Achievable, Relevant/Realistic, Timely/Timebound
SpLD	Specific Learning Difference
SWOT	Strengths, Weaknesses, Opportunities, Threats
TASO	Transforming Access and Student Outcomes in Higher Education
TEF	Teaching Excellence Framework
TEQSA	Tertiary Education Quality and Standards Agency
THE	Times Higher Education
UCAS	University and Colleges Admissions Service
UDL	Universal Design for Learning
UUK	Universities UK
VLE	Virtual Learning Environment
WAM	Workload Allocation Model

Illustrations

Figures

4.1	Gibbs' reflective cycle (1988)	63
5.1	Bloom's Taxonomy of learning	82
5.2	Slide with workshop objectives	84
5.3	Slide outlining workshop structure	84
5.4	Starter activity: an interactive poll	85
5.5	Starter activity: an interactive word shower	85
5.6	Gauging students' stances: an interactive poll	86
5.7	Example workshop task (a)	88
5.8	Example workshop task (b)	88
5.9	Assessing understanding: an interactive poll	89
5.10	The jigsaw approach to group work	93
7.1	Slide one	129
7.2	Slide two	129
7.3	Using images: a rollercoaster	137
7.4	Using images: a veggie burger to illustrate the PEEL approach to paragraph structure	138
7.5	Slide explaining the PEEL approach to paragraph structure	139
7.6	A concept cartoon	140
9.1	The five stages of networking capital accumulation	177

Tables

3.1	UK degrees by level and the powers to award them	30
3.2	Office for students' conditions of registration	32
3.3	Common leadership roles in a university and their function	34
4.1	A tutorial log sheet	52
4.2	An adapted summary of the 5Ps formulation approach to conducting tutorials	59
6.1	Planning template for embedded teaching	110
7.1	Materials and resources for a specific intended learning outcome	128

7.2	Response to task	130
8.1	Three UK statutory provisions relevant to 'working with respect for diverse learners' in the HE context	157
9.1	Adapted summary of Buckley and Frith's categorisation of networking capital	177
9.2	Example of an informal CPD log	180
9.3	Identifying developmental needs in relation to the ALDinHE values	181
9.4	Example SWOT analysis on delivering workshops	181
9.5	Example SMART goal	182
10.1	KWL chart	201

Chapter 1

Introduction

1. Introduction

> **Chapter overview**
>
> This chapter provides an overview of the following:
>
> - What the book is about.
> - Who the book is for.
> - The rationale for the book.
> - How the book is structured and how it might be used.

What is this book about?

In my initial three months working in Learning Development (LD), I was sitting in a café with an acquaintance. We had been discussing our jobs – he worked in a sector outside of higher education (HE) and LD – and he asked, 'I know that you work with students but what is it that you *do exactly?*' Finding it hard to articulate and being an inexperienced (and nervous) new Learning Developer (LDer), I answered in a rote-like way, 'I support students with developing their academic skills'. My acquaintance slurped his latte, gave an all-knowing look, and said, in a disparaging manner, 'That's easy'.

I sometimes reflect on that interaction and wish I had said something, anything, that better expressed the complexity of what we do as LDers. Maybe I should have said that LD involves reflecting, researching, creating, developing, learning, reading, refiguring, trialling, trying again, teaching, tinkering, tooling, diagnosing, questioning, negotiating, failing, and a myriad of other tasks in an intricate web of decision-making, all with the aim to aid students to better understand and succeed in navigating the complexities of the academic

DOI: 10.4324/9781003604266-1

context. But that would have been a mouthful. At that time, I lacked the understanding and confidence in my professional role so; instead, I said nothing and sipped my lukewarm tea. Since then, with time and experience, I have learned that what we do as LDers is enjoyable, interesting, impactful, and amusing at times. But easy? Most certainly not.

Due to the complex nature of the role, as a new LDer, you may be seeking a manual, like a recipe book, telling you how to 'do' LD. The issue is that doing LD typically entails learning on the job through 'trial and error', practice, and experience (Syska and Buckley, 2024a, p. 2). This can be affirming in the sense that there is the scope and autonomy to make the role your own. However, in your early years in LD, this lack of 'instruction' can quickly lead to the feeling that you are trying to wallow through a swamp, wading through bit by bit, never quite knowing whether you are headed in the right direction.

As such, this book provides guidance to new and early career LDers, and those in similar roles, who feel a little adrift. Its focus is on the practical day-to-day functions that LDers undertake in their role. It offers ideas, suggestions, and examples of 'good' practice and addresses the questions that you may have but feel reluctant to ask for fear of looking silly, including the following:

- What exactly is LD and what are its values?
- What are tutorials, workshops, and embedded sessions, and how might these be structured?
- How do I find, create, and adapt teaching and learning materials?
- What can I do if I face challenges when teaching or delivering skills sessions?
- What types of people might I work with as an LDer?
- How do I work effectively with students and colleagues?
- Help! I feel like an imposter. What should I do?
- What professional development opportunities are available to me?
- How do I advocate for LD and begin to get my voice heard as a new LDer?

The book is intended as a professional friend and guide. It is written as if we were having an exchange about effective LD practice and is designed to help with navigating those early years in the role. It takes as its premise the view that relationships are integral to the practice of LD. As relationships are complex, this means that whilst there may be general approaches to LD that are effective in the pedagogical sense, there can be no 'one-size-fits-all' method. As such, it will be important to think about how you might adapt, refine, and apply (or discard) the guidance and ideas contained here to your specific professional context. There are tasks and activities in each main body chapter to aid you to do this.

An important principle of effective LD practice is that of collaboration, with students, staff, and colleagues, both in your immediate institution and within the wider LD community. In this collaborative spirit, the book includes several reflections from experienced LDers providing encouragement and insight into the role from different voices. It is hoped that you too will become a voice in the field as your understanding of LD evolves.

Who is this book for?

Doing Learning Development in Higher Education is intended to aid new or early LDers, and those in associated roles, working in HE contexts. For clarity, I define new or early career as those at the emergent stage; that is, within their first one to five years, or those with little to no experience of teaching and tutoring students in a university context. Early career professionals such as academic or subject librarians, subject lecturers, academic advisers, and Educational/Academic Developers working in student-facing or teaching-related roles in HE may also find the suggestions and guidance in this book relevant to their teaching practice. Other professionals, such as subject lecturers seeking to transition into LD, teaching staff working in further education offering HE level qualifications, or graduate and postgraduate students considering a career in LD should find the ideas contained here valuable. Senior LDers and educational leads or managers might use this book as an aid for training and developing new and early career teaching staff, including academic and professional services staff with teaching and LD remits.

The book is written from the perspective and experience of an LDer working in and situated in the UK, specifically in England, in a London-based higher education institution (HEI). Therefore, reference to professional LD and HE bodies and organisations such as the Association for Learning Development in Higher Education (ALDinHE), or the Office for Students (OfS), the regulatory body for HE in England, are UK-based. However, new LDers – and those in similar roles – working internationally should still be able to draw parallels and resonance with their own practice and their comparable professional bodies, such as the Association of Tertiary Learning Advisors of Aotearoa in New Zealand, the Learning Specialists Association of Canada (LSAC), the South African Association for Academic Literacy Practitioners (SAAALP), the Association for Academic Language and Learning (AALL) in Australia, and the European Association for the Teaching of Academic Writing (EATAW).

Whilst the focus is on providing advice to new and early career LDers, experienced practitioners will also find the book a helpful reference tool and supplementary resource.

What is Learning Development?

Although job titles and the contexts in which LDers practise differ, Hilsdon, a highly significant figure in LD for his seminal work in the field, offers an overarching and influential definition. He describes it as:

> a complex set of multi-disciplinary and cross-disciplinary academic roles and functions, involving teaching, tutoring, research, and the design and

production of learning materials, as well as involvement in staff development, policy-making and other consultative activities.

(Hilsdon, 2011, p. 14)[1]

As an LDer, you will be involved in teaching and tutoring. You will work with a diverse student body who are undertaking varied degrees or programmes or study. Your role will entail developing, creating, and adapting teaching materials, and you will work collaboratively alongside staff with the aim to aid students to better understand sometimes complex academic practices. You may work under an academic or professional services contract, or in a 'hybrid' role straddling the line between a disciplinary academic or subject lecturer and an LDer (see Grayson and Syska, 2024, pp. 43–50). As you develop experience, you could find yourself involved in research, supporting staff and academics, undertaking policy-related activities, and engaged in consultative-style practices.

Whilst this book takes as its focus the day-to-day functions of the LD role, it is important to acknowledge and be aware of the scholarly activity and theory that underpins this practice.[2] As a new LDer, the word 'theory' may seem very abstract, and possibly even overwhelming, when all you really want to know is where to find a good handout on essay writing. This is normal, particularly when you are caught up in the minutiae of the day-to-day role. However, once you start to dig a little deeper into some of the values and foundational principles that underpin LD practice, it will become clearer as to why theory is the bedrock of LD work.

As an example of why theory is important, Johnson and Bishopp-Martin, both established LDers, posit that the 'crucial delineating hallmark' of LD is its focus on, 'understanding HE *as the student experiences it* [original emphasis], or learning to walk in students' shoes' (Johnson and Bishopp-Martin, 2024, p. 16). To be able to 'walk in students' shoes', we clearly need to empathise with the students we work with which in part relates to understanding how our own values, identity, and belief systems influence our interactions with students, also known as being reflexive. That is, our everyday practice needs to be underpinned by an awareness of *why* we do things in the way we do. This is where theory comes in: it aids us with becoming 'thinking' educational practitioners, critically reflecting on our actions and behaviours (Cohen et al., 2007) which should, hopefully, translate into improving our LD practice. Theory, then, becomes an oar, gently guiding us, even though it may not always be at the forefront of our minds when we are navigating the day-to-day role. This is where theory meets practice, that is, praxis. Therefore, throughout this book, as well as considering the 'what' and 'how' of LD, you are also encouraged to think about 'why' you do things in the way you do. At the end of each chapter, there are ideas for further reading if you wish to explore the theoretical and scholarly activity related to LD practice in more depth. However, the focus in this book is on enabling you to better understand the everyday functions of LD. As such, it takes a pragmatic approach, providing practical suggestions and guidance from first-hand experience, so that you will be able to embark confidently upon your role.

What's in a name?

There is no single job title for an LDer. Indeed, if your job title does not specifically use the words 'Learning Developer', you may question whether you are indeed one at all. For example, a quick search on an academic jobs board reveals a non-exhaustive list of job titles related to the LD function. These include 'Learning Development Tutor', 'Study Skills Tutor', 'Learning Development Lecturer', 'Academic Skills Adviser', 'Student Success Tutor', 'Academic Developer', 'Learning Skills Co-ordinator', 'Study Development Tutor', 'Associate Lecturer in Learning Development', and 'Academic Guidance Tutor'. To add to the confusion, job titles ascribed to the LDer role can differ significantly even *within* institutions. For instance, in my immediate institution, a London-based university, job titles for our team of LDers include 'Learning Developer', 'Student Success Tutor', 'Learning Skills Co-ordinator', and, as in my case, 'Learning Development Tutor'. Along with these variations in terms of 'what' we call ourselves, there is ongoing debate within the LD community about our professional identities, that is, who we are and what we are for (Briscoe and Olson, 2024) and existing misconceptions about what LD is in the wider HE sector in which we work.

LD is also sometimes confused and conflated with educational development, sometimes also referred to as academic development. Whilst this field has overlap and synergies with LD, the key distinction is that educational developers usually focus on developing the teaching and educational practices of academics (lecturers and teaching staff) as opposed to students. Further, LD as a field or profession is also, at times, mistaken for a quite distinct but similarly named occupation, 'Learning *and* Development', which focuses on human resource development and training typically within corporate and commercial companies.

In addition to complexities in terms of 'what' we are called, the everyday practice of an LDer can also vary significantly according to the university context in which you find yourself. You may be based in a specific school, department or faculty; you may operate more centrally in a study skills centre; you might be located in the library or an information centre; or as is increasingly common in HE contexts, you may be part of a 'hub and spoke' model where specialist tutors work as part of a larger core or central team or 'hub' providing specialist support (the 'spoke' element) to specific faculties or departments. You may find that related functions within your university also overlap with the LD function. For instance, in your institution, you might work alongside digital education or information technology specialists and subject librarians with teaching or student-facing remits that involve developing students' learning.

Whilst job titles, remits, and contexts for LDers vary, one key element that binds our work is the principle of 'working in partnership with students and staff to make sense of and get the most out of higher education' (ALDinHE, 2024). If working with students and staff in this way is a significant aspect of what you do, your role will fall under the umbrella of LD, or at the very least you will be working in the 'spirit' or with an ethos of an LDer. Throughout this book, I use the 'uppercase' for LD and LDer, to reflect the distinction that Johnson and Bishopp-Martin (2024, p. 20) propose, that there is a 'lowercase' Learning Development 'mindset' that many might adopt which is driven by the 'uppercase Learning Development', a profession and field in its own right. Throughout, I use the collective terms LD and LDer to refer to roles and responsibilities that encompass what LDers do, bearing in mind our shared values, yet varied titles, within our distinct, contextualised practices.

Why this book?[3]

Prior to LD, I worked as a teacher. In the first nerve-wracking year as newly qualified, there had been a wealth of information and mandates clothed as guidance about how to do the job 'correctly'. Even with this preponderance of guidance, teaching was never easy and most of the time, I was simply 'trying to figure out how not to fail quite so much, with not quite so many students' (Blaisdell, 2013, p. iii). However, the 'guidance' reassured me that I was doing okay and enabled me to feel a little less lost.

In contrast, as a new LDer, I recall vividly the feeling that I was having to flounder and find my own way, doing my best to navigate the job without a map. My best laid plans would fall apart, carefully thought out workshops would go completely awry, and what worked well with a student in a tutorial one day would leave another student (and myself) completely bemused the next. It felt like I was constantly failing, and I was reluctant to ask for help from colleagues for fear of looking incompetent. So, I began to search for guidance. Although I found resources and support on the ALDinHE website, I was having to do a lot of 'digging' when all I was really hoping for was a one-stop manual advising me on how to do the job 'right'. I could not find it, so I began jotting down ideas for resources and teaching so that I would have a record of what worked well in my own practice. These thoughts were published in an ALDinHE #Take5 blog titled *What the Learning Developer Needs to Know*. Feedback from members of the LD community prompted me to consider developing my ideas in a more substantive way into a book. Whilst this seemed daunting, I was motivated by the thought that if I would have found it helpful to have had such a 'manual' available in my initial years in LD then so too might other new LDers.

In 2024, Syska and Buckley published an edited collection, *How to be a Learning Developer in Higher Education* (Syska and Buckley, 2024b). This followed its seminal precursor, *Learning Development in Higher Education*, also an edited collection, published in 2011 (see Hartley et al., 2011). With chapter contributions from members and practitioners within the LD community, both books explore and offer critical perspectives on the historical origins, debates, practices, and theoretical underpinnings of LD. Both are referred to in this book as they are influential texts within the field. However, rather than attempting to compete with their work, this book is intended to serve as a complement, aiding you as a newer LDer to gain a sense of the practical elements of LD whilst providing reassurance that you are doing just fine. Throughout, I offer ideas and guidance rather than a prescriptive approach in the recognition that, as LDers, we need to be responsive to the needs of the specific students we work alongside.

How is the book structured?

Each chapter in the book, whilst interconnected, is also self-contained. This means you can use it as a reference guide, to dip in and out when a particular section is relevant to your needs, or it can be read in its entirety. Due to its concise nature, it is not possible to cover all facets of doing LD in depth. As such, the book focuses on providing guidance for the main student-facing aspects new LDers are likely to encounter in the role, namely, tutorials, workshops, and embedded provision. It also provides ideas and suggestions for other aspects of the role including how to develop teaching and learning materials, working with students and colleagues, ideas for ongoing learning and continuing professional development (CPD), and further sources of inspiration to pursue.

Chapters 2 and 3 are more theoretical in nature. Chapter 2 is a short contextual chapter. It begins by exploring what LD is, what LDers do and, briefly, how LD emerged as a practice in higher education (HE). It asks the reader to reflect on what brought them into LD and considers the varied routes that people enter LD, positing that this variety is a strength of the field but is also perhaps a double-edged sword. The chapter situates LD as a responsive, emerging, and exciting field in which to work but one with its own unique challenges. It includes reflections from experienced LDers on the nature of the LD role. The chapter explores the five guiding community-driven principles of LD as espoused by ALDinHE. It emphasises how these values can guide the LDer in their day-to-day role and points to the importance of new LDers familiarising themselves with this underlying ethos. Finally, the chapter provides suggestions for further reading on the historical and theoretical foundations of LD.

Chapter 3 aims to begin to contextualise for new and early career LDers what working in higher education institutions (HEIs) involves. It provides an explanation of the key characteristics and functions of a university as relevant to LD. It then outlines some of the wider contextual issues influencing the HE sector including increased regulation and competition. The chapter also highlights the impact of emerging generative artificial intelligence (GenAI) technologies on LD practice. It is not the purpose of this book to provide a comprehensive theoretical discussion on GenAI or of these wider contextual matters; for this, readers might wish to explore the recently published edited collection *How to Be a Learning Developer in Higher Education* (Syska and Buckley, 2024b). Instead, the chapter outlines, in brief, examples of the practical day-to-day impact of these developments in relation to LD practice.

Chapter 4 offers guidance for conducting tutorials which are an important student-facing aspect of the LD role. It explains what tutorials are, why they are commonplace in LD practice, and suggests ways they can be structured. It offers pragmatic ideas on how to prepare for tutorials, what to do during and after, and how to deal with challenges. Given the wider regulatory context in which LDers work, it also highlights ways to assess and evaluate the impact of tutorial provision. The chapter finishes with a review of the key points and signposts to relevant resources and further reading.

Chapter 5 offers ideas for another of the core student-facing functions of the LDer role: extra-curricular (or optional) academic skills workshops. It begins by explaining what workshops are and why they are widespread practice in the field of LD. The chapter looks at practical matters including how to promote workshops to students, ways to structure an online or in-person workshop, how to encourage engagement and participation, how to deal with classroom challenges that arise, and means to assess the impact of workshops. The chapter concludes with a summary of the key points and a list of relevant resources and further reading.

Chapter 6 explores what embedded LD work is and why LD scholars and practitioners advocate for such provision. The chapter provides guidance on how to plan for and deliver embedded teaching, discusses how to deal with classroom management issues, and presents ideas on how to advocate for embedded work in your university context.

Chapter 7 concerns the development of teaching and learning materials for LD practice. It provides guidance for creating, adapting, and developing materials for synchronous and asynchronous use. The chapter discusses the importance of building a toolkit of 'go-to' resources whilst emphasising the need to remain flexible about use and choice of materials in response to the needs of diverse student cohorts. It explores why it is important to make materials inclusive and accessible and suggests how to do so. The chapter provides brief examples of how GenAI tools might be used to develop and create teaching materials. It ends with a review of the key points and signposts to relevant resources such as the LearnHigher resource bank from ALDinHE.

Chapter 8 provides guidance on working effectively with students and staff. It highlights the importance of understanding the wider regulatory HE landscape. The chapter suggests ways to adopt inclusive practices when working with students from diverse backgrounds and with varied needs. It outlines approaches to working with students, such as co-creation, which encourage student agency and involvement with LD. The chapter considers the range of colleagues that LDers are likely to work with, providing suggestions on how to make these professional relationships effective. It concludes by providing pragmatic tips on how LDers can look after their professional wellbeing, emphasising the importance of establishing boundaries.

Chapter 9 outlines various avenues for professional development that new and early career LDers might choose to pursue. It explores the benefits of informal continuing professional development (CPD) such as observing colleagues, reading, listening to podcasts, attending conferences, and writing and blogging. It then highlights formal opportunities for professional development including involvement with ALDinHE and related professional bodies, professional recognition, and ideas for CPD within the LDer's own institution. The chapter ends with a self-reflection activity whereby new LDers are asked to consider their professional development goals for the short to medium term and what CPD opportunities might be helpful to pursue.

Chapter 10, the concluding chapter, summarises the key points from the earlier chapters. It reminds the new LDer that LD is an emerging and exciting field with scope to add their own voice and make impact. The chapter posits to the reader that whilst it is important to develop effective practice, making mistakes as a new LDer is also an inescapable (and positive) aspect of growing in the role. It reminds the new LDer that this is a book that can be dipped in and out of as relevant to their future needs – a guiding friend to return to, as necessary. Finally, the chapter signposts to further reading and resources and asks the reader to think about next steps in their own development.

How might you use this book?

There is no obligation to read this book from cover to cover – as LDers, we are by the nature of our jobs often time poor – so browse through or read sections in depth that might be most pertinent to you in the moment. If you are short on time, each chapter ends with a summary of the key points which you can refer to quickly as and when needed. To avoid repetition, acronyms and abbreviations are used where required and a list explaining these is provided at the start of the book. As far as possible, I avoid jargon to make the ideas accessible. Where jargon is necessary, I explain what these terms mean. There are tasks, exemplars, and reflective activities throughout the main body chapters to aid with developing your understanding of the role. As you read, feel free to note down your responses, questions, or thoughts on the page. You might find that your jottings provide a useful starting point for your own burgeoning writing, professional development, and growing confidence as an LDer. With all that said, let us begin to explore the wonderful, yet complex, world of doing LD.

Summary

- This is a book for new and early career LDers, or those in associated roles, working in HE or tertiary education. Other teaching and learning professionals, LDers working in international contexts, and experienced LDers should also find value in this book.
- LDers work in a myriad of contexts, with a range of functions, responsibilities, and job titles. However, we aim to 'work in partnership with students and staff to make sense of and get the most out of HE' (ALDinHE, 2024). This fundamental value is at the core of LDers' practice.
- The book provides guidance on the main functions of LD including teaching and delivering workshops and tutorials, embedded provision, developing teaching and learning materials, working with students and colleagues, and professional development.
- Whilst the focus is on the practical aspects of LD, it highlights the importance of theory and scholarly activity in situating this practice.
- The central premise of this book is that relationships are crucial to LD practice. As such, there can be no one-size-fits-all approach. Therefore, the suggestions and ideas contained in the following chapters should be adapted to your own professional context. There are examples and tasks throughout the book to help you to do so.

Notes

1 Hilsdon (2011, p. 14) quote used by permission of Bloomsbury Publishing Plc.
2 See 'Ideas for further reading' at the end of this chapter for readings that explore the theoretical and foundational underpinnings of LD practice.
3 This section is adapted from my ALDinHE #Take5 20 April 2023, blog post, 'What the Learning Developer needs to know'. Available at: https://aldinhe.ac.uk/take5–84-what-the-learning-developer-needs-to-know/.

References

ALDinHE (2024) *About ALDinHE*. Available at: https://aldinhe.ac.uk/about-aldinhe/ (Accessed: 9 April 2024).

Blaisdell, B. (2013) 'Note', in B. Blaisdell (ed) *Essays on Teaching*. Mineola, New York: Dover Publications, Inc, iii–v.

Briscoe, H. and Olson, C. (2024) 'Who are we? An autoethnographic investigation into professional role identity of the learning developer', *Journal of Learning Development in Higher Education* [Preprint], 32. https://doi.org/10.47408/jldhe.vi32.1430

Cohen, L., Manion, L. and Morrison, K. (2007) *Research Methods in Education*, 6th edn. Abingdon, Oxon: Routledge.

Grayson, N. and Syska, A. (2024) 'Hybrid learning developers: Between the discipline and the third space', in A. Syska and C. Buckley (eds) *How to be a Learning Developer in Higher Education: Critical Perspectives, Community and Practice*. Abingdon: Routledge, 43–50.

Hartley, P., Hilsdon, J., Keenan, C., Sinfield, S. and Verity, M. (eds) (2011) *Learning Development in Higher Education*. Basingstoke: Palgrave Macmillan.

Hilsdon, J. (2011) 'What is learning development?', in P. Hartley, J. Hilsdon, C. Keenan, S. Sinfield and M. Verity (eds) *Learning Development in Higher Education*. Basingstoke: Palgrave Macmillan (Red Globe Press), 13–27.

Johnson, I. and Bishopp-Martin, S. (2024) 'Conceptual foundations in learning development', in A. Syska and C. Buckley (eds) *How to be a Learning Developer in Higher Education: Critical Perspectives, Community and Practice*. Abingdon: Routledge, 15–24.

Syska, A. and Buckley, C. (2024a) 'Introduction', in A. Syska and C. Buckley (eds) *How to be a Learning Developer in Higher Education: Critical Perspectives, Community and Practice*. Abingdon: Routledge, 1–4.

Syska, A. and Buckley, C. (eds) (2024b) *How to be a Learning Developer in Higher Education: Critical Perspectives, Community and Practice*. Abingdon: Routledge.

Ideas for further reading

Historical and Theoretical Foundations of Learning Development

Abegglen, S., Burns, T. and Sinfield, S. (2019) 'It's learning development, Jim – but not as we know it: Academic literacies in third space', *Journal of Learning Development in Higher Education [Preprint]*, 15. https://doi.org/10.47408/jldhe.v0i15.500

ALDinHE (2024) *About ALDinHE*. Available at: https://aldinhe.ac.uk/about-aldinhe/ (Accessed: 9 April 2024).

Hilsdon, J. (2011) 'What is learning development?', in P. Hartley, J. Hilsdon, C. Keenan, S. Sinfield and M. Verity (eds) *Learning Development in Higher Education*. Basingstoke: Palgrave Macmillan (Red Globe Press), 13–27.

Johnson, I. and Bishopp-Martin, S. (2024) 'Conceptual foundations in learning development', in A. Syska and C. Buckley (eds) *How to be a Learning Developer in Higher Education: Critical Perspectives, Community and Practice*. Abingdon: Routledge, 15–24.

Lea, M. R. and Street, B. V. (1998) 'Student writing in higher education: An academic literacies approach', *Studies in Higher Education*, 23(2), 157–172. https://doi.org/10.1080/03075079812331380364

Murray, L. and Glass, B. (2011) 'Learning development in higher education – community of practice or profession?', in P. Hartley, J. Hilsdon, C. Keenan, S. Sinfield and M. Verity (eds) *Learning Development in Higher Education*. Basingstoke: Palgrave Macmillan, 28–39.

Slawson, T. and Eyre, J. (2024) 'Theory in learning development: We are all players', in A. Syska and C. Buckley (eds) *How to be a Learning Developer in Higher Education: Critical Perspectives, Community and Practice*. Abingdon: Routledge, 7–14.

Chapter 2

What does it mean to 'do' Learning Development?

Overview

This chapter provides the following:

- A discussion of what Learning Development (LD) is and what Learning Developers (LDers) do.
- An outline of how LD emerged as a practice in higher education.
- A consideration of the five community-driven values underpinning LD practice.
- Suggestions as to where you can read more about the historical and theoretical foundations of LD.

As a starting point

The first question that you may ask as a new LDer is, 'What exactly is Learning Development (LD)?', the second being, 'What precisely am I meant to be *doing*?' Such questions relate to professional identity and reflect ingrained and ongoing debate in the wider LD community, namely, questions of who we are and what we are for (Briscoe and Olson, 2024). Whilst you will have a job description, this might not offer a nuanced or comprehensive answer to the question of what it means to do LD. However, to do LD well and to be able to articulate its worth to those who may not understand it, you need to have a clear grasp of what LD is, what its values are, and why it matters to your everyday practice. As a starting point then, this chapter introduces the practice of LD, outlines its origins, and discusses its community-driven ethos to aid with providing greater clarity about the role.

What does it mean to 'do' Learning Development?

In the introductory chapter, we saw that Hilsdon (2011), a highly influential figure in LD for his pioneering work in the field, offers an overarching description which it is helpful to be reminded of here. He conceptualises LD as:

> a complex set of multi-disciplinary and cross-disciplinary academic roles and functions, involving teaching, tutoring, research and the design and production of learning materials, as well as involvement in staff development, policy-making and other consultative activities.
>
> (Hilsdon, 2011, p. 14)[1]

From this, we can begin to get a sense of the variety of tasks that are involved in LD. As an LDer, your primary responsibilities will involve teaching academic skills workshops, providing embedded support, delivering one-to-one and group tutorials, and developing teaching and learning resources. Your work will involve supporting students across the student 'journey' from pre-arrival (or pre-sessional) support through to induction, across different transition stages (e.g. those progressing from the first year of an undergraduate degree to the second), and beyond. You will attend meetings, undertake administrative tasks, and collect and evaluate data about your service. You will undertake scholarly activities such as research, writing for publication, and disseminating ideas at conferences. You will work with colleagues, such as subject lecturers, to plan LD support and may be involved in providing guidance to staff on teaching and learning-related matters like assessment design. These myriad tasks, designed to aid students to study successfully, are multi-layered, complex, and may vary daily. This means there is no typical day for an LDer. The purpose of undertaking such activities is to aid the students you work with to develop successful learning strategies, to further their self-agency, and improve their academic skills, such that they 'get the most out of HE' (ALDinHE, 2024a).

LD clearly involves something to do with learning and something to do with development. But who is learning and what are we developing?

Reflective task

- What does it mean to learn? How do you know you have learned something?
- Do you view learning as a process, as the outcome, or something else?

At its simplest, learning involves the 'acquisition' of skills or knowledge (Oxford English Dictionary, 2025). However, what it means 'to learn' is contested and there are different interpretations and theories about the factors that influence learning.[2] LD work takes as its focus students' learning. This is approached holistically: we are interested in the student experience, the learning and teaching 'practices' of those involved in students' learning (Hilsdon, 2011, p. 18), the social context in which the learning happens, the student's identity and its influence on learning, and the implications of institutional 'processes', 'practices', and pedagogy on that learning (Hilsdon, 2011, p. 16). Learning is also viewed as a process over which students have and can develop self-agency. As such, LD adopts a developmental ethos, working with students' strengths to aid them to succeed with their studies (whatever success means to the learner). This distinguishes LD from a traditional 'study skills' approach which has associations with being remedial or 'deficit' oriented (Wingate, 2006; Hilsdon, 2011, p. 16).

In LD, you will meet with students in the classroom, lecture, or tutorial space where you will work alongside them to develop the skills and 'academic literacies' (Lea and Street, 1998) (more on this later in the chapter) that they need to be effective learners in the university context. LD work done well is underpinned by empathy for the student (Johnson and Bishopp-Martin, 2024) alongside a respect and willingness to understand their experience. The relationship between a student and an LDer is often quite distinct from that between students and their subject lecturers. As LDers, we do not typically assess or grade students' work (unless we work in a hybrid academic/LDer role) and we are not the gatekeepers deciding whether a student progresses in their programme. Instead, we take on a mediating role to help students 'make sense of' (ALDinHE, 2024a) aspects of their study including assessment practices, disciplinary expectations, markers' feedback, and their classroom experience. Given this, the balance of power between an LDer and student as compared to that between student and subject lecturer could be viewed as more equal in nature. Indeed, as we shall see later in the chapter, a core LD value promotes the idea of working 'in partnership with students' (ALDinHE, 2024a) highlighting the egalitarian relationship that we seek to develop with learners.

LD practice is student-centred. It is respectful of students' circumstances and existing knowledge. This might mean, for instance, exploring a student's previous experience of essay writing in a one-to-one tutorial, or adapting learning materials to make them accessible for students who identify as having a visual impairment, or giving a student time to express their joys and worries about the studying process. Whilst as an LDer you will develop expertise in effective learning and teaching practices, students can be viewed as 'expert' in their own learning experience (Webster, 2023, p. 4). Given this, rather than aiming to be the fount of all knowledge, your role as an LDer might best be thought of as a guiding one, working collaboratively with students to develop their skills so that they can successfully navigate the complexities of academia.

Learning Development as a 'third space'

You will also hear LD referred to as occupying a 'third space' (Whitchurch, 2008). What might this mean? LD work is academic related. We work closely with students, teaching and tutoring, and carry out similar functions to academics such as scholarly research. However, many LDers work under a 'professional services' contract rather than an academic one. Whilst LDers provide a specialist service in the form of advice and guidance, given our teaching remit, our work does not fit solely under the professional services umbrella. As such, many LDers identify with the notion of being 'third space' professionals, in-between an academic/teaching and a professional services role (Whitchurch, 2008). The 'third space' can also be thought of as the mediating role that LDers play between the student and unfamiliar conventions in HE. For instance, lecturers will have expectations in terms of class and seminar contribution or norms around disciplinary writing that students might be unfamiliar with or find difficult to understand. LDers aim to bridge the gap, for example, by working with a student during a tutorial to understand and clarify feedback that they have received on their coursework, or running workshops on how to prepare for and interact in a seminar or lecture, or by working alongside lecturers to devise clear marking criteria that students understand.

> **Reflective task**
> - Do you see your role as an LDer as occupying an in-between or 'third space'?
> - If so, what elements of your work for you operate in this 'third space'?

Should we define Learning Development?

It is important to note that there are different perspectives in the field about what it means to do LD. Eyre and Slawson (2018) have argued that seeking a 'fixed' or sole definition reduces LD's ability to remain dynamic and responsive to the students we work alongside. Instead, they argue that the essential thing is to consider what distinguishes our practice as LDers (Eyre and Slawson, 2018). As we saw in Chapter 1, for Johnson and Bishopp-Martin (2024, p. 16) the crux and distinctive element of LD practice is 'understanding HE *as the student experiences it* [original emphasis] or learning to walk in students' shoes'. Sinfield et al. (2011, p. 55) emphasise LD as a 'socio-political' and 'emancipatory' practice the purpose of which is to 'empower' and promote students' autonomy. From a social justice viewpoint, LD practice can play a role in aiding with issues of equity and equality in education (see, e.g. Zamora and Bali, 2025). LD might also be viewed as a caring and compassionate practice (see, e.g. Huzar, 2025), or from a 'reparative' perspective as a means of mending 'legacies of institutional harms' perpetuated in the HE context (see Altunbas et al., 2025, p. 2). These examples are not exhaustive but give a sense of the multiplicity of perspectives about what LD is and could be for.

Reflective task

- What *for you* captures the essence of your role as an LDer?
- Do you think there should be a universal definition for LD?

By reading this section, you should have begun to get a sense of what LD is about and what it entails. We have seen that there are varied ways of conceptualising and thinking about LD. In later chapters, we will look at practical suggestions for 'doing' LD. However, this necessitates having a grasp of the main drivers and underpinning values for LD practice and why it matters to your everyday practice. To better understand this, it is helpful to go back in time a little to see how LD emerged as a field of practice and profession. As such, the next section briefly explains the historical foundations of LD. If you are keen to gain a more in-depth understanding of LD's historical basis and key theoretical debates in the field, additional readings are signposted at the end of the chapter.[3]

How did Learning Development emerge in higher education?

LD is a relatively new field (Webster, 2023). In the UK HE context, LD-type work has been evident since the 1970s (Hilsdon, 2011). However, several key developments galvanised LD as a profession. First, in 2002, a professional email discussion group, the Learning Development in Higher Education Network (LDHEN), was established (Hilsdon, 2011). This forum enabled practitioners to discuss, debate, and share understandings around students' learning and development. This was followed, in 2005, by the inception of the Centre for Excellence in Teaching and Learning, known as LearnHigher, which was funded by the Higher Education Funding Council for England (HEFCE)[4] (Hilsdon, 2011; Webster, 2023). LearnHigher is a resource bank of free peer-reviewed materials for use in supporting students' learning (ALDinHE, 2024b). In 2007, the Association for Learning Development in Higher Education (ALDinHE) was formed (Hilsdon, 2011). This is a UK-based, though international in-scope, professional membership organisation for LDers or those with an interest in LD. Subsequently, in 2008, the *Journal of Learning Development in Higher Education* (JLDHE) which publishes scholarly research and literature pertinent to LD was established (Hilsdon, 2011).

In the UK, the 1990s saw a drive by Tony Blair's Labour government to increase the proportion of 18- to 30-year-olds participating in HE (Hilsdon, 2011; Webster, 2023). This drive, commonly referred to as the 'widening participation' agenda led to increased numbers of students in HE from 'non-traditional' or underrepresented backgrounds, particularly in newer post-1992 institutions (Hilsdon, 2011). LD developed from this growth in the sector, with its aim to aid students to understand the expectations of academia, thereby playing a key role in enhancing the student experience and feeding into wider institutional concerns around student retention, completion, and progression (Webster, 2023). LD has since shifted in emphasis away from a remedial focus towards a strength-based, non-deficit approach, working with all students, not solely those deemed as 'non-traditional' or lacking readiness or skills for HE (Webster, 2023). However, there is still a perception by some outside the LD community that LD is a remedial service – an additional and sometimes unnecessary add-on, rather than a fundamental and integral part of students' learning (White and Webster, 2023; Johnson and Bishopp-Martin, 2024).

What is 'academic literacies' theory and how does it link to Learning Development?

LD work is strongly influenced by 'academic literacies' theory (see Lea and Street, 1998; Lillis et al., 2015). Academic literacy concerns students' understanding of the skills of academic reading and writing (literacy) required for their discipline. The academic literacies approach adopts a critical and 'socially situated' view of academic reading and writing (Lillis et al., 2015, p. 13). It considers questions of 'power and identity' at all levels of the institution and how these impact 'literacy practices' (2015, p. 13). Adopting this approach, academic literacies can be considered from multiple perspectives including that of the students, lecturers, and the 'institution' itself (2015, p. 13). Critical questions might include: what are students' understanding of disciplinary writing? What do lecturers look for in an effective piece of writing and why? How do lecturers' and students' identities and previous writing experiences impact their understanding of what is expected in academic writing? What are the barriers that students face in developing their academic literacies' understanding? What are the university's expectations around academic writing and how is this communicated to students? Academic literacies theory posits that it is the HE context itself which is 'alienating' and unfamiliar and which should be put under scrutiny rather than the issue being students' 'deficits' or lack of understanding of literacy practices (Johnson and Bishopp-Martin, 2024, p. 17, citing Lillis, 2001). In a similar vein, LD practice takes its own critical stance, acknowledging that it is often the learning context or HE itself which is 'alienating' or 'inadequate' for students (Hilsdon, 2011, p. 17). As such, LD can play a 'scaffolding' or supporting role (Johnson and Bishopp-Martin, 2024, p. 17) in aiding students to 'make sense' of it (ALDinHE, 2024a). For instance, in LD we recognise that there are often unspoken, unwritten, and confusing aspects to being a university student that learners are expected or assumed to know but may not (referred to as the 'hidden curriculum'). Students need to become literate at many levels in the workings of the academy to succeed and LD, through its intermediary role, can aid them to navigate this (Johnson and Bishopp-Martin, 2024).

How do people become learning developers?

> **Reflective task**
>
> - What is your previous educational background and career experience?
> - What led you to become an LDer or, if you are not yet one, what interests you in LD work?

There is currently no set qualification path or entry route to becoming an LDer in HE. LDers often have a previous teaching or training background in schools, colleges, universities, or other educational or work-based settings. Many hold master's level and doctoral degrees. Some LDers work under an academic contract with a research expectation (Bickle et al., 2022), whilst others are employed under a professional services contract. Some also work in a 'hybrid' role as both LDer and subject lecturer (Grayson and Syska, 2024, p. 43). Some LDers work under fixed-term or casual contracts, whilst some are employed under permanent contracts or on an ongoing basis. You will meet LDers who have transitioned into LD from related fields such as English for Academic Purposes (EAP) teaching, librarianship, digital education, counselling, coaching, and educational development roles. Others have arrived at LD through a non-linear, or completely unrelated career or educational route. The diversity of entry routes into LD is a strength of the field, allowing for multiple perspectives about what effective teaching and learning in LD should look like. However, it might also be viewed as a double-edged sword as the lack of a specific entry route can lead to questions about LD's status as a profession.[5]

What do learning developers do on a day-to-day basis?

> **Task**
> - What does a working day as an LDer look like for you? What do you do?
> - Go to the shared ALDinHE collective diary at https://aldinhe.ac.uk/collective-diary/. This is an online diary where on the 15th day of each month, or thereabouts, LDers can write a reflective entry about their day. Browse through two or three entries in the collective diary. If you are unable to access the collective diary, then you can read the example entries in Appendix 1. What types of tasks and activities are mentioned?
> - Can you see similarities between your working day and the entries that you have read?

The role of an LDer is varied and involves complex interactions with students, colleagues, academics, and other professional staff. Maybe today you met with a student (or several) for one-to-one appointments. You may have completed some administrative tasks. Perhaps your day involved developing resources for an upcoming skills workshop. Possibly you spoke with a subject lecturer about the benefits of running some in-class skills sessions, or you worked with other LD colleagues to develop a strategy on how to reach more students. This variety is partly what makes LD an interesting field in which to work. However, it can also make it difficult to get a coherent sense of what doing LD 'well' should look like.

We saw earlier that a significant aspect of doing the LD role is to aid students to develop the academic skills and literacies necessary for them to be successful in HE. This typically relates to the development of academic literacy (reading and writing), planning and organisation, presentation and communication, research, critical thinking, digital, note-taking, and revision skills. However, as much as doing LD encompasses this day-to-day function, it also embodies the way in which we interact with and communicate with students, as emphasised in these reflections by experienced LDers:

> [To do LD means] cheering students on and challenging them in equal measure. Being interested, listening, showing attention, encouraging students to generate their own solutions, and creating space for thinking and reflecting. Supporting innovative approaches to educational and social justice interventions.
>
> Dr Katharine Jewitt, Associate Lecturer,
> The Open University

> [To do LD] is [t]o 'meet' the student close to whatever their starting point is; to open their mind to different perspectives – including their own, the (sometimes imagined or inferred) perspective of the assessment-setter, and everything in-between; to encourage their agency to decide. We are more 'well-travelled guide' than 'all-knowing sage'.
>
> Dr Ian Johnson, Teaching Fellow in Learning Development, University of Portsmouth

These thoughts capture the idea that LD involves much more than the practical elements of the job. It is the entire approach we take to our work with students. It is an ethos that aims to promote students' agency and autonomy, their questioning and critical faculties, and their ability for them to view themselves as empowered learners. It is evident in our championing of students' strengths and abilities. LD done well has the potential to be 'transformative' in the lives of the students we work alongside (Hilsdon, 2011, p. 35). It is both a profession and a 'mindset' (Johnson and Bishopp-Martin, 2024, p. 22) as well as a privilege and responsibility. Such ideas might seem abstract to you. This is where the guiding ALDinHE community-driven values can help to anchor and direct your practice. We will turn to look at these values and consider their meaning in the next section.

What are the guiding values of Learning Development?

A starting point for thinking about why LDers work in the way they do is to explore LD's community-driven set of values. These values emerged from a 2017 keynote speech at the ALDinHE annual conference delivered by Buckley and Briggs (Johnson and Bishopp-Martin, 2024, p. 16). The values are listed on the ALDinHE website, a UK-based professional LD body, and espouse the following as a guide to what underpins effective LD practice:

1. Working in partnership with students and staff to make sense and get the most out of HE.
2. Embracing and respecting diverse learners through critical pedagogy and practice.
3. Adapting, sharing, and advocating effective LD practice to promote student learning.
4. Critical self-reflection, ongoing learning, and a commitment to professional development.
5. Commitment to a scholarly approach and research related to LD.

(ALDinHE, 2024a)

> **Task**
> - What is your understanding of these five ALDinHE values?
> - List your five core values. These are principles that are important to you in your professional or personal life (e.g. teamwork, independence, integrity, kindness). Are your values reflected in the ALDinHE values?

The first value is fundamental to LD practice. It emphasises working 'in partnership' with students and staff. This is to enable students to 'make sense of' and 'get the most out of HE'. Underpinning this value is the idea that LD can have a tangible benefit on students' experiences of HE, particularly in helping them to become familiar with what might be unfamiliar. Getting the most out of HE can of course mean different things to individual students. For many, it will mean passing their degree or programme of study and moving or transitioning into a desired career. For others it might mean developing in confidence, communication, and social skills. For others still it may mean feeling a sense of belonging and community during their studies. Being aware of students' purpose(s) and respectful of meeting them at the stage they are at is a crucial element of working successfully in partnership with them. For instance, mature students may have different priorities to 18-year-olds who have progressed to HE straight from college or sixth form studies. Keeping the students' needs and motivations at the forefront can act as the driver for offering relevant and personalised LD support.

Value two refers to 'embracing' and 'respecting diverse learners'. It indicates that this should happen through 'critical pedagogy and practice'. What might this mean? First, your work as an LDer will involve working with students of different social, cultural, and linguistic characteristics and with a range of learning needs. Being respectful of and 'embracing' diversity is important so that all students can access your service in a way that is helpful and meaningful to them. This might entail, for instance, ensuring that learning materials are easily accessible for students with auditory difficulties. It might mean making sure that the language you use during workshops is inclusive and not derogatory or stereotypical such that students feel a sense of belonging and respect. Adopting a questioning or critical stance to your LD practice and pedagogy can aid you to be deliberate about the choices you make and to be conscious of the impact such choices might have on learners. Chapter 8 will continue to consider what value two might look like in practice.

The third value, 'adapting, sharing, and advocating effective learning development practice to promote student learning' highlights the collaborative nature of LD work. We know that LD is often undervalued or misunderstood by some working in the wider HE sector (Verity and Trowler, 2011; White and Webster, 2023). By sharing good practice with colleagues in our institutions and beyond and articulating the need for LD, we seek to improve perceptions of LD and its impact on students.

Value four is an important one. It refers to 'critical self-reflection, ongoing learning, and a commitment to professional development'. As LDers, we aim to adopt a critically reflective stance to our work, seeking opportunities for developing our professional skills through learning and continuing professional development (CPD). The underlying reason for this is to improve practice and for our own sense of professionalism. Chapter 9 considers this value and prospects for professional development in more depth.

Value five concerns a 'commitment to a scholarly approach and research related to LD'. As you learn more about the role, you might start to read the literature on LD in publications such as the *JLDHE* which offers research papers, case studies, opinion pieces, and other scholarly commentary. You might also wish to get involved in conducting research, writing for publication, or speaking at conferences in a specialist area of your practice. Chapter 9 considers some of the potential avenues for professional development in this area.

Your daily practice will likely be underpinned by these five values (and your own personal values) in the way you 'do' LD and in the everyday professional decisions that you make. For example, a focus of mine over my first few years as an LDer was to ensure that all students, regardless of disability, could access our services. My office was located on the second floor of an old building with steep, winding steps, and no lift – inaccessible to those with mobility impairments. I made a simple adjustment so that students could meet with me in an accessible space on campus. Whilst it was not taken by me consciously with it in mind, this decision reflects value two, that of 'embracing' and 'respecting diverse learners'. The decisions you make in your role *are* value-laden regardless of whether these values are at the forefront of your mind.

Throughout this book, you will see reference to the ALDinHE values. By beginning to articulate your thoughts and understandings of what these values mean, perhaps in conversation with colleagues, you will begin to clarify whether aspects of your practice reflect these. This does not mean to say that the ALDinHE values themselves should not be the subject of 'scrutiny' and questioning (Dhillon, 2024, p. 112). Indeed, it will be important to think critically about your stance in relation to them and how this impacts your practice. At times, you may feel that your work 'falls short' of these guiding principles. This is okay. We are humans working closely with other humans and will make mistakes or face unpredictable and difficult situations in our practice. This book will consider ways to manage such challenges. Working as an LDer also involves giving a lot of self, so in Chapter 8 we look at practical suggestions for looking after yourself in your professional role.

What is the best way to 'do' Learning Development?

The answer to this question (frustratingly perhaps) is that there is no one best way to do LD. You will find research-informed approaches demonstrating good pedagogical practice provided in the LD and HE scholarly literature. There is also access to a vast range of teaching ideas from colleagues in more informal contexts such as on the LDHEN JiscMail professional email discussion list[6] and teaching and learning resource banks such as LearnHigher (ALDinHE, 2024b). As we have seen, LD work is also underpinned by the five community-driven values that can inform your day-to-day work, and which can be used as a framework to assess whether your practice is pedagogically sound. However, even with this understanding of what works well, this book does not propose one 'best' approach. Given the complexity of working in HE, and the diversity of students with whom we work, a prescriptive guide would be particularly meaningless and would soon be invalid. Rather, this book takes as its stance that the practice of LD is multi-dimensional, relationship-driven, symbiotic, and evolving. It is also context specific. Given this, there is much scope as a new LDer to forge your own unique, pedagogically informed, way of doing LD that works for your circumstance. This book therefore offers ideas in relation to the primary student-facing aspects of the role that you can use, adapt, refine (or disregard) for your specific situation.

Where can I learn more about the context of Learning Development?

In this chapter, we began by considering what LD is and how it emerged as a field. We saw that LD is a distinct profession and can also be considered more broadly as a 'mindset' (Johnson and Bishopp-Martin, 2024, p. 22). We also saw that LDers enter the profession from a diversity of backgrounds. Reading this chapter should have brought to light some of the wider concerns in the field and the underlying rationale and values that drive LD work. You should now hopefully have a clearer sense of what doing LD involves. It should be apparent that the nature of LD practice is context specific but that the community-driven values can act to guide your work regardless of institutional difference. We have seen that LD is a responsive, emerging, and exciting field in which to work but one with its own unique challenges.

This book focuses on the practical aspects of the LD role. However, the practice of LD cannot, and should not, be completely removed from its theoretical foundations. We can think of this as praxis, that is, our practice and how it intertwines with theory. This chapter has therefore provided an overview of the historical drivers for the development of LD as a field and profession so that you can begin to understand some wider debates and contextual issues. However, it serves only as an initial introduction. If you are interested in learning more about the origins of LD and in further exploring its theoretical underpinnings, then a good place to start is with the edited collection *Learning*

Development in Higher Education (see Hartley et al., 2011). Chapter 1 in that collection is titled *What is Learning Development?* and explores how LD emerged and looks forward to how it might evolve. Another good critical text is *How to be a Learning Developer in Higher Education* (see Syska and Buckley, 2024) which is a collection of edited chapters by different LD contributors. Chapter 1 focuses on *Theory in Learning Development* and Chapter 2 provides a detailed analysis of the *Conceptual Foundations in Learning Development*.

We saw earlier in this chapter that LD work is developmental by nature. Whatever your starting point, this developmental ethos also applies to your growth as an LDer. You are not expected to know everything there is to know about LD. Indeed, similarly to the students we work with, some of the practices and conventions of the HE sector may at first seem bewildering and alien which can lead you to question your self-efficacy. As a starting point, this book should aid with increasing your awareness of the key functions of LD work such that you feel more confident about the value you provide. Part of this will be to understand what it means to work in HE. Therefore, in the next chapter, we will consider what a university is, what it is for, and outline some contemporary issues impacting HE. The remaining chapters in the book then turn to focus on the practicalities of undertaking the role.

Summary

- This chapter began by considering what Learning Development (LD) is and what it entails. We saw that LD is complex and that it involves a range of tasks and responsibilities including 'teaching', 'research', 'tutoring', and the development of materials (Hilsdon, 2011, p. 14).
- The chapter situated LD as a 'third space' role (Whitchurch, 2008) having both an academic and professional services remit and playing an intermediary function.
- It outlined the historical foundations of LD noting how it stemmed from, in the UK context, the widening participation agenda.
- It highlighted the developmental nature of LD practice and its key theoretical influences including Lea and Street's (1998) 'academic literacies' approach and rejection of a traditional study skills or deficit model.
- The chapter considered how people enter LD and what Learning Developers (LDers) do on a day-to-day basis. It framed this within the five LD community-driven values as espoused by the Association for Learning Development in Higher Education (ALDinHE). It began to explore what these values mean and how they might emanate in practice.
- It emphasised that there is no single best approach to do LD and that whilst LD practice is context specific our work can be guided by the community-driven values.
- Finally, the chapter signposted to key texts to learn more about the historical and theoretical foundations of LD.

Notes

1 Hilsdon (2011, p. 14) quote used by permission of Bloomsbury Publishing Plc.
2 Some major theories of learning that you may be aware of include behaviourism, constructivism, and cognitivism, but there are many others. See 'Ideas for further reading' for a selection of texts discussing and explaining learning theories in depth.
3 The Association for Learning Development in Higher Education (ALDinHE) has created a 'Learning Development Scholarship Library' with key readings to enhance your understanding of LD. It is available at: https://aldinhe.ac.uk/resource-bank/scholarship-library/.
4 The HEFCE has since been replaced by the Office for Students (OfS) which is the regulatory body for universities and colleges providing higher education qualifications in England. More on the OfS in Chapter 3.
5 There is some debate as to whether LD might be better thought of as a community of practice – a group of practitioners with a shared concern about enhancing the learning experience for students (see Murray and Glass (2011) under 'Ideas for further reading').
6 JiscMail lists can be accessed at https://www.jiscmail.ac.uk/. These are professional email discussion lists for practitioners in the education and research community. It is a UK-based site but has many subscribers worldwide. The lists cover a range of professional interests including the Learning Development in Higher Education Network (LDHEN). You can sign up to as many JiscMail email lists as you wish.

References

ALDinHE (2024a) *About ALDinHE*. Available at: https://aldinhe.ac.uk/about-aldinhe/ (Accessed: 9 April 2024).

ALDinHE (2024b) *LearnHigher*. Available at: https://aldinhe.ac.uk/learnhigher/ (Accessed: 9 April 2024).

Altunbas, H. G., Guo, X., Liu, Y., Knowler, H. and Wright, T. (2025) 'Can education heal? Staff and students exploring reparative pedagogies in the context of institutional harms in higher education', *Journal of Learning Development in Higher Education [Preprint]*, 35. https://doi.org/10.47408/jldhe.vi35.1337

Bickle, E., Allen, S. and Mayer, M. (2022) 'Learning development 2030', *Journal of Learning Development in Higher Education [Preprint]*, 25. https://doi.org/10.47408/jldhe.vi25.972

Briscoe, H. and Olson, C. (2024) 'Who are we? An autoethnographic investigation into professional role identity of the Learning Developer', *Journal of Learning Development in Higher Education*, 32. https://doi.org/10.47408/jldhe.vi32.1430

Dhillon, S. (2024) 'Critical self-reflection in learning development', in A. Syska and C. Buckley (eds) *How to be a Learning Developer in Higher Education: Critical Perspectives, Community and Practice*. Abingdon: Routledge, 109–117.

Eyre, J. and Slawson, T. (2018) 'Dramatising learning development: Towards an understanding without definition', *Journal of Learning Development in Higher Education [Preprint]*. https://doi.org/10.47408/jldhe.v0i0.472

Grayson, N. and Syska, A. (2024) 'Hybrid learning developers: Between the discipline and the third space', in A. Syska and C. Buckley (eds) *How to be a Learning Developer in Higher Education: Critical Perspectives, Community and Practice*. Abingdon: Routledge, 43–50.

Hartley, P., Hilsdon, J., Keenan, C., Sinfield, S. and Verity, M. (eds) (2011) *Learning Development in Higher Education*. Basingstoke: Palgrave Macmillan.

Hilsdon, J. (2011) 'What is learning development?', in P. Hartley, J. Hilsdon, C. Keenan, S. Sinfield and M. Verity (eds) *Learning Development in Higher Education*. Basingstoke: Palgrave Macmillan (Red Globe Press), 13–27.

Huzar, T. J. (2025) 'Practising vulnerability; presuming equality: Towards a pedagogy of care', *Journal of Learning Development in Higher Education [Preprint]*, 35. https://doi.org/10.47408/jldhe.vi35.1349

Johnson, I. and Bishopp-Martin, S. (2024) 'Conceptual foundations in learning development', in A. Syska and C. Buckley (eds) *How to be a Learning Developer in Higher Education: Critical Perspectives, Community and Practice*. Abingdon: Routledge, 15–24.

Lea, M. R. and Street, B. V. (1998) 'Student writing in higher education: An academic literacies approach', *Studies in Higher Education*, 23(2), 157–172. https://doi.org/10.1080/03075079812331380364

Lillis, T. (2001) *Student Writing: Access, Regulation and Desire*. London: Routledge.

Lillis, T., Harrington, K., Lea, M. R. and Mitchell, S. (eds) (2015) *Working with Academic Literacies: Case Studies Towards Transformative Practice*. SC: Parlor Press.

Murray, L. and Glass, B. (2011) 'Learning development in higher education – community of practice or profession?', in P. Hartley, J. Hilsdon, C. Keenan, S. Sinfield and M. Verity (eds) *Learning Development in Higher Education*. Basingstoke: Palgrave Macmillan, 28–39.

Oxford English Dictionary (2025) *Learning*. Available at: https://www.oed.com/dictionary/learning_n?tab=meaning_and_use (Accessed: 9 April 2025).

Sinfield, S., Holley, D., Burns, T., Hoskins, K., O'Neill, P. and Harrington, K. (2011) 'Raising the student voice: Learning development as socio-political practice', in P. Hartley, J. Hilsdon, C. Keenan, S. Sinfield and M. Verity (eds) *Learning Development in Higher Education*. Basingstoke: Palgrave Macmillan, 53–63.

Syska, A. and Buckley, C. (eds) (2024) *How to be a Learning Developer in Higher Education: Critical Perspectives, Community and Practice*. Abingdon: Routledge.

Verity, M. and Trowler, P. (2011) 'Looking back and looking into the future', in P. Hartley, J. Hilsdon, C. Keenan, S. Sinfield and M. Verity (eds) *Learning Development in Higher Education*. Basingstoke: Palgrave Macmillan, 241–252.

Webster, H. (2023) 'The five Ps of LD: Using formulation in learning development work for a student-centred approach to study skills', *Journal of University Teaching & Learning Practice*, 20(4). https://doi.org/10.53761/1.20.4.07

Whitchurch, C. (2008) 'Shifting identities and blurring boundaries: The emergence of third space professionals in UK higher education', *Higher Education Quarterly*, 62(4), 377–396. https://doi.org/10.1111/j.1468-2273.2008.00387.x

White, S. and Webster, H. (2023) 'Hey you! They're calling you Tinkerbell! What are you going to do about it?', *Journal of Learning Development in Higher Education* [Preprint], 29. https://doi.org/10.47408/jldhe.vi29.1120

Wingate, U. (2006) 'Doing away with "study skills"', *Teaching in Higher Education*, 11(4), 457–469. https://doi.org/10.1080/13562510600874268

Zamora, M. and Bali, M. (2025) 'From socially just care to socially just distributed ecosystems of care', *Journal of Learning Development in Higher Education* [Preprint], 35. https://doi.org/10.47408/jldhe.vi35.1333

Ideas for further reading

Conceptualisations of Learning Development

Hilsdon, J. (2011) 'What is learning development?', in P. Hartley, J. Hilsdon, C. Keenan, S. Sinfield and M. Verity (eds) *Learning Development in Higher Education*. Basingstoke: Palgrave Macmillan (Red Globe Press), 13–27.

Johnson, I. and Bishopp-Martin, S. (2024) 'Conceptual foundations in learning development', in A. Syska and C. Buckley (eds) *How to Be a Learning Developer in Higher Education: Critical Perspectives, Community and Practice*. Abingdon: Routledge, 15–24.

Murray, L. and Glass, B. (2011) 'Learning development in higher education – community of practice or profession?', in P. Hartley, J. Hilsdon, C. Keenan, S. Sinfield and M. Verity (eds) *Learning Development in Higher Education*. Basingstoke: Palgrave Macmillan, 28–39.

Syska, A. and Buckley, C. (eds) (2024) *How to Be a Learning Developer in Higher Education: Critical Perspectives, Community and Practice*. Abingdon: Routledge.

Wingate, U. (2006) 'Doing away with "study skills"', *Teaching in Higher Education*, 11(4), 457–469. https://doi.org/10.1080/13562510600874268

Academic Literacies

Lillis, T. (2019) '"Academic literacies": Sustaining a critical space on writing in academia', *Journal of Learning Development in Higher Education*, 15, 1–18. https://doi.org/10.47408/jldhe.v0i15.565

The 'Third Space' and Learning Development practice

Whitchurch, C. (2012) *Reconstructing Identities in Higher Education: The Rise of 'Third Space' Professionals*. Abingdon: Routledge.

White, S. (2025) 'On third space and critical paralysis: The case for a pragmatic conception of third space to advance Learning Development in higher education', *Journal of Learning Development in Higher Education [Preprint]*, 33. https://doi.org/10.47408/jldhe.vi33.1260

Learning theories

Drew, C. (2024, 12 May) *Every Major Learning Theory (Explained in 5 Minutes)* [YouTube]. Available at: https://youtu.be/SH15sqpqy_Q?si=SDezEenjhf_mqvJN (Accessed: 2 August 2025).

Giannoukos, G. (2024) 'Main learning theories in education', *European Journal of Contemporary Education and E-Learning*, 2, 93–100. https://doi.org/10.59324/ejceel.2024.2(5).06

Illeris, K. (ed) (2009) *Contemporary Theories of Learning: Learning Theorists . . . in Their Own Words*. Abingdon: Routledge.

Schunk, D. (2013) *Learning Theories: An Educational Perspective: Pearson New International Edition*, 6th edn. Essex: Pearson.

Learning Development: Looking forward

Hood, S. and Powell, E. (2024) 'Raising the profile of learning development: Thinking forwards', *Journal of Learning Development in Higher Education [Preprint]*, 32. https://doi.org/10.47408/jldhe.vi32.1416

Chapter 3

New to Learning Development in Higher Education

This chapter provides

- An outline of the key function(s) of a university.
- An overview of the role of regulatory bodies such as, in England, the Office for Students (OfS).
- A 'who's who' of leadership roles in a university and their function.
- An outline of some topical issues affecting the higher education (HE) sector.
- A provocation to the reader as to what role Learning Development (LD) should play amidst these complexities.

New to Learning Development in Higher Education

It is 2018. I am a new Learning Developer (LDer) sitting in a three-hour school meeting. There are about 20 other academic and professional services colleagues in attendance. Unfamiliar acronyms and words are being thrown about – 'OfS this' and 'QAA that'[1] – and I am focused on biting my breakfast croissant delicately so as not to make any sound or to drop any obvious crumbs on the oak table. An academic asks me a question, something to do with 'student engagement'. Hands trembling, I plaster on a smile and answer 'Yes'. I get strange looks and shift uncomfortably in my seat. I have no clue what it is that I have just been asked or, to be frank, what this meeting is about. Queue tumbleweed.

The above is not a good look in a professional context. To establish credibility amongst colleagues and students, you will need to become familiar with the practices, language, and norms of working in the HE sector or at the HE level.[2] It will be important to form an understanding of the primary function(s) of a university and how your role fits into this. You will also need to be aware of topical issues that are impacting the sector and how this affects your work as an LDer. If you are new to working in an HE context, acclimatising to all this can be difficult.

This chapter sets out to develop your awareness of what working in HE entails. It begins by explaining what a university 'is' and what it 'does'. Given that universities are increasingly regulated, we look at the OfS, the regulator for institutions in England, as an example of its function. The chapter then outlines issues affecting HE, including the 'marketisation' of the sector, and the impact of emerging generative artificial intelligence (GenAI) technologies on LD practice. The focus is on highlighting some of the practical implications of such matters on your day-to-day work rather than to offer detailed debate or theoretical exposition on these issues.[3] The chapter refers mainly to the UK context – regulatory practices and sector concerns may differ internationally. Whilst the ideas here should provide an indication as to the nature of what working in HE entails, it is a complex sector, and familiarisation will come through your immersion into the culture and workings of your specific institution.

Working in the HE sector can feel very unfamiliar as a new LDer. As a starting point, it is important to have a basic sense of what universities do and so the next section provides an indication of their main purpose. However, the function of a university is much more complex than the following part suggests: HE is contested terrain and there are ongoing debates as to what a university should be for. The chapter therefore ends by considering some of these tensions and points to additional readings should you wish to learn more about these wider discussions.

> **Task**
>
> - Have you previously worked in HE or a university?
> - How would you describe the role of a university? What do universities do?

What do universities do?

Most universities in the UK are classed as charitable bodies though there are also a small number of private institutions (Stephenson and Dandridge, 2019). However, universities in the UK are not governed or regulated in the same way as a typical charity. They are considered 'exempt' charities meaning that they are not required to register with the Charity Commission which regulates charities (HowCharitiesWork, 2023). Instead, universities are regulated by independent bodies (more on this later in the chapter). Institutions receive most of their income from tuition fees, research grants, funding from the government, and other sources such as donations (QAA, 2018; Universities UK, 2023). Their primary function is to provide education and undergo research and scholarship for the social good rather than to make profit (Synge, 2023).

Universities (and further education (FE) colleges) in the UK are entitled to award degrees if they have degree awarding powers and those that do are referred to as 'recognised bodies' (QAA, 2018, p. 2). Institutions in Scotland, Wales, and Northern Ireland are granted degree awarding powers under Royal Charter by the Privy Council in consultation with the Advisory Committee on Degree Awarding Powers which is part of the Quality Assurance Agency for Higher Education (QAA) an independent membership body monitoring the quality of HE (QAA, 2018; QAA 2023). In England, the Privy Council originally granted degree awarding powers, but this is now the responsibility of the OfS (QAA, 2018). Table 3.1 lists type of degree by level and the required power necessary to award them for the four UK nations.

The Framework for Higher Education Qualifications of UK Degree-Awarding Bodies (FHEQ) published by the QAA provides a set of 'sector-wide' standards and requirements for HE qualifications (QAA, 2024a). HE institutions with degree awarding powers in Scotland, Wales, and Northern Ireland must adhere to the FHEQ standards (QAA, 2024a). In England, institutions registered with and regulated by the OfS must also meet these 'sector-wide' standards as part of the conditions of their registration (QAA, 2024a).

Table 3.1 UK degrees by level and the powers to award them.

Type of Degree	Level in UK Qualifications Frameworks		Powers Necessary
	England, Wales, and Northern Ireland	Scotland	
Doctoral degree (or doctorate)	Level 8	Level 12	Research degree awarding powers
Research master's degree	Level 7	Level 11	Research degree awarding powers
Taught master's degree	Level 7	Level 11	Taught degree awarding powers
Bachelor's degree with honours	Level 6	Level 10	Taught degree awarding powers
Ordinary bachelor's degree	Level 6	Level 9	Taught degree awarding powers
Foundation degree	Level 5		Foundation degree awarding powers

Source: QAA, 2018, p. 2; reproduced with permission *from The Right to Award UK Degrees*, 2018, Quality Assurance Agency for Higher Education.

Who regulates universities?

In England, as mentioned earlier, it is the OfS that regulates universities (Universities UK, 2023). The devolved nations of the UK have similar regulatory bodies: the Scottish Funding Council (SFC) for Scottish universities (SFC, 2023; Universities UK, 2023); in Wales, the Higher Education Funding Council for Wales (HEFCW); and in Northern Ireland, the Higher Education Division of the Department for the Economy (Universities UK, 2023). LD is practised widely in Australian and Canadian institutions and increasingly across South African universities. In South Africa, universities are regulated by the Council on Higher Education and the South African Qualifications Authority (Department of Higher Education and Training, 2024). The Tertiary Education Quality and Standards Agency regulates Australian universities, and, in Canada, universities are regulated by their relevant province (Universities Canada, 2025). In the next section, we will look at the OfS as an example of the regulatory body for universities in England. Regulatory bodies for institutions in the devolved UK nations and those internationally will differ in their practice and requirements.

Task

- Where is your institution based? Who is its regulator?
- Find the regulator's website and go to the 'About' section. What is their purpose?

What does a regulator do?

The OfS originated under the Higher Education and Research Act 2017. It is a 'non-departmental public body' answerable to the UK Parliament (OfS, 2025a) and is supported by the Department for Education, the ministerial department of the UK government responsible for education from early years to tertiary level (Amos, 2023). Registration with the OfS is optional; however, English HE providers need to register if they want to call themselves a 'university' and if they wish to have the power to award degrees (Institute for Government, 2023; OfS, 2025a). The OfS works in the interests of students. Its primary aim is to ensure that institutions meet their conditions of registration such that students have a 'high-quality academic experience' and 'receive value for money' (OfS, 2025a). Universities[4] that are registered must fulfil certain conditions including providing data when requested (OfS, 2025b). These conditions are listed in Table 3.2.

If your institution is regulated by the OfS, it is likely that conditions A and B will have most direct bearing on your role as an LDer. Under condition

Table 3.2 Office for Students' Conditions of registration[a]

Condition	What Is the Condition?
A	Access and participation for students from all backgrounds
B	Quality, reliable standards and positive outcomes for all students
C	Protecting the interests of all students
D	Financial sustainability
E	Good governance
F	Information for students
G	Accountability for fees and funding

Source: OfS, 2025b.
[a]Contains public sector information licensed under the Open Government Licence v3.0.

A, registered universities (or FE colleges) are required to have an access and participation plan (OfS, 2025c). These plans stipulate how institutions will provide equal access and opportunity to students from 'disadvantaged' backgrounds (OfS, 2025c). As an LDer, you may be directly involved in working with colleagues responsible for access and participation; for instance, by contributing to initiatives or providing relevant data about use of your service that may feed into access plans. Under condition B, institutions must provide quality education and 'positive outcomes' (OfS, 2025b). Condition B2 specifies that universities must provide access to 'resources and support' and 'effective engagement', and B3 refers to 'successful outcomes' for students (OfS, 2025c, p. 1). B3 outcomes are set out as 'baseline standards' (OfS, 2025d) that universities must meet in relation to four areas:

- *Continuation and completion* (measures students moving on from year to year and those successfully finishing their programme).
- *Degree outcomes* (measures degree classification, e.g. First/2:1/2:2).
- *Awarding gaps* (measures different outcomes between students of diverse backgrounds).
- *Progression* (related to students' outcomes post degree in relation to employability and further study).

(OfS, 2025c, p. 1)

Registered universities in England who fail to fulfil the requirements of their registration may be subject to heavy fines, investigations, disqualification, closure, limitations to the numbers of students recruited, and other serious consequences (OfS, 2025b). The stakes for institutions and their members are, therefore, extremely high.

The OfS also runs the Teaching Excellence Framework (TEF). This is a quality assessment scheme open to institutions across the UK (not solely England) provided they meet the baseline quality standards for their home nation (OfS, 2025e). The TEF 'assesses and rates' institutions against a 'minimum' set of standards regarding quality and student outcomes (OfS, 2025e). Universities provide data as evidence and once assessed are given a rating from the lowest, 'requires improvement', to 'Gold', the highest (OfS, 2025e). As an LDer, if your university participates in the TEF scheme, you may be asked to provide data on your teaching to feed into evidence for a TEF submission; for instance, demographic data on who attends your workshops and tutorials or student feedback on the use of your service. In addition, the OfS administers the national student survey (NSS) which collates feedback from final year undergraduate students across all UK HE institutions and colleges about the quality of their course (OfS, 2025f). Data from the NSS are collected and made publicly available on an annual basis.

The Research Excellence Framework (REF) is another quality assessment scheme run by the four UK HE funding bodies: Research England, the Scottish Funding Council (SFC), the Higher Education Council for Wales (HEFCW), and the Department for the Economy, Northern Ireland (UKRI, 2025). The REF scheme rates and assesses universities for excellence in relation to research (OfS, 2025e). For universities, such schemes are high stakes. For instance, having a TEF rating enables universities in England to charge a higher tuition fee than that set by the government[5] and an REF rating can impact the level of research funding allocated to a university (OfS, 2025e).

Given such regulatory requirements and external measures of performance, it should be clear that universities tend to be data driven. We will come to see in later chapters that a key part of your role as an LDer will also involve collating and evaluating data to provide evidence of the 'impact' of your service. This data will inform and feed into wider institutional concerns around student outcomes and experience. Chapters 4–6 include suggestions for how you might go about showing the impact of your work.[6]

Who oversees what in a university?

It is helpful to have a basic understanding of who oversees what in a university context. Table 3.3 lists common administrative leadership roles in a university and their typical function.

On a day-to-day basis, you are unlikely to work directly with senior leadership staff. You will though encounter Heads of Faculty or School, and programme/module leads in wider staff meetings and in strategic discussions around LD provision. Alongside this, you will work with staff with varied remits and responsibilities. This will include academic and professional services colleagues such as those in administrative roles and information technology. To familiarise yourself with what other colleagues do, it can be helpful to attend any sessions of relevance to your role that are arranged by staff in different teams. For instance, you might attend training, webinars, and meetings with colleagues working in access and engagement, wellbeing and mental health, disability services, digital education, and so forth. In these forums, it

Table 3.3 Common leadership roles in a university and their function.

Role	Typical Function
University Chancellor	Honorary head/leader of a university
Vice Chancellor/Vice Principal	Day-to-day and administrative head/leader of a university
Pro/Deputy Vice Chancellor	Senior head/leader of a specific area (e.g. Pro Vice Chancellor for research/education/student experience)
Governing body/Board of Governors/Board of Trustees	Part of the governance structure of a university. Provides strategic oversight, for instance, in relation to finances and regulatory compliance
Academic Senate	Part of the governance structure of a university. Provides strategic leadership for all academic concerns including research and education quality
Registrar/Registry Office	Responsible at a senior/strategic level for the administration of the university (e.g. student records/course data)
Dean/Head	Head of a specific remit/area of work (e.g. Head of School/Dean of Education/Undergraduate Lead)
Programme Lead	Academic head of a specific programme or course (e.g. Programme Lead for the BA in English)
Subject/Module Lead	Academic head of a specific module/subject (e.g. Module Lead for Legal Systems)

is fine to ask questions of colleagues' work if you need clarification. It shows interest and it will help you to get a sense of what other teams do and how you might work alongside them. We will consider ways to work effectively with staff (and students) in Chapter 8.

What are some topical issues impacting the HE sector?

As a new LDer, your primary focus will be on acclimatising to the role and improving your day-to-day practice. However, as well as these immediate priorities, it is important to be aware of wider concerns impacting HE. Here I outline in brief some topical issues, namely, the impact of neoliberalist thinking on the sector, financial precarity of institutions, and the rapid emergence of GenAI and digital technologies. This serves only as a starting point. Reading publications such as WonkHE, Times Higher Education (THE), or University World News is a way of staying aware of matters impacting the sector as these provide in-depth analysis and commentary.

You will hear the term 'neoliberalism' used frequently when working in HE. Neoliberalist thinking emphasises individualism and competitiveness. It is 'a free-market ideology based on individual liberty and limited government that connect[s] human freedom to the actions of the rational, self-interested in the competitive marketplace' (Ball, 2021, p. 2, citing Jones, 2016, p. 2). Ball (a sociologist of education) argues that, in the UK, successive educational policies have created a *neoliberal education system . . . driven and justified by results/outputs rather than any moral principles*' (Ball, 2021, p. 210). 'Outputs' include, for instance, workplace 'readiness' – the skills students leave university with that will enable them to function effectively at work in a capitalist system. From a neoliberal perspective, universities are businesses, selling a commodity (education), and competing for scarce resources (the students or 'customers') to retain market share. This commodification of HE has prompted much debate as to whether the idealist purposes of a university education – to 'advance knowledge and scholarship' for the 'public good' (Synge, 2023) – are still being achieved.

Increased competition in a neoliberal system has also had direct bearing on universities' finances. We saw earlier that, in the UK, universities get most of their income from tuition fees, research grants, and government funding (Universities UK, 2023). The combined impact of having to compete for students and research funding, reductions in student admissions following the COVID-19 pandemic, changes to visa requirements affecting the number of international students, inflationary pressures, and less public funding, has left many HEIs in the UK in a financially precarious position and, at the extreme end, unable to continue operating and having to exit the 'market' (Jarvis, 2024; THE, 2025). This is a sector-wide problem (OfS, 2024; THE, 2025). Many universities have simply not been able to bring in enough income resulting in significant deficits and leading to steps to cut costs, often through redundancies, employment of staff on cheaper, 'precarious' fixed-term or zero-hours contracts, and reduction to services (THE, 2025).

In the UK, neoliberalist thinking has been partly fuelled by increased globalisation – the growing interrelationship between countries in relation to its companies, goods, people, information, and technologies (Oxford Reference, 2025) – with successive governments looking to international competitors, systems, and workplaces, and prioritising how to retain competitiveness in the global marketplace (Ball, 2021). One consequence of globalisation for universities has been the need to consider how to ensure that they are providing education that meets the needs of diverse students (Tikly, 2025). Wider global concerns such as worldwide conflicts, climate change, advancements in technology, and polarised political views have also led to questions about the role of HE in a changing world. Should the aim be to prepare students for employability and to meet the demands of the economic workforce or should the emphasis be on developing critically, socially informed citizens well placed to address such societal concerns? These are big questions and the more you become familiar with working in HE, the more confidently you will be able to articulate your stance in relation to such issues. In the next section, we turn to look at another pressing concern in the sector: the impact of GenAI technologies on teaching and learning practices.

What is all this talk about GenAI?

There seems to be no escape from the noise about GenAI. It permeates our news reports, clutters our professional (and personal) inboxes with calls to attend webinars, talks, and symposia on the topic, and seems to involve two quite polarised camps: those who embrace it wholeheartedly and those who are sceptical, suspicious, or afraid of it (D'Agostino, 2023). It has been hailed as the next major revolution in technology (Time, 2023) and regardless of whether you have strong feeling towards it or not, it is difficult to disregard the constant discourse around its use and misuse.

Artificial intelligence (AI) has existed in usable form since the 1950s (Maryville University, 2023). However, since the emergence, in particular, of GenAI technologies like ChatGPT, Claude and Quill Bot, which can generate content such as text, images, and video, there has been a proliferation of debate, discussion, and, at times, panic over what this might mean for HE as we know it (QAA, 2024b). As HE adjusts to the rapid changes and advancements in such technologies, questions abound concerning the impact on assessment, academic integrity, critical thinking, and the ethics surrounding its use. How might students use and misuse such technologies? What might the effect be on assessments? Will students be aware of how GenAI can recreate and perpetuate existing inequalities and societal stereotypes? Will universities be necessary in a GenAI age? Will developments in GenAI lead to a growing digital literacy divide? Can GenAI level the playing field for students with specific learning differences (SpLDs) and/or disabilities?

Debate and discussion have not wavered, but many universities, whilst initially having a piecemeal or knee jerk reaction to these issues, have now adopted institutional-level approaches to dealing with the impact of GenAI technologies. For instance, universities have created GenAI policies and guidance for students and staff, and many universities and professional bodies such as ALDinHE have established specific working groups or committees to debate, discuss, and devise solutions for addressing the issues GenAI raises. These are big concerns and given the relative newness of such technological developments we cannot yet be certain of what the long-standing impact might be. Regardless of where you stand in relation to the use of GenAI, such significant developments require you to think about the potential impact on your practice as an LDer.

> **Task**
> - Have you used GenAI tools in your LD practice, for instance, to create materials?
> - How confident do you feel about using GenAI tools?
> - What do you think (if anything) might be the main impact of GenAI on your work with students and staff?

GenAI advancements will impact many aspects of your LD work. For instance, you will need to consider how to approach student questions and concerns around legitimate uses of GenAI tools and how to avoid plagiarism. In your consultative-style work with staff, you may be asked for guidance about appropriate uses of GenAI for assessment and about how to design GenAI 'proof' or 'resilient' assignments – if such a thing exists. In your development of learning and teaching materials, you will need to consider the ethics around using GenAI tools to create resources. Regarding research and scholarly activity, you may need to think about how to keep updated with the vast and changing literature on the topic. With CPD, you might wish to explore seminars and conferences on the topic, and to share good practice or examples of its use with colleagues in your institution and beyond. All this does not mean that you must necessarily be an 'expert' in the use of GenAI. However, it is advisable to develop a general awareness of how GenAI is affecting the sector and how HE institutions (and other LD colleagues) are responding. This could involve, for instance, attending digital education training or keeping up to date with discussion on the Learning Development in Higher Education (LDHEN) or Staff Educational Development Association (SEDA) on JiscMail which are professional email lists where colleagues across the sector ask questions, and share practice and ideas.[7] You might also think about joining the ALDinHE GenAI Working Group if this is an area of interest to you.[8]

It will be important to think about whether and how you choose to engage with GenAI tools in your own LD practice. You may welcome all such use of new tools and actively experiment with what is on offer. On the other hand, such tools may be unethical to you, and you might choose to avoid their use or promotion. You might be fearful of the technologies and feel reluctant to engage with them. Perhaps you are sceptical but interested in exploring the options and functionality of GenAI tools for use in teaching and learning. Even if the idea of using GenAI tools does not sit well with you, try to develop some level of understanding of its capabilities, as many students are engaging with such technologies. You can then ask yourself critical questions to decide how and whether to use

GenAI for teaching and learning purposes. Questions might include the following:

- What is the purpose of this tool/app/technology? What does it do?
- Who created this tool? For what purpose?
- Is the tool free or behind a paywall?
- How will my data be used with this tool? Where could I find this information? Does the tool have any privacy issues? Can I control how I interact with the tool?

Tip: always check the settings.

- Will the tool enable me to do something better, more efficiently, or to a higher quality than if I were to create the material myself? Is this important to me?
- Does using such a tool sit well with me? Does it seem ethical?
- Is the use of the tool for teaching and learning purposes pedagogically sound?
- What is my university policy or stance on the use of the tool?

If you do wish to engage with GenAI technologies and are not confident with their use, then it is advisable to seek guidance from or to collaborate with digital education colleagues who may be able to provide training and ideas for its use in your teaching. Concerns around the ethics of GenAI can also provide useful material for engaging students' critical thinking in relation to the use of such tools. For instance, Keshishi and Hossein offer a replicable workshop for educators based on Hosseini's (2023) blog which explores how GenAI images might perpetuate and recreate existing gender, race, and ethnic stereotypes. Zhou and Schofield (2024) also offer a practical framework of activities for teaching and developing students' AI literacy in the areas of knowledge and understanding, use and application, evaluation and creation, and ethics. By adopting a critically self-reflective and scholarly approach towards the use of GenAI, you will be demonstrating a core LD value. Chapter 7 provides further discussion around ways to incorporate GenAI materials into your teaching and learning practice if this is something that you wish to explore.

Really, what is the purpose of a university?

This chapter began by setting out some of the functions and purposes of a university. Yet this was merely scratching the surface. On a rudimentary level, we have seen that the aim of a university is to 'advance education, research' and 'scholarship' for the 'public good' (Synge, 2023). However, this definition might be considered simplistic, not accounting for ongoing ideological debates around what a university is and what it is for. For instance, we saw earlier that from a neoliberal perspective, universities are commodified: they are businesses and 'business-like' providing a service to 'customers' (Ball, 2021, p. 59). This, Ball (2021, 59) argues, fosters an environment of 'terror' where 'performativity' (being seen to be 'doing' or being seen to be productive) in a 'performance management' culture is the status quo. As the antithesis to this, for critical pedagogues such as Paulo Freire and bell hooks, education and universities can be sites of transformation, even of love – a means to liberate from oppression and change the world (Freire, 1970; hooks, 1994).

The above are only some ways of thinking about what a university (and education) is and what it should be for. Given the state of flux in the sector and rapid advancements in digital technologies the purpose(s) of a university will need to be fundamentally reimagined. As an LDer, the more you begin to acclimatise to working within HE, the more you will start to ask yourself questions as to your position in relation to such debates. This positioning is not just theoretical in nature. It will impact the way in which you interact with students and your practice of 'doing' LD. Adopting a critical stance to such issues will also become increasingly necessary as you navigate the everyday job of being an LDer.

Where does Learning Development fit in all of this?

The chapter should have given you a sense of the high-stakes nature of working in universities and a flavour of some of the topical issues impacting HE. Given this, what part might we play as LDers in our student-centred third space role? How can we mediate these ever-changing dynamics and external pressures such that our practice reflects LD's community-driven values?[9] Should we be aiming to fit into the existing systems and structures or are we well placed to – and should we – disrupt it? You are not expected to have all the answers to these questions, but by reading this book you should hopefully start to develop a clearer grasp of the role LD might play amidst these complexities.

Through the suggestions in the remaining chapters, it is hoped that you will get a sense of the positive impact that your everyday work as an LDer can make in a sector with ongoing and complex challenges. The better you understand the practical elements of the role, the more you will start to contextualise your work and think about where it fits in relation to these wider concerns. This, combined with a growing theoretical and scholarly appreciation of what LD is about, will aid you on the way to becoming a 'critically reflective' (ALDinHE, 2024) and *reflexive* practitioner, asking questions of your own beliefs, values, and assumptions, to guide your decision-making in relation to 'doing' LD. So, let us get started.

Summary

- This chapter began by providing a basic overview of the primary functions and purpose of a university. We saw that many universities in the UK context are charities and are primarily involved in education, research, and scholarship for social good (Synge, 2023).
- Most universities in the UK are regulated by independent bodies, and we looked at an example of the regulator for England, the OfS, as an illustration of a regulator's function. We saw that the higher education (HE) sector is one of high stakes and that this is a key driver for data collation and evaluation. Given this, data collection and analysis are also a necessary part of the LD role.
- To give a sense of who is responsible for what in a university, the chapter highlighted key leadership roles in a university context and their responsibilities.
- We looked at topical issues impacting the sector including marketisation and competition amongst providers and how emerging generative artificial technologies might affect LD practice.
- The chapter ended by positing that better understanding the practical elements of the LD role as well as developing an appreciation for the theory that underpins this will aid you with becoming a reflective and reflexive HE practitioner.

Notes

1 These acronyms are explained later in the chapter and also included in the list of acronyms and abbreviations provided at the beginning of the book.
2 A large number of Further Education (FE) colleges in the UK provide qualifications at higher education (HE) level.
3 Readers interested in exploring some of the issues in further depth should refer to 'Ideas for further reading' at the end of the chapter.
4 Or FE colleges providing HE level qualifications.
5 In England, tuition fee limits are set under the Higher Education and Research Act (HERA) 2017.
6 Transforming Access and Student Outcomes in Higher Education (TASO) is a UK-based charity, funded by the Office for Students, that specialises in evidence-informed approaches to evaluation to improve student success and equality gaps (www.taso.org.uk). They provide guidance and helpful frameworks for evaluating the impact of your work or a specific intervention.
7 JiscMail lists can be accessed at https://www.jiscmail.ac.uk/. These are professional email discussion lists for practitioners in the education and research community. It is a UK-based site but has many subscribers worldwide. The lists cover a range of professional interests including the Learning Development in Higher Education Network (LDHEN). You can sign up to as many JiscMail email lists as you wish.

8 See Chapter 8 on 'Professional Development' for an explanation of what Working Groups are and what they do.
9 See Chapter 2 'What does it mean to do Learning Development in Higher Education?' for an overview of the five LD community-driven values.

References

ALDinHE (2024) *About ALDinHE*. Available at: https://aldinhe.ac.uk/about-aldinhe/ (Accessed: 9 April 2024).

Amos, N. (2023, 26 July) *Office for Students*. Institute for Government. Available at: https://www.instituteforgovernment.org.uk/explainer/office-for-students (Accessed: 8 June 2025).

Ball, S. J. (2021) *The Education Debate*, 4th edn. Bristol: Policy Press.

D'Agostino, S. (2023, 13 September) 'Why professors are polarized on AI', *InsideHigherEd*. Available at: https://www.insidehighered.com/news/tech-innovation/artificial-intelligence/2023/09/13/why-faculty-members-are-polarized-ai (Accessed: 9 March 2025).

Department of Higher Education and Training (2024, 26 April) *Policy for the Recognition of South African Higher Education Institutional Types Determined in Terms of Section 3 of the Higher Education Act*. Available at: https://www.gov.za/sites/default/files/gcis_document/202404/50569gon4757.pdf/ (Accessed: 30 July 2025).

Freire, P. (1970) *Pedagogy of the Oppressed [Reprint]*. London: Penguin Classics, 2017.

hooks, b. (1994) *Teaching to Transgress*. New York: Routledge.

Hosseini, D. (2023, 8 August) 'Generative AI: A problematic illustration of the intersections of racialized gender, race, ethnicity', *Dustin Hosseini Blog*. Available at: https://www.dustinhosseini.com/blog/2023/08/08/generative-ai-a-problematic-illustration-of-the-intersections-of-racialized-gender-race-ethnicity (Accessed: 17 February 2025).

HowCharitiesWork (2023) *Why are Universities, Churches and Private Schools Charities?* Available at: https://howcharitieswork.com/about-charities/what-is-a-charity/why-are-universities-churches-and-private-schools-charities/ (Accessed: 7 February 2025).

Jarvis, A. (2024, 3 July) *Tough questions for government and institutions to fix higher education's finances*. WonkeHE. Available at: https://wonkhe.com/blogs/how-do-we-start-to-fix-university-funding/ (Accessed: 8 June 2025).

Maryville University (2023, 19 May) 'History of AI: Timeline and the future', *Maryville University Blog*. Available at: https://online.maryville.edu/blog/history-of-ai/ (Accessed: 9 March 2025).

Office for Students (OfS) (2024) *Financial Sustainability of Higher Education Providers in England: November 2024 Update*. Available at: https://www.officeforstudents.org.uk/publications/financial-sustainability-of-higher-education-providers-in-england-november-2024-update/ (Accessed: 14 February 2025).

Office for Students (OfS) (2025a) *What the OfS does for Students*. Available at: https://www.officeforstudents.org.uk/for-students/ofs-and-students/what-the-ofs-does-for-students/ (Accessed: 20 February 2025).

Office for Students (OfS) (2025b) *Registration with the OfS*. Available at: https://www.officeforstudents.org.uk/for-providers/registering-with-the-ofs/registration-with-the-ofs-a-guide/conditions-of-registration/ (Accessed: 20 February 2025).

Office for Students (OfS) (2025c) *Access and Participation Plans*. Available at: https://www.officeforstudents.org.uk/for-providers/equality-of-opportunity/access-and-participation-plans/ (Accessed: 14 February 2025).

Office for Students (OfS) (2025d) *Condition B3: Baseline for Student Outcomes Indicators*. Available at: https://www.officeforstudents.org.uk/media/490d884f-03aa-49cf-907d-011149309983/condition_b3_baselines.pdf (Accessed: 20 February 2025).

Office for Students (OfS) (2025e) *About the Teaching Excellence Framework (TEF)*. Available at: https://www.officeforstudents.org.uk/for-providers/quality-and-standards/about-the-tef/ (Accessed: 20 February 2025).

Office for Students (OfS) (2025f) *National Student Survey – Guide for Students*. Available at: https://www.officeforstudents.org.uk/for-students/teaching-quality-and-tef/national-student-survey/ (Accessed: 30 June 2025).

Oxford Reference (2025) *Globalisation*. Available at: https://www.oxfordreference.com/display/10.1093/oi/authority.20110803095855259 (Accessed: 29 June 2025).

QAA (2018, August) *The Right to Award UK Degrees*, 3rd edn. Available at: https://www.qaa.ac.uk/docs/qaa/guidance/the-right-to-award-degrees-18.pdf?sfvrsn=4a2f781_16 (Accessed: 20 February 2025).

QAA (2023) *Advisory Committee on Degree Awarding Powers Specific Terms of Reference*. Available at: https://www.qaa.ac.uk/docs/qaa/about-us/acdap-terms-of-reference.pdf?sfvrsn=2cead681_16 (Accessed: 14 February 2025).

QAA (2024a) *The Frameworks for Higher Education Qualifications of UK Degree-Awarding Bodies*. Available at: https://www.qaa.ac.uk/docs/qaa/quality-code/the-frameworks-for-higher-education-qualifications-of-uk-degree-awarding-bodies-2024.pdf?sfvrsn=3562b281_11 (Accessed: 20 February 2025).

QAA (2024b, 19 February) *Navigating the Complexities of the Artificial Intelligence Era in Higher Education*. Available at: https://www.qaa.ac.uk/docs/qaa/news/quality-compass-navigating-the-complexities-of-the-artificial-intelligence-era-in-higher-education.pdf (Accessed: 20 February 2025).

Scottish Funding Council (2023) *Learning and Quality*. Available at: https://www.sfc.ac.uk/assurance-accountability/learning-quality (Accessed: 7 February 2025).

Stephenson, H. and Dandridge, N. (2019, 27 June) *Educational Charities Must Behave Charitably*. Charity Commission. Available at: https://charitycommission.blog.gov.uk/2019/06/27/educational-charities-must-behave-charitably/ (Accessed: 7 February 2025).

Synge, M. (2023, 7 June) *Most Universities are Charities: So What?* HEPI. Available at: https://www.hepi.ac.uk/2023/06/07/most-universities-are-charities-so-what/ (Accessed: 7 February 2025).

THE (2025) *UK University Redundancies: Latest Updates*. Available at: https://www.timeshighereducation.com/news/uk-university-redundancies-latest-updates (Accessed: 19 June 2025).

Tikly, L. (2025, 16 January) *Supporting Learning in a Multicultural Environment: The Richness and Challenge of Diverse Universities [Lecture] Inspiring Learning New Year Lecture*. Heriot Watt University [Online].

Time (2023) *How the AI Revolution will Reshape the World*. Available at: https://time.com/6310115/ai-revolution-reshape-the-world/ (Accessed: 9 March 2025).

UKRI (2025) *How Research England Supports Research Excellence*. Available at: https://www.ukri.org/who-we-are/research-england/research-excellence/research-excellence-framework/ (Accessed: 31 May 2025).

Universities Canada (2025) *How Quality Assurance Works in Canada*. Available at: https://univcan.ca/about-universities-canada/membership-and-governance/quality-assurance/ (Accessed: 14 February 2025).

Universities UK (2023, 31 March) *What's Happening in Higher Education Regulation and What Does This Mean for Transnational Education (TNE)?* Available at: https://www.universitiesuk.ac.uk/universities-uk-international/insights-and-publications/uuki-blog/whats-happening-higher-education (Accessed: 14 February 2025).

Zhou, X. and Schofield, L. (2024) 'Developing a conceptual framework for artificial intelligence (AI) literacy in higher education', *Journal of Learning Development in Higher Education [Preprint]*, 31. https://doi.org/10.47408/jldhe.vi31.1354

Ideas for further reading

The Higher Education context

Ball, S. J. (2021) *The Education Debate*, 4th edn. Bristol: Policy Press.

Komljenovic, J., Sellar, S. and Birch, K. (2025) 'Turning universities into data-driven organisations: Seven dimensions of change', *Higher Education*, 89, 1369–1386. https://doi.org/10.1007/s10734-024-01277-z

Syska, A. and Buckley, C. (eds) (2024b) *How to be a Learning Developer in Higher Education: Critical Perspectives, Community and Practice*. Abingdon: Routledge.

Wood, K. (2011) *Education: The Basics*. Abingdon: Routledge.

Generative Artificial Intelligence and Learning Development practice

Bobula, M. (2024) 'Generative artificial intelligence (AI) in higher education: A comprehensive review of challenges, opportunities, and implications', *Journal of Learning Development in Higher Education [Preprint]*, 30. https://doi.org/10.47408/jldhe.vi30.1137

Hosseini, D. (2023, 8 August) 'Generative AI: A problematic illustration of the intersections of racialized gender, race, ethnicity', *Dustin Hosseini Blog*. Available at: https://www.dustinhosseini.com/blog/2023/08/08/generative-ai-a-problematic-illustration-of-the-intersections-of-racialized-gender-race-ethnicity (Accessed: 17 February 2025).

Zhou, X. and Schofield, L. (2024) 'Developing a conceptual framework for Artificial Intelligence (AI) literacy in higher education', *Journal of Learning Development in Higher Education [Preprint]*, 31. https://doi.org/10.47408/jldhe.vi31.1354

Chapter 4

Teaching tutorials

> **This chapter provides an overview of**
> - What a Learning Development (LD) tutorial is.
> - Why tutorials are commonplace in LD practice.
>
> **You will be guided on**
> - How to deal with practical concerns such as location, attendance, and timing.
> - How to encourage students to attend tutorials.
> - Ways to structure a tutorial.
> - How to deal with challenges that you might encounter during a tutorial.
> - Ways to evaluate and measure the impact of tutorials.

What are tutorials?

LD tutorials are one-to-one sessions (although they can also be conducted in groups) held with students to discuss a specific aspect of their academic skills development.

> **Task: what I know about tutorials**
> - What is your experience of tutorials (as a student or a tutor)?
> - What do you think is the purpose of a tutorial?

You may have attended tutorials either as a student at university or you might have experience of leading tutorials in a previous educational context.

Personal tutorials in academia are distinct from LD tutorials in that they are usually led by an academic who specialises in the subject that the student is undertaking. Personal tutors are often assigned a small group of personal tutees who they support throughout the academic year and sometimes for a longer duration. Tutorials of this nature tend to focus on pastoral-, professional-, or academic-related concerns that the tutee may have. The academic acting as personal tutor may signpost to relevant services as appropriate. Academics taking on a personal tutor role can experience similar issues that arise for Learning Developers (LDers) in terms of understanding the scope of their remit (Dobinson-Harrington, 2006). As such, there has been a movement in some higher education institutions (HEIs) towards professionalising the personal tutor role, with structured training and development provided to carry out this important function.

LD tutorials, in theory, focus on developing an aspect of a student's learning typically related to understanding and completing assignments, academic writing and reading, or general study skills (Turner, 2011). However, in practice, you may find that the discussion during a one-to-one extends far beyond a dialogue about skills development. You might, for instance, meander into conversation about a student's motivations, their previous study experiences, and personal joys and challenges that they are facing. Such exchanges, whilst often fruitful, mean that the boundaries between being an LDer and being a personal tutor, counsellor, or coach, for instance, can easily become blurred (Webster, 2023). Whilst coaching and mentoring methodologies (and even counselling models) have been employed or used as frameworks in LD work (see, e.g. Gurbutt and Gurbutt, 2015; Delderfield and McHattie, 2018; Hillman and Lochtie, 2024), it is important to only use such an approach if you understand its method and rationale. As such, aim to be clear as to what your professional role is during a tutorial and sensitively manage students' expectations about what you can and cannot provide. We will consider professional boundaries later in this chapter in the sections, 'How might I structure a tutorial?' and 'How do I deal with a challenging tutorial?' and again in Chapter 8, 'Working with Students and Colleagues'.

Students who attend LD tutorials usually opt to do so, although they may also be referred by academic teaching staff or specialist colleagues working in university departments or functions such as wellbeing, disability, or mental health. This means that, unless the student has previously used the service, you will see different students each time and must quickly establish an environment where they feel safe, secure, and confident to discuss their concerns. In this regard, a tutorial can encapsulate the 'third space' nature of our role (Webster, 2023; Johnson and Bishopp-Martin, 2024) with the LDer 'bridging the gap' and acting as intermediary between the student and their lecturers by providing room to discuss and negotiate understandings of academia together.[1] This chapter will provide guidance around structuring and delivering an effective tutorial. However, the chapter does not attempt to prescribe one correct way of 'doing' an LD tutorial as it is always important to be led by students' needs.

Why are tutorials commonplace in Learning Development?

Tutorials are a useful way of providing personalised support to individual students. The provision of tutorials clearly aligns with two of the guiding Association for Learning Development in Higher Education (ALDinHE) values; that is:

1. Working in partnership with students and staff to make sense and get the most out of HE, and
2. Embracing and respecting diverse learners through critical pedagogy and practice.

(ALDinHE, 2024a)

Although they can be time-intensive, tutorials are standard practice in the field of LD as they can be used to explore, in depth, an area of concern that the student feels the need to discuss. Whilst there have been concerns expressed about parity and equity of access to tutorials (Shackleton and Peel, 2023), and a gradual movement in some HEIs away from provision of one-to-ones due to their time and labour-intensive nature (Turner, 2011), there are many potential benefits for students and LDers from partaking in the tutorial process, and they continue to be commonplace practice for many working in LD.

Effective LD tutorials enable students to negotiate understandings of what it is to learn and 'be' in the academy with less restraint than they might have in another setting. They afford students the time and space to clarify misconceptions about difficult concepts or topics, to receive personalised feedback on work, to clarify subject markers' feedback in a non-threatening way, and to grow students' confidence in seeing themselves as valued members of their academic community (Turner, 2011). Further, they provide scope for students who may be feeling alienated in the HE environment to establish a positive professional relationship with a 'friendly face' as they develop trust in your service (Turner, 2011). LD tutorials may also impact positively on attainment levels (Loddick and Coulson, 2020). Tutorials may be particularly beneficial for students who have come to university from a 'non-traditional' educational background, who lack confidence, or who face barriers in terms of developing the independent learning techniques required at university level (Turner, 2011). However, it is important to reiterate that LD aims to take a strengths-based, developmental approach to student learning rather than a remedial or deficit perspective (Hill et al., 2010; Brazant, 2023). This means that rather than LD tutorials being used as places to 'fix' or remedy students who are struggling, instead they are best reimagined and used as spaces that any student – even those referred to colloquially as the 'worried well' – can access to openly discuss and develop their learning, understanding, and skills.

Compared to a classroom environment, LD tutorials, on the face of it, offer an informal and 'neutral' student-centred space to discuss issues that students may be having with their studies, such that they can openly express their fears, concerns, and triumphs about academia. However, Webster (2023, p. 2) highlights the conflict that LDers may face between the 'participatory' and 'collaborative' values that LD espouses and that of working in HE, 'a community of practice . . . which has its own norms, values and standards and [which] is strongly hierarchical, with issues of power and authority' (Webster, 2023, p. 2 in reference to Lea and Street, 1998, p. 159). This suggests that the tutorial space is never, indeed, 'neutral'. Instead, tutorials can easily become a site where LDers simply diagnose and 'fix' the students 'ills', similarly to a doctor giving a prescription, thereby 'pathologising' and disempowering the student (Webster, 2023). To address this, Webster (2023) offers a useful 'formulation' model as a framework for structuring a tutorial such that the 'prescribing' approach can be avoided. This model is outlined within this chapter as one approach you might take. We will also consider the practicalities of delivering tutorials and answer questions that you may have as a new LDer.

Where should I hold a tutorial?

As with workshops (see Chapter 5), tutorials can be held in a variety of locations. Typically, they will be held in an office or room on campus that allows space for discussion and for students not to be overheard, so that the students feel free to speak. However, tutorials might also be held online on video conferencing platforms such as Teams or Zoom, by telephone or an online chat, or, more experimentally, off-site in the form of walking tutorials, or in informal environments such as a campus coffee shop.

If you are holding tutorials on an online platform such as Zoom or Teams, it is important to make sure that the student knows how to access the platform, that they have sufficient bandwidth to do so, and that the communication will be clear. If the technology might be problematic for the student, offer alternatives such as a telephone or in-person tutorial. If you wish to hold tutorials off-site or walking tutorials, make sure that you have checked that these are permitted by your institution, and that you have carefully assessed any potential health and safety risks to students and yourself. Your university should have a policy in place about off-site work, so do ensure that you follow it. If you are not sure about the process for such work, ask an experienced colleague for guidance, or check with your line manager or a senior manager. Also, ensure that such tutorials are accessible to all students. For instance, a walking tutorial that involves a route climbing steep steps might not be possible for students with physical disabilities, so you may need to make adaptations or provide alternatives. Provided you have carried out due diligence, do not be afraid to be experimental in your approach to tutorial (or indeed workshop) location as you never know who might benefit (see Psaros (2022) for a discussion around the use of urban walks in LD).

How long should a tutorial last?

Tutorials can be very time consuming (Turner, 2011). One positive of this, as mentioned, is that they afford space for in-depth discussion with a student about their individual experience of their studies, which may not be readily available for the student in other arenas. However, this time-intensive nature means that they can be demanding for you, physically and emotionally, as a new LDer. As such, it will be important to think carefully about how many tutorials you wish to offer on a daily or weekly basis and how long such tutorials will last. It may be that the number of tutorials you provide and their duration are already mandated in your job or role description or it may be that there are established methods and processes for tutorials in your institution or team. However, if this is not the case, you will need to consider and decide how many to offer and an appropriate duration.

In terms of the ideal length of time for a tutorial to run, this is not prescribed. There has been discussion on the Learning Development in Higher Education Network (LDHEN) JiscMail[2] about appropriate length of time with some LDers positing that tutorials lasting under an hour may not allow enough time to adopt a 'student-centred' approach and instead end up being prescriptive (LDHEN, 2019). You may find a duration of less than 30 minutes insufficient for giving time for students to talk in enough depth about their concerns, and anything over an hour may be emotionally and physically taxing for both the student and you. When I started in LD, my sessions ran for 50 minutes as a legacy from the outgoing LDer's practice, but over time, I have adjusted these to 40-minute sessions with 20-minute gaps in between tutorials to allow for overrunning if necessary. Depending on the time of year, I offer anything between four and eight sessions a week which, in my practice, is manageable. Your institution and LD unit may offer significantly more (or fewer) tutorials per week depending on the allocation of time between these, workshops, and your embedded practice. If it is up to you to decide, you may need to experiment to see what timing and number of sessions work best in your specific context. Remember that if time does run out during the tutorial, you can also remind students that they can book follow-up sessions or contact you by email (or whatever communication method is standard in your institution) with additional queries.

You could also trial shorter drop-in sessions (of about 10–20 minutes) where students with 'quick' queries, for instance, on essay writing or the mechanics of referencing, can get their questions answered. This might take the form of a 'helpdesk' approach, if your institution currently has these, which is a centrally located physical or online 'desk' where students across the university can drop-in, or it may take the form of students being able to drop by your office, whether online or in-person, during your designated office hours (i.e. standard hours where you are available for students). Given that these by their nature are shorter sessions, they might necessitate you taking a more prescriptive approach than a longer, in-depth tutorial.

How do I get students to attend tutorials?

Students may be unfamiliar with the term 'tutorial' so it can be helpful to explain clearly what this is on your virtual learning environment (VLE) or website or to use terminology that might be more meaningful to them such as one-to-one or small group appointment.

Tutorials can be advertised similarly to workshops, for instance, through the students' VLE, through email and notifications, via social media platforms, through physical posters displayed on campus that include the use of easy access QR codes, via promotion by academics, and through word-of-mouth. It can be helpful to include a link in your email signature that connects directly to your tutorial booking form and that allows students to easily book a one-to-one session. You might design a page on your VLE or LD website that clearly explains what to expect during a tutorial and how students should prepare.

> **Task: promoting tutorials**
>
> - What do you think students might want to know prior to attending an LD tutorial?
> - What information could you include on your website or VLE to aid students attending a tutorial?

You could provide general information, in 'student-friendly' accessible language, on the VLE, about what a tutorial is, how long sessions should last, what help your service can provide during a tutorial, how to book a tutorial, expectations around behaviour during a tutorial, and whether students need to do anything in preparation such as emailing a draft of work or preparing specific questions. Including visuals or a video tutorial explaining the tutorial process and student testimonials about the benefits of attending can be an effective, and creative, way of promoting tutorials and increasing attendance.

It is also important to manage students' expectations by being upfront about the limits of your tutorial service. Be clear as to what you can and cannot cover in a tutorial. For instance, in relation to student assignments, you might make clear that you can provide guidance and feedback on academic writing, including style, cohesion, and language, but cannot comment on the accuracy of subject content. You should also stipulate whether you are able to look at repeat drafts of work. You might choose to specify that you cannot provide proofreading or editing services but can give guidance about revising and editing work and can comment on structural, language, and grammatical issues. In such cases where you have stated what you *cannot* provide during a tutorial, it can be helpful to provide links to resources that *can* aid students, for example, links to resources and guidance about editing and proofreading a draft.

An online booking form can be created via your VLE, or you could set one up through an online calendar tool such as Microsoft Bookings. Alternatively, the approach in your institution might be for students to email the LD team directly to organise a tutorial. Whichever approach is taken, your booking form (or email communication) should allow students to select a date and time for an appointment and should make clear the location of the tutorial. You might wish to make it compulsory for the student to state the reason for booking a tutorial as this can aid with your planning and preparation. For this, you could include a drop-down menu on the booking form that lists common topics or areas of concern, or the student could respond free hand to express their reasons for booking a tutorial in their own words (see the following box).

Example drop-down menu that could be used on a booking form

Please select the main area of concern you wish to discuss

- Essay and assignment writing
- Referencing skills
- Academic reading
- Critical thinking
- Avoiding plagiarism and academic integrity
- Digital skills
- General study skills
- Other (please specify)

Remember that students may not always have a clear sense of what they wish to discuss. Conversely, although students might state that they wish to talk about a specific topic when they book a tutorial, you might end up involved in quite a different topic of conversation in the tutorial itself. As such, allow for flexibility during the tutorial. Once booked, to ensure that students attend the session, it is advisable to send a reminder message the day or week before reiterating the time, date, and location of their appointment.

What can I do in preparation for the tutorial?

As mentioned earlier, aim to send the student an email or communication in advance of the tutorial confirming the date and time of their session. This email can also set out any preparation that they may need to do. For instance, you might wish the students to send you an essay draft or extract from their work to read and comment on in advance, or you might ask them to provide more detail about the specific nature of their query. See the example pre-tutorial email below:

An example pre-tutorial email

Dear [student name]
I hope you are well.
Thanks for booking an online/in-person appointment for [state date and time].
Here are the address details for your appointment [state address/provide visual map]
or
Here is the Teams/Zoom link/for your appointment [include link].
Please could you let me know what it is you wish to discuss in the session as this will help us to make the best use of time during the appointment.
or
To be able to make the best use of time during your tutorial, please could you send me a draft of your work by [date] so that I can read it in advance.
If you need to cancel your appointment, please let me know via email or by cancelling directly on the booking form [provide hyperlink].
I look forward to meeting with you on [date and time].

Prior to the tutorial, it can be helpful to make some brief notes about the student and the areas of concern they wish to discuss, alongside suggested resources and signposting. You could use an online or paper template to log details such as the one in Table 4.1. The log could be used as a prompt or discussion sheet during the tutorial to remind you of the student's key areas of concern and of which resources to signpost. It is important though to be led by the student during the tutorial rather than your notes, so do be responsive

Table 4.1 A tutorial log sheet.

Date of appointment:
Time of appointment:
Name:
Student ID number:
Programme:
Personal tutor:
Year of entry:
Year of study:
Current modules:
Upcoming assessments:
Student support needs:
Email:
Topic(s) to discuss:
Suggested resources:

to the discussion that is taking place rather than sticking rigidly to a proforma. Remember to also follow your university policy regarding handling data and keep any physical or digital copies of such forms stored in a safe location if they contain confidential student information.

Thoughts on effective tutorials

As a new LDer, I lacked confidence in how to structure an effective tutorial. I would panic that I had little to offer in terms of guidance, teaching, and good practice, particularly as each tutorial involved meeting new students with different concerns. I would over prepare pages of notes with reams of guidance and suggestions, sometimes quite literally copied from *The Study Skills Handbook* – shout out to Stella Cottrell! – and read verbatim from these. This meant that rather than being led by the students' needs and concerns, I was being led by my 'tutorial plan'. It meant that rather than providing personalised guidance, I was offering general advice that they might receive from reading a generic study skills book. And it meant that at times students were left dissatisfied with the service they received. Something needed to change.

Since then, with time, research, and experience, I have learned that the most effective tutorials are not a one-way monologue where you prescribe ways to redeem the student of their 'ills', as if in a doctor's surgery (Webster, 2023). The effectiveness of our LD practice pivots on our professional relationships with the students we work alongside. Relationships can, of course, be unpredictable. This means that our most expertly prepared and planned tutorials can go completely awry if we are not alert to and responsive to the human being in front of us. In a tutorial then, rather than aiming to be the all-knowing sage, instead try to focus on establishing a space where the student feels a sense of belonging and safety to communicate with you, and this should set the conditions whereby some form of teaching and learning takes place.

With this in mind, you might view yourself more of a critical friend during the tutorial, asking pertinent questions, listening, and responding with guidance where relevant; that is, your role might be focused on helping the student to better navigate their understandings of academia, their subject, and academic practices (ALDinHE, 2024a). You might also view the tutorial space as a place for the student to 'play' – that is, where they feel able to experiment and test out ideas, strategies, and approaches without fear of 'doing it wrong'. This shift in focus to the student and their needs can help to allay some of the anxieties around conducting tutorials in your initial few years as an LDer. As we shift the focus away from our own 'performance' and 'advice', we allow space for authentic dialogue and learning *alongside* the student. Later in the chapter, we will consider some practical suggestions for structuring tutorials in a way that promotes dialogue and students' willingness to engage with you during the tutorial.

How might I structure a tutorial?

Prepare beforehand

Although tutorials should be student-led, this does not negate you preparing beforehand. Ease of preparation will depend on what access you have to student data and whether you work for a particular faculty or department or across your institution with students from many different disciplines. As a minimum, particularly in your early years as an LDer, ensure that you know the student's name, including its correct pronunciation, what programme of study the student is undertaking, what year or level they are working at, and that you have some notion of what it is they would like to discuss. You can get most of this information by asking students to complete a short form prior to their tutorial, as suggested in the section above, 'What can I do in preparation for the tutorial?'. Remember, though, that during the tutorial itself it will be important to be flexible and responsive to the student's immediate concerns as discussions may take very unexpected tangents.

> **Case Study One: preparing for a tutorial**
>
> A first-year undergraduate student books an appointment with you for a one-to-one tutorial. They state on their booking form that they wish to discuss essay writing as it is an area that they struggle with. They also mention that they are dyslexic and would like guidance on effective reading strategies and time management. You are not a dyslexia specialist and have limited experience of working with students with dyslexia. What might you do to prepare yourself and the student for the session?

> **Suggested response to Case Study One**
>
> Prior to the tutorial, contact the student with an email to introduce yourself and set out the scope of your role. This will help to set expectations and enables the student to have a clearer understanding of what you will cover in the tutorial. You may explain that although you are not a dyslexia or autism specialist, you are happy to talk to the student about general strategies for essay writing, time management, and academic reading. You might ask the student to send you a sample of their essay writing ready to be discussed during the tutorial. In your introductory email, you might also wish to make the student aware of relevant services in your university, for instance, if there are specialist LDers in your team that work with students with specific learning differences (SpLDs) or to signpost to disability and dyslexia services.
>
> When thinking about your own preparation, you might think about general concerns around essay writing, reading strategies, and time management that the student may raise. For instance, typical queries that may arise might relate to how to structure an essay, how to organise paragraphs, and how to show evidence of argument. You might write a list of essay writing resources to signpost to within the session. The same could be said when thinking about effective reading strategies and time management. What generic or subject-specific resources are you aware of to signpost the student towards? If possible, you could read the student's essay draft or sample and provide written comments ready to discuss with the student. You might also see if there are any available resources or guidance specifically for students with dyslexia available on professional body sites such as the Dyslexia Association or on the ALDinHE neurodivergence resource bank (ALDinHE, 2024b). However, remember as a non-specialist, your role is to work within your own professional remit, so do not steer into providing advice about dyslexia in the tutorial itself. This might, however, be an area that you choose to develop your understanding of through future continuing professional development.[3]

As a new LDer, it can feel very disconcerting to be unable to plan for what the student wants to discuss. This can result in tutorials that end up quite generic rather than personalised as you attempt to stick rigidly to your pre-tutorial notes or to steer the conversation to 'safe' topics with which you are familiar. However, whilst common themes may come up in tutorials (e.g. concerns around essay writing, referencing, or academic reading), each student brings their unique questions and concerns and, therefore, having a rigid or detailed plan that you stick to might end up being quite detrimental to promoting the ALDinHE core value of 'working in partnership with students to help students make sense of higher education' (ALDinHE, 2024a). With experience, it is likely that you will become increasingly comfortable with allowing the sessions to be 'led' by the student. However, at this stage, you may wish to have a 'safety net' that will provide structure to the tutorial but still enable the student to express their concerns and needs fully. The next section provides guidance on this.

Structure the tutorial so that you have an introduction, main body, and conclusion

Much like a workshop, tutorials need to have a clear structure. That is not to say that you should not be flexible and responsive during the tutorial, but you should have a clear idea of how to start, what to cover in the main part of the session, and how to draw it to a conclusion.

How to start a tutorial

As a starting point, it can help to settle your nerves (and those of the student) to have a routine way that you begin tutorials. For instance, whether online or in-person, you could begin by introducing yourself and briefly explaining your remit if you have not previously met the student. If you have met the student previously, you could check-in with them on how things have been going since you last met. You might then ask how the student is, explain how the tutorial will be structured, and clarify what they would like to focus on or get out of the session. Having a familiar way of starting the session can help to establish rapport, boundaries, and expectations. If the tutorial is a drop-in style tutorial and you have not been able to gather information about the student's programme and what they wish to discuss, you may choose to start the session by introducing yourself and asking the student to briefly provide this information which you can record.

What to do during a tutorial

In the main part of the tutorial, try to ensure that the student is engaged in doing something. For instance, if the student is concerned about how to write clear paragraphs, you could model or scaffold the process for them, for example, by writing a clear topic sentence or by visually illustrating how paragraph structure tends to move from general to specific with a sample paragraph relevant to their discipline or within the student's own work. You can then check their understanding either by getting them to try themselves or by asking them to explain back to you what they understand. If their concern is about the structural elements of writing, you could look at an extract of their writing and focus on a specific aspect, for example, sentence-level concerns, talking through their thought processes and providing suggestions for improvement. After you explore or talk through concepts avoid asking, 'Do you understand?' or 'Does that make sense?' as this might place the student under pressure to respond 'Yes' even if they have no idea what you mean. Instead, check understanding in an active and developmental way, such as asking the student to explain it back to you in their own words, or, as suggested earlier, scaffolding a process and getting them to then try it themselves.

Another way to deliver the main part of a tutorial that not only allows for flexibility but also provides an element of structure is to ask specific questions to explore the student's concerns so that you can aid them to articulate their thought process and think through strategies that might assist them. Adopting a Socratic-style or dialogic approach can be a useful technique to use for this. Socratic questioning, derived from the ancient Greek philosopher Socrates, is an approach that enables questioning and unearthing of underlying values, beliefs, and understandings. It involves a dialogue between you and the student which gives an opportunity to question underlying assumptions and to arrive at reasoned understandings; namely, it enables you to engage in a critically reflective process with the student. The student's responses can then serve as a prompt to lead and guide the discussion. Whilst it is not advisable to simply work your way through a list of questions which may be overwhelming for the student, targeted questioning intermixed with discussion and application (i.e. getting the student to do something) can be an effective way to structure a tutorial.

Adopting a questioning/dialogic approach to tutorials

Examples of questions or prompts that you might ask

- Tell me more about what you mean by . . .
- What led you to that conclusion?
- Tell me about why you chose that strategy or approach.
- What do you understand by . . .?
- What do you like about your writing/draft? What do you think you have done well?
- What puzzles you about the writing/reading/assignment process?
- What would you now do differently?

Using a questioning approach entails listening carefully to the student's responses so that you can build upon their ideas and develop a dialogue that demands them to think deeply about their thought processes. It can be helpful, when asking questions, and if in a suitable environment, to take notes about what the student says. However, avoid scribbling away without focusing on the student as it is important to show active listening through appropriate body language and signalling of verbal cues. If you wish to use a questioning approach during the main part of the tutorial, aim to ask open questions, that is, exploratory questions that encourage more than a yes or no response. Remember to also intersperse this with discussion and other forms of dialogue such as guidance and building on the student's response so that they do not experience a barrage of questions. You might create a ready-made 'bank' of questions in advance that can be used and adapted according to a student's specific concerns.

If during the tutorial the conversation strays into a topic that is outside the scope of your remit, do not feel pressured into giving advice or suggestions. Having clear professional boundaries is important and, in such cases, it is advisable to steer the student towards the relevant services that are best placed to aid with their query. We will consider this some more in the section on *Dealing with challenging tutorials*.

How to end a tutorial

To end a tutorial, you can summarise what was covered, ask students what they gained from the session, and if they have any final questions. Be ready for students to ask final questions that diverge onto a different topic and, in this instance, do not be afraid to say to the student that it is best for them to book a follow-up tutorial to have adequate time to discuss the topic in depth. You might also ask the student to explain their next steps.

Follow up after the session with the student with relevant resources

It can be helpful to follow up with the student with an email summary outlining what was covered during the appointment. You might also provide a list of resources that the student can work through independently. This can help the student to take ownership of their learning and can also serve as a 'toolbox' of materials that they can come back to as and when they need. In addition, you can remind the student that they can contact you again (if services permit) if they want to talk further about an aspect of their studies. You might use an email such as the following one:

Example tutorial follow-up email

Dear [student name]

Thank you for attending your appointment earlier today. It was a pleasure speaking with you and well done on the progress you have made so far on your draft.

During the tutorial, we discussed [summarise the key points].

> **As promised, I have attached**
>
> - [List resources and provide relevant links]
>
> **Next steps for you**
>
> [Write one or two next steps that might be helpful for the student to remember] e.g.
>
> - Create a summary plan of each main body chapter. Use subheadings if it helps. Plan how many words you will use for each section.
> - Try to incorporate three to four reflective sentences in each main body paragraph. Use the reflective writing phrases handout (attached) to help you with this.
> - Think about how you can reduce or cut out sentences which are descriptive.
> - Remember to use the 'read aloud' tool in Word to check your sentences are clear and make sense. If sentences are over 25 words or so, try to break them down into shorter sentences.
>
> I hope that helps. If you have any more questions about the resources or about your assessments, please feel free to email me or to book another appointment.
>
> [Signed]

A formulation model for structuring tutorials

Webster (2023) offers a practical framework for conducting tutorials which she refers to as the 5Ps. This approach is based on the 'formulation' model or approach typically used in the 'helping' industries such as counselling and psychology and emphasises positioning the individual (in this case, the student) at the centre of the discussion and as expert in their own experience (2023). This model moves away from a prescriptive approach that can be the inclination during LD tutorials and instead emphasises LD's collaborative and participatory values. Webster (2023) makes clear that the five stages or 5Ps do not need to be followed in a particular order. As such, if you use this approach, aim to be flexible, open, and responsive to the student you are working with.

In Table 4.2 I outline the approach briefly, with examples, as a useful method for structuring tutorials.[4]

Table 4.2 An adapted summary of the 5Ps formulation approach to conducting tutorials.

The 5Ps	Meaning	Example	Points to Highlight for the LDer
Presenting problem	The student presents the 'problem' they are having with their learning. The aim is to establish what the 'underlying need' is and to reach a joint understanding of the problem: 'what it is, why it matters to the student, and the extent to which it is a problem for the student'.	The student is a final year undergraduate and expresses that they are having issues with understanding the essay question and do not know whether they are fulfilling the assessment requirements. They explain that they are on track for a 2:1 but are worried they will 'mess this up' because they 'just don't get the assignment' and are struggling with getting started.	Avoid making assumptions. Let the student explain the presenting problem in their own way/language. Students might use the feedback they have received from lecturers to explain their problem rather than their own words. Aim to seek a shared understanding of what the issue is with the student.
Pertinent factors	This P concerns any important 'holistic or contextual' issues that impact a student's learning. These may be 'major/minor, short-term or long-lived, current or historical, systemic or individual'. Pertinent factors might come up organically in the discussion, may be held 'unspoken' by the student, may be something the student is not aware of or finds hard to articulate, or may be conclusions or diagnoses made by friends or health and other support services.	The student explains that they are completing their master's degree part-time ten years after their first degree. They have recently started a new full-time job and have caring responsibilities. They are currently undergoing a dyslexia assessment.	Pertinent factors are tied up with issues of identity and students' experiences/histories. For instance, the student may say 'I've always been terrible at essay writing'. Aim to 'acknowledge', explore and 'negotiate' with the student the meanings they give to these factors. Exploring pertinent factors also 'positions the LDer as part of the pastoral network of support around a student'. This requires working in a joined-up way with colleagues in relevant services such as wellbeing, disability and dyslexia and students' personal tutors.

(Continued)

Table 4.2 (Continued)

The 5Ps	Meaning	Example	Points to Highlight for the LDer
Perception of task	This P relates to the student's understanding and insight into the assignment or learning activity	You work together with the student to gauge their understanding of the essay question	LDers can play a mediating role between academics' expectations and a student's perception of the task at hand
Process	This P is about the process the student undertook to create the finished 'product'.	You explore with the student the steps they took to draw up an essay plan thinking through the choices they made and why.	LDers can explore with the student their reasons for choosing a particular approach and their thoughts on what they think is 'working well' for them in the process.
Product	This P is the product or 'artefact' or event' that is produced (the 'outcome'). It does not necessarily need to be a written product (e.g. the product could be the student talking to you about their experience of an exam or a presentation they had to give).	The student shows you their first draft for a 2,000-word assignment.	This P should be explored whilst being mindful of the other 5Ps. LDers might wish to think through the other Ps first with the student so to place focus on the developmental nature of learning rather than the end 'product'. The LDer should explore meanings with the student (e.g. How do they feel about their work? What state is the work in draft or edit? Did the student achieve what they wanted to achieve?) The 5Ps formulation approach encourages the student to think through the disciplinary conventions themselves.

Source: This adapted summary is based on material originally published in the *Journal of Learning Development in Higher Education* by Helen Webster and is licensed under CC-BY 4.0.

How do I deal with a challenging tutorial?

You may experience various challenges in tutorials. For instance, a student may want to divulge very personal information about their life; you may have students become frustrated, tearful, or upset; students might appear hostile or defensive; or you may meet a student who does not understand your role and asks you for advice or help outside your remit. It is important to recognise such situations when they do occur and to think, in advance, about appropriate steps to take to ensure that you maintain your professional boundaries.

With a student who is becoming frustrated, upset, or tearful, be human and give them the space and time to express their emotions, and, if in a physical setting with them, offer them a drink or tissue. Once you have done so, acknowledge their feelings, and then ask them if they wish to continue the tutorial. For example, you may say, 'I can see you are upset. Do you need a moment, or would you like us to continue the tutorial?' or 'Thank you for sharing that with me. Is this something that you feel you would like further support with? If so, I can signpost you to services in the university that can offer relevant support such as [wellbeing/counselling]'. If they persist in wanting to discuss personal or sensitive issues that fall outside your remit, this is where it becomes necessary to establish boundaries and make clear the scope of your role. For example, you may say something like,

> Thank you for sharing that. It sounds like a really difficult situation and I'm glad that you felt able to express that with me. I'd like to be able to support and the way I can do that is to contact [state service] if you are happy for me to do so.

In my experience, it is extremely rare for a student to become overtly hostile or verbally or physically aggressive in an LD tutorial. However, if you perceive that a student is behaving in a way that is unacceptable or that threatens your dignity or other students' dignity and you are in a physical location with them, try to move yourself to a place, if possible, where other colleagues or staff are in the vicinity. If you are online, you can remind the student that you can only continue the tutorial if they remain respectful of the space. This will be easier to do if you refer to your university or LD service code of conduct. Try to maintain your professionalism and complete the tutorial if possible and if you judge it is safe to do so. If not, explain that you will be ending the tutorial. Afterwards, make a detailed written record of what happened and then feedback to your line manager or a senior colleague who should be able to advise on next steps. Such situations, however, are exceptional rather than the norm.

A common issue that may occur is when students ask you for advice outside your remit. For instance, they may ask your guidance about financial or housing issues they are facing, about wellbeing concerns, or about other personal concerns. If questions arise that clearly fall outside your remit, do not be tempted to fall into a rabbit hole of trying to provide guidance as you may end up giving misleading or wrong advice. Instead, explain clearly that this is something that is not within your remit but that you can put them in contact with the relevant person or service who should be able to help with their query. You can then follow up with the student during or after the tutorial with an email providing links or details to the relevant service(s).

Students may also ask you what 'mark' you think their essay will get. This question is often asked by students who are anxious about their assignment and who are seeking reassurance. Do not be tempted to give them a mark ('Oh, I think it looks like a 2:1 level', 'This is definitely an excellent, first-class piece of work') as it may be problematic for you if they do not end up with this as their actual assessment result. Instead, if students ask you to give their essay a mark, use it as a learning opportunity by, for instance, looking at the marking criteria relevant to their assignment, clarifying its meaning, and getting them to identify which elements of the criteria they feel are evident (or not) in their work.

Case Study Two: dealing with challenges in tutorials

You are talking to a mature student about time management in an in-person tutorial. They become very tearful and explain that they have always been 'rubbish' at managing their time and that a previous schoolteacher made them feel that they were 'useless' at studying. They say that they have been out of education for so long and that they feel they know 'nothing' and are depressed and 'feel life is not worthwhile'. How might you respond?

Suggested response to Case Study Two

First, it is important to give the student time and space to express their emotion in their own way. Offer them a drink or tissue. You might then express to them that you are sorry that they are feeling this way and have a dialogue around difficulties with adjusting to studying as a mature student and carrying others' negative words into our existence. Be careful not to veer into 'counselling' mode as is important to stay within the scope of your role, but it is okay to empathise and show concern about their emotions. You might also talk to them about general strategies and approaches for developing confidence in studying such as acknowledging small steps, giving themselves little rewards, reminding themselves of the end goal, using past negative feedback as motivation, using positive affirmations or quotes, having a support network, and so forth. Again, even if you are a trained counsellor, remember your role in this instance is that of LDer, so try not to steer into counselling mode as you may end up in difficulties in terms of stepping outside the scope of your responsibilities.

> Make the student aware of any wellbeing and counselling services that they can access via the university. If you feel there are any safeguarding concerns, you can express this to the student and explain that you will need to follow up with the relevant safeguarding officer in your institution.

What else can I do after a challenging tutorial?

LD tutorials involve a significant investment in time and emotional labour. This means that it will be important to think about your wellbeing following emotionally demanding or difficult tutorials. If you have a particularly challenging tutorial, it can be helpful to check-in with a more experienced colleague to debrief and feedback about how things went. This can be done informally, or you could organise a formal meeting. This will allow you the space and time to share your experience so that you can reflect on what went well and how you might do things differently next time.

It can help to diarise or write down your thoughts and reflections on how the tutorial went (both positive and negative aspects) as it can serve as a useful learning point. You may wish to use an established model, such as Gibbs' (1988) reflective cycle to think through a challenging tutorial. Although this reflective model has been subject to critique and amendment, it offers a structured way for critically reflecting on tricky situations that may arise in your LD practice and of evidencing the value of 'critical self-reflection, and ongoing learning' (ALDinHE, 2024a). The model is illustrated in the following:

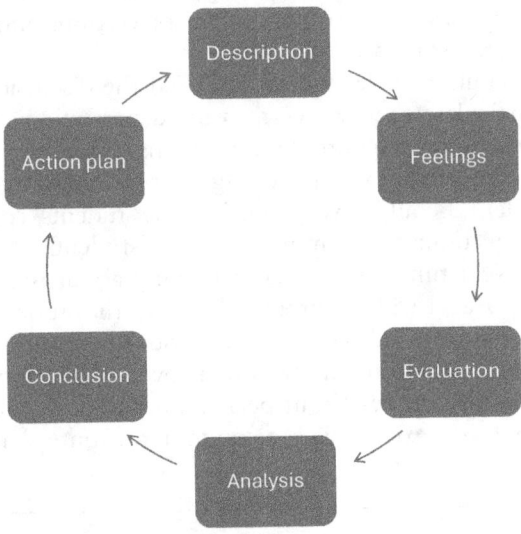

Figure 4.1 Gibbs' reflective cycle (1988).

At the description stage, ask yourself, 'What specific situation happened in the tutorial that I want to think through?' At the feeling stage ask, 'What were my feelings and thoughts when this happened?' At the evaluation stage, 'What was positive and negative about the situation?' At the analysis stage ask yourself, 'What do I understand by the situation?' At the conclusion stage ask, 'What else would I have done?' For the final stage, ask 'What is my action plan? What would I do if it happened again?' The following provides an example of the reflective cycle in action.

> **Example reflection following Gibbs' reflective cycle model**
>
> *Description*: Today, I met with a postgraduate student studying towards a master's in English. It was a difficult tutorial as the student said they struggle with feelings of perfectionism and that they have been having difficulty in making contributions during seminars as they do not want to look 'stupid' in front of their peers.
> *Feelings*: At the time, I was not sure what advice to give the student, and it felt out of my depth. I did think, I know how it feels to be a perfectionist, but thought it best not to say so.
> *Evaluation*: It was good that I allowed the student to express their concerns about perfectionism and how it is impacting their participation and sense of confidence. However, I felt that I did not offer much in terms of advice and was just there nodding along with occasional murmurs to show that I was listening.
> *Analysis*: From this, I can now see that perfectionism is a common trait, and that my own sense of perfectionism was preventing me from focusing on the student.
> *Conclusion*: I could have let the student lead the discussion by getting them to articulate their concerns around perfectionism in relation to their studies by asking guiding questions. I do not always need to offer 'advice' – sometimes just having the space to talk can be helpful for the student. I could have normalised the students' concern by saying that perfectionism is common amongst students.
> *Action plan*: Next time, rather than worrying about my performance or how I appear, I will continue to listen to the students' concerns. If I am not sure of advice to give, I could continue to use guiding questions to help them reach their own conclusions. I will also look up some resources about perfectionism and managing this in the academic context as this is a common attribute shared by other students.

Whilst this section has outlined certain challenges that you may encounter, running tutorials tends to be a very enjoyable part of the role. They offer a learning opportunity for both the student and you, are a place to connect in a human way, and provide the means to offer personalised, timely support to the student.

Other tips for conducting effective tutorials

Have a list of go-to-resources and guidance

As you gain more experience with conducting tutorials, you will find that student concerns tend to be similar or fall into a pattern. Typical areas of concern include questions about essay writing, referencing, time management and organisation, academic reading and note making, and struggles or concerns about the course. Whilst it is important to provide tailored support during tutorials, it can be helpful to create a bank or list of frequently asked questions (FAQs) that may arise and some potential responses or generic resources that you could point the student towards. This can help to alleviate the feeling of being in the unknown or being unsure of how to respond. For example, FAQs might include: how do I write an essay? How do I improve my marks? Is my writing any good? Can you explain how this referencing system works? How do I make good notes? I have failed an assignment, can you help? Remember to be prepared for concerns which you have not thought about to arise – this is the nature of LD tutorials. Indeed, you might find that students simply want to vent or share their struggles (or triumphs) with studying and are not really seeking advice or guidance as such. In this situation, remember to have clear boundaries and signpost students to relevant services (e.g. disability services, counselling, or student services) if they need support outside the scope of your role.

Show your human side

One of the key hallmarks of LD practice is to 'understand HE *as the student experiences it* [original emphasis]' (Johnson and Bishopp-Martin, 2024, p. 16). This requires a level of empathy and compassion (de Silva and Dempsey, 2022), and potentially even embracing a 'pedagogy of kindness' (Gilmour, 2021) towards our work with students. Given this, to aid with approachability and to nurture a level of trust, it can be helpful to share short anecdotes of your own experiences of studying with students (whilst maintaining boundaries and only to the extent that you feel secure doing so). For instance, if a student is discussing struggling with motivation for dissertation writing, I may tell them a short story of my own struggles with procrastination during my undergraduate dissertation and how I overcame this through giving myself mini-deadlines and short daily word counts. Sharing short excerpts of your own experiences with studying and strategies to overcome them can help the student to see that you are human and relatable and can demonstrate empathy. This can be particularly helpful for a student who is finding it hard to find connections or a 'friendly face' during their time at university and can help to engender a sense of belonging. Another way to demonstrate empathy is by modelling to students the idea that making mistakes when learning is fine (Delderfield and McHattie, 2018). For instance, when talking through a process or explanation with the student, if you make an error, acknowledge this and use it as a learning point by talking through how you will rectify it (Delderfield and McHattie, 2018). This can aid with establishing trust and can be helpful for the student who might view university staff as 'all-knowing' and unapproachable sages.

The literature on self-disclosure in the field of LD (i.e. sharing personal and professional experiences with students) is limited; however, in fields such as psychology, it is widely researched. Self-disclosure might come in the form of more 'frivolous' topics such as sharing a favourite sports team or food you enjoy eating and, of course, more serious or sensitive topics. There are advantages and disadvantages to sharing something of yourself with students, and it will be to you to decide whether this is an appropriate pedagogical tool (see Thompson-Cook, 2024). Self-disclosure can potentially build rapport and trust, can be used as a learning tool, and allows the student to view you as human (Tobin, 2010; Thompson-Cook, 2024). On the other hand, self-disclosure, even if done with the right intention rather than as a 'self-indulgence', can make you vulnerable, can unintentionally decentre the student's experience, and might appear 'unprofessional' if not handled sensitively (Tobin, 2010). When choosing whether to self-disclose, you might begin by asking yourself questions such as: 'Will sharing something of my experience aid with the student's learning?' 'What is my relationship with the student? Do I know them well enough to self-disclose? Might self-disclosure do more harm than good?' 'What is the likely impact of self-disclosure on the student at hand and on me as a new LDer?' 'Are there other approaches that I could use rather than self-disclosure to reach the same learning outcome?' There is no right answer as to the question of whether to self-disclose; it very much depends on your context and specific situation (Tobin, 2010). Whilst it is not a prerequisite of an effective tutorial, self-disclosure used as a pedagogical tool in certain circumstances might be something you wish to explore in your practice (Thompson-Cook, 2024).

Use storytelling

Storytelling can be an invaluable method of communicating with students in an empathetic, impactful, and clear manner (hooks, 2010; Jewitt, 2024). Stories help us to connect and make meaning and can be a way of managing difficult conversations or trying to convey complex topics. Stories or anecdotes can be from your own personal or professional experiences (see Thompson-Cook, 2024), or from others' stories that you have read or heard. They should relate to the student's specific concern and can be used to illustrate a concept or provide some form of advice or guidance. One story I tell students struggling with procrastination is based on my personal experience of being a student at undergraduate level. I would often leave essays to the last minute and be sat furiously typing a 3,000-word essay in the campus 'computer room' at 3 am when the assignment was due imminently at 9 am. I use this to illustrate that procrastinating is normal, and it also provides a way in to discuss with the student reasons why we might procrastinate and strategies for dealing with it.

What stories do you recall from personal or professional experience? What stories do you tell yourself? How do these help you to learn? Be creative and experiment with anecdotes and storytelling approaches as you develop greater confidence.

Be flexible

Students often come to tutorials with a specific concern, for example, to ask for guidance on how to write a clear essay introduction. However, as the tutorial progresses you may find that there are other fundamental issues that are important to discuss. For instance, a student may want to discuss how to improve their essay marks, but in the process of the tutorial, through questioning, you may come to see that there are underlying concerns such as issues with time management and organisation, procrastination, and low self-esteem. Without discussing and addressing some of these underlying matters, you risk simply addressing the surface concerns rather than dealing with the core issue impacting the student.

Being flexible and responsive to what the student is 'really saying' in tutorials is a skill and can be one of the most daunting aspects as a new LDer. To aid with this, it can be helpful, particularly in the early days, to develop that bank of exploratory questions mentioned earlier that you can refer to, as needed. The crucial thing will be to listen carefully to what is said, look out for what is unsaid, and allow the student to express their concerns in their own words. However, do not be overly harsh on yourself if you end a tutorial feeling as if you did not really help the student. The student might have benefitted from the session in a way that is not obvious to you. Also, you will not always be able to solve the student's concerns. There could be many intersecting and complex factors requiring a joined-up, holistic, and multi-agency approach to supporting the student. Remember too that there will be other services that the student can seek out or that you can signpost to if they require additional support. Whilst our work as LDers can certainly be transformative for the student, it does not all need to fall to you.

How do I evaluate the impact of tutorials?

Impact can seem a slippery concept. How do we know that the actions that we take as LDers have directly affected or been of benefit to the students (and staff) we work with? What precisely are we impacting? Should we focus on 'objective', quantifiable measures like student attainment or also consider more elusive concepts such as belonging and confidence? Is all impact of equal weight? In relation to tutorials which are student-centred and revolve around building a trusting, open space for students to share their experience of HE, does measuring 'hard' impact undermine the work we have done to establish such spaces? And why should we need to measure impact anyway?

Task: thinking about impact

Key points

- How do you define impact? What would demonstrate impact to you?
- How would you know you had impacted an individual student or group of students?
- What would you need to measure to gauge impact?
- What steps do you already take to measure the impact of tutorials in your practice?

There are no easy answers to these questions, and there are few studies in LD focused specifically on impact that we might turn to for guidance.[5] However, given that HE is a highly regulated sector (see Chapter 3), as LDers, measuring and evaluating impact is a necessary aspect of the role.

It may be that the way in which you undertake evaluation and measure impact is already prescribed by your institution or LD service. If this is the case, then do follow the required processes and seek guidance from colleagues if needed. If you have choice about how to evaluate and measure impact then, as a starting point, you could aim to capture demographic data about who uses your tutorial services. This data can inform you of who is accessing and engaging with LD provision. You could create a simple tracking table or spreadsheet via a tool like Microsoft Excel or even Microsoft Word. Using this, you might gather data such as student identification number, course or programme, level of study, demographic data, type of tutorial (i.e. whether online or in-person), any specific student needs or support plan, and a record of what was discussed. This information should be kept securely according to your university's data compliance and retention policy, as required, for instance, by the European General Data Protection Regulation (GDPR) or the equivalent UK GDPR.

You could also gather qualitative data to find out how students experience tutorials. For example, following a tutorial, you could send a survey asking students about their experience of the tutorial and whether they feel the tutorials have had any impact on their study. You might pose questions such as whether the tutorial covered what they expected, what they gained from attending the tutorial, and provide a section for them to add any additional comments. Surveys could be sent out immediately after a tutorial or a few weeks post tutorial as this may produce a more accurate representation of their experience. Such data, both qualitative and quantitative, could then be evaluated and analysed according to your specific purposes. For instance, you might choose to scrutinise who is attending in terms of demographic data such as gender, or you might look for patterns of attendance based on programme level. You might track and compare attendance at tutorials with attainment over time or compare your current data to a previous year's data. Such evaluation provides a useful basis for demonstrating impact and can be shared with academic colleagues and senior management via a report in wider departmental or faculty meetings.

Impact can also be seen in the positive interactions you will have with individual students, the authentic and respectful relationships you develop over time, students' anecdotal feedback ('Thank you so much, it was really helpful!') and when you know they have finally understood – that 'lightbulb' moment. These moments are intangible and might not provide you with quantifiable 'data', but they should serve as a reminder of the positive and influential work you are doing.

Concluding comments

Conducting tutorials as a new LDer can be daunting, particularly if you are meeting new students each time. This chapter will have given you some ideas on how to conduct and structure an effective LD tutorial. In this chapter, we thought about how planning and preparation can help you to feel more confident in carrying out tutorials. We saw that whilst tutorials are time and labour intensive, they are also hugely beneficial for students (and you) as an arena to explore, in depth, experiences of being a student. We looked at ways of structuring a tutorial, including via a dialogic approach and a 'formulation' model.

Reflective task

- What are your next steps in terms of developing your experience of conducting tutorials?
- What would you like to learn more about?

It is important to emphasise that there is no one 'right' way to run a tutorial and there are many approaches that can be taken which have not been explored in this chapter. However, what does matter is the way in which you interact with the student to establish a space where they feel respected and safe to communicate authentically with you. Following your next tutorial, try to reflect on what worked well and what you found difficult, either using a model such as Gibbs' (1988) reflective cycle model (see Figure 4.1) or in any way that works for you. The more tutorials you experience running, the more your confidence should slowly grow in dealing with a range of student queries. By centring the student, rather than your 'performance' in the tutorial you will also be very much reflecting ALDinHE core values of 'working in partnership with students and staff to make sense and get the most out of HE' and 'embracing and respecting diverse learners through critical pedagogy and practice' (ALDinHE, 2024a).

Summary

- In this chapter, we looked at what tutorials are, why they are common in LD practice, and how to structure an effective tutorial.
- The chapter provided guidance on a range of topics including different approaches to running an online or in-person tutorial, tips for timing and structuring tutorials, ways to encourage and promote attendance, what to do when tutorials present difficulties, and how to respond to student questions.
- You had the opportunity to reflect on your next steps in terms of developing your understanding of running effective tutorials.

Notes

1 See Chapter 2 for extended discussion on LD as a third space 'intermediary' role.
2 JiscMail lists can be accessed at https://www.jiscmail.ac.uk/. These are professional email discussion lists for practitioners in the education and research community. It is a UK-based site but has many subscribers worldwide. The lists cover a range of professional interests including the Learning Development in Higher Education Network (LDHEN). You can sign up to as many JiscMail email lists as you wish.
3 See Chapter 9 on 'Professional Development'.
4 For detailed explanation and discussion of the 5Ps approach, see Webster (2023) and Webster (2024).
5 Transforming Access and Student Outcomes in Higher Education (TASO) is a UK-based charity, funded by the Office for Students, that specialises in evidence-informed approaches to evaluation to improve student success and equality gaps (www.taso.org.uk). They provide guidance and frameworks for evaluating the impact of your work or a specific intervention.

References

ALDinHE (2024a) *About ALDinHE*. Available at: https://aldinhe.ac.uk/about-aldinhe/ (Accessed: 9 April 2024).

ALDinHE (2024b) *Neurodivergence Resource Bank*. Available at: https://aldinhe.ac.uk/resource-bank/neurodivergence/ (Accessed: 9 April 2024).

Brazant, K. (2023) 'Going beyond remedial learning support: Reframing learning development as a catalyst for practice learning. A case study exploring father involvement in social work education', *Journal of Learning Development in Higher Education [Preprint]*, 29. https://doi.org/10.47408/jldhe.vi29.1140

de Silva, D. and Dempsey, E. (2022) 'Empathy and compassion: Towards wellbeing in learning development', *Journal of Learning Development in Higher Education*, 25. https://doi.org/10.47408/jldhe.vi22.988

Delderfield, R. and McHattie, H. (2018) 'The person-centred approach in maths skills development: Examining a case of good practice', *Journal of Learning Development in Higher Education [Preprint]*, 13. https://doi.org/10.47408/jldhe.v0i13.447

Dobinson-Harrington, A. (2006) 'Personal tutor encounters: Understanding the experience', *Nursing Standard: Official Newspaper of the Royal College of Nursing*, 20(50), 35–42. https://doi.org/10.7748/ns2006.08.20.50.35.c4485

Gibbs, G. (1988) *Learning by Doing: A Guide to Teaching and Learning Methods*. Further Education Unit. Oxford: Oxford Polytechnic.

Gilmour, A. (2021) 'Adopting a pedagogy of kindness', *Journal of Learning Development in Higher Education [Preprint]*, 22. https://doi.org/10.47408/jldhe.vi22.798

Gurbutt, D. J. and Gurbutt, R. (2015) 'Empowering students to promote independent learning: A project utilising coaching approaches to support learning and personal development', *Journal of Learning Development in Higher Education [Preprint]*, 8. https://doi.org/10.47408/jldhe.v0i8.225

Hill, P., Tinker, A. and Catterall, S. (2010) 'From deficiency to development: The evolution of academic skills provision at one UK university', *Journal of Learning Development in Higher Education [Preprint]*, 2. https://doi.org/10.47408/jldhe.v0i2.54

Hillman, J. and Lochtie, D. (2024) 'Evaluating our "impact": Reflections from the personal learning advice service', *Journal of Learning Development in Higher Education [Preprint]*, 32. https://doi.org/10.47408/jldhe.vi32.1447

hooks, b. (2010) *Teaching Critical Thinking: Practical Wisdom*. New York: Routledge.

Jewitt, K. (2024, 27 June) *LD@3: The Art of Storytelling for Learning Developers: How to Transform Complex Ideas into Compelling Narratives [Webinar]*. ALDinHE [Online].

JiscMail (2025) *What is JiscMail?* Available at: https://www.jiscmail.ac.uk/about/whatisjiscmail.html#:~:text=JiscMail%20is%20the%20national%20academic,discussions%2C%20knowledge%20exchange%20and%20collaboration (Accessed: 5 April 2025).

Johnson, I. and Bishopp-Martin, S. (2024) 'Conceptual foundations in learning development', in A. Syska and C. Buckley (eds) *How to be a Learning Developer in Higher Education: Critical Perspectives, Community and Practice*. Abingdon: Routledge, 15–24.

LDHEN (2019) *LD Tutorial Time Query*. Available at: https://www.jiscmail.ac.uk/cgi-bin/wa-jisc.exe?A3=ind1901&L=LDHEN&E=quoted-printable&P=9832343&B=-000000000000d3eb0b05809bd855&T=text%2Fhtml;%20charset=UTF-8&pending= (Accessed: 1 April 2024).

Lea, M. R. and Street, B. V. (1998) 'Student writing in higher education: An academic literacies approach', *Studies in Higher Education*, 23(2), 157–172. https://doi.org/10.1080/03075079812331380364

Loddick, A. and Coulson, K. (2020) 'The impact of learning development tutorials on student attainment', *Journal of Learning Development in Higher Education*, 17. https://doi.org/10.47408/jldhe.vi17.558

Psaros, C. (2022) '"Walk me through your dissertation": Using urban walks to develop students' thinking about research', *Journal of Learning Development in Higher Education [Preprint]*, 25. https://doi.org/10.47408/jldhe.vi25.968

Shackleton, E. and Peel, K. (2023) 'Enhancing attainment and belonging at the London College of Fashion: A proactive personalised approach to address limitations of the academic support provision', *Journal of Learning Development in Higher Education [Preprint]*, 29. https://doi.org/10.47408/jldhe.vi29.1109

Thompson-Cook, S. (2024) 'What if I am the story? Using self-disclosure as a teaching tool', *Journal of Learning Development in Higher Education [Preprint]*, 32. https://doi.org/10.47408/jldhe.vi32.1410

Tobin, L. (2010) 'Self-disclosure as a strategic teaching tool: What I do – and don't – tell my students', *College English*, 73(2), 196–206. Available at: https://www.jstor.org/stable/25790469 (Accessed: 1 April 2025).

Turner, J. (2011) 'The case for one-to-one academic advice for students', in P. Hartley, J. Hilsdon, C. Keenan, S. Sinfield and M. Verity (eds) *Learning Development in Higher Education*. Basingstoke: Palgrave Macmillan, 91–101.

Webster, H. M. (2023) 'The five Ps of LD: Using formulation in learning development work for a student-centred approach to study skills', *Journal of University Teaching & Learning Practice*, 20(4). https://doi.org/10.53761/1.20.4.07

Webster, H. M. (2024) 'The five Ps of LD in practice: Student partnership approaches in one-to-one, workshops and online work', *Journal of Learning Development in Higher Education [Preprint]*, 32. https://doi.org/10.47408/jldhe.vi32.1457

Ideas for further reading

Coaching models in Learning Development

Gurbutt, D. J. and Gurbutt, R. (2015) 'Empowering students to promote independent learning: A project utilising coaching approaches to support learning and personal development', *Journal of Learning Development in Higher Education [Preprint]*, 8. https://doi.org/10.47408/jldhe.v0i8.225

The Five Ps of LD: a formulation approach (in detail)

Webster, H. (2023) 'The five Ps of LD: Using formulation in learning development work for a student-centred approach to study skills', *Journal of University Teaching & Learning Practice*, 20(4). https://doi.org/10.53761/1.20.4.07

Chapter 5

Teaching and delivering workshops

> **This chapter provides an overview of**
> - What is meant by an optional or extra-curricular skills workshop.
> - Why workshops are commonplace in Learning Development (LD).
>
> **You will be guided on how to**
> - Encourage students to attend and participate in your workshops.
> - Structure an online or in-person workshop.
> - Plan and develop ideas for workshop content.
> - Deal with classroom management issues.
> - Assess the impact of workshops.

What do I already know about workshops?

One of the main student-facing aspects of the LD role is to teach or 'deliver' optional or extra-curricular academic skills workshops. As such, as a new or early career Learning Developer (LDer), much of your time will be spent planning, creating, designing, and delivering or leading such sessions. This chapter aims to provide clarity on what workshops are, what they are for, and why they are everyday practice in LD, and suggests ways to structure an effective workshop.

> **Reflective task**
> - What do you understand by the term 'workshop'?
> - Do you have any experience of teaching or delivering workshops?
> - Have you attended any workshops as a participant?

DOI: 10.4324/9781003604266-5

You might already have extensive experience of delivering workshops in a context outside of LD. Perhaps, as is common, you have entered LD from a teaching or training background and are aware of the parallels and distinctions between these and workshops. If you have attended workshops in the past as a participant, it can be helpful to reflect on your subjective experience of these:

> **Reflective task**
>
> - What was the 'best' workshop you attended? What was the 'worst'?
> - Did you feel that the workshop was well structured and clear?
> - Did the tutor or facilitator do a lot of talking or did they manage the session so that you did most of the work?
> - Was there anything you particularly liked/disliked about the tutor's approach?
> - Did you learn anything from the workshop? Did you enjoy it?

Recalling your past experiences as a workshop participant can be a useful starting point when planning your own sessions as it can help you to reflect on what works well. If you have little idea of what an effective LD workshop might look like, this chapter will hopefully aid you to better understand how to plan and structure one. It also covers how to encourage students to attend, how to deal with classroom management challenges that may arise and suggests ways to assess and evaluate the impact of your workshops.

What are workshops?

An LD workshop is a session in which students (and you!) work to better understand or develop a particular study skill, academic literacy, or other aspect of their learning. Workshops can be generic, covering common academic skills such as time management and organisational skills, academic writing and reading, critical thinking and reflection, note making, and referencing and research skills. They can also be discipline specific if, for instance, you work with students from a particular faculty or have a specialism. For example, an LDer specialising in working with maths students might teach workshops covering statistics, basic maths skills, and improving understanding of maths vocabulary. An LDer supporting students undertaking chemistry degrees might deliver workshops on subject-relevant skills such as laboratory skills and scientific writing.

LD workshops can be optional or extra-curricular, such that students choose or self-select whether to attend the sessions as 'extra' to their main studies or degree programme, or they can be embedded into students' curriculum.[1]

Whilst extra-curricular workshops are typically standalone, one-off sessions, they can also be developed as a series, sometimes with a specific theme, building upon previous learning, or as targeted workshops, for example, a suite of workshops preparing new students to higher education (HE) (Burns et al., 2024, p. 57).

Extra-curricular workshops can raise a challenge in terms of whether students will show up. In addition, you will have different students attending each time, with whom you have no existing relationship and must quickly establish an effective teaching and learning environment. Though this might seem daunting as a new LDer, there is significant potential for such workshops to be a physical or virtual space where you can actively demonstrate 'working in partnership with students . . . to make sense and get the most out of HE' (ALDinHE, 2024a). If students have a positive experience of your sessions, the likelihood is that they will return and will talk encouragingly about them with others which can act as endorsement for your service. Given the potential for well-run workshops to improve students' perception of and engagement with LD, it will be important to think carefully about workshop design, how to boost attendance, and ways to ensure that your sessions are engaging, accessible, and inclusive.

With workshops, the emphasis is 'work'. Ideally, they should involve students actively 'doing' something rather than a didactic 'chalk and talk' approach. As such, workshops (and teaching in general) tend to be most effective, when there is opportunity for 'doing' through practice, interaction, questioning, and discussion. Workshops that do not include a high level of interaction might be better thought of as online seminars (webinars) or in-person lectures/talks. There is nothing intrinsically wrong with running a taught session as a webinar or in-person talk, but where these are titled 'workshop' students attending will expect that they will be active rather than solely listening to you speak. This does not mean that you cannot incorporate periods of explanation and lecturing but, for it to be a workshop in its truest sense, much of the session should allow for students' active involvement. The next section briefly considers why workshops are commonplace in LD. Given that you may have questions about where to begin with planning and teaching engaging, interactive and well-structured sessions, the remainder of the chapter focuses on practical suggestions that should aid with this.

Why are workshops commonplace in Learning Development?

Workshops are common practice in LD. First, as compared to tutorials, they offer a convenient way to provide LD support to many students. In an hour-long workshop, you will encounter significantly more students than in a tutorial. In a workshop, you work alongside students to develop their understanding of the key literacies and skills they need to succeed on their course.

Effective workshops then, like tutorials, can become a space whereby students are enabled to actively contribute, participate, and engage in the process of metacognition or 'learn[ing] how to learn' (Burns et al., 2024, p. 57). As such, they provide the means to enact a fundamental value of LD, that is, 'to work in partnership with students . . . to make sense and get the most out of HE' (ALDinHE, 2024a).

How might I promote Learning Development workshops?

The most important thing is to make sure that students attend your workshops. It may be that your university actively supports you in promoting your sessions, for instance, by advertising LD sessions through its institutional website. If you work in a team of LDers, is there a pre-existing established suite of workshops that are well advertised such that you do not need to worry too much about promotion and can simply 'deliver' them? Or will you need to create workshops and publicise them yourself? If so, there are many approaches that could be taken to make your service visible.

You will likely already have an LD presence on your university website. If this is the case, then promoting optional skills workshops through your institutions' website is an obvious starting point given a websites' potential to reach the entire student community and beyond.

> **Task**
>
> - Go online and find three or four examples of LD/study skills websites from universities.
> - How do they promote their workshops (and other resources)?
> - What are the strengths/weaknesses of the layouts?

If your LD service does not already have a website presence, it will be important to discuss the need for this with the digital or marketing team in your institution or a senior manager with remit to push for creating this. Workshops can also be publicised through social media if your university policy allows, via your university's virtual learning environment (VLE), or through digital newsletters. Do not forget offline promotion. Physical 'study skills' posters, which are displayed in a visible place around campus, incorporating a quick booking QR code, can be highly effective. Recommendations or testimonials from students can provide an additional means to advertise the benefits of attending workshops. With students' permission, you could display such testimonials in written form or get students to speak on a video or podcast to be viewed on your LD website or the student VLE. Subject lecturers could also be asked to promote skills workshops to students within classes or in their communications. This could be as simple as them displaying a 'study skills' slide with contact and booking details for the LD service at the end of their seminar or lecture presentation.

However you publicise your workshops, it will be important to make it clear what the session will cover, who the workshop is aimed at, the duration of the session, and its location. The following provides an example of a blurb published on a university events website to promote a workshop for law students:

Workshop blurb

Academic skills workshop: Reading cases and statutes for beginners
  When: 8 October 2024, 16:00–17:00 GMT
  Venue: Online

- Do you find reading cases and statutes overwhelming?
- Are you unsure of where to start when reading cases and statutes?
- Do you struggle with understanding the different elements of a case or statute?

If you answered yes to any of the above questions, then you may find this workshop useful. In this beginner's level workshop, we will consider why reading cases and statutes (as opposed to solely casebooks or textbook summaries) is important. We will learn about how to read a case or statute, by considering its different elements and the importance of taking an active approach. You will go away with useful tips for your reading of cases and statutes.

In the blurb above, questions are included to get the students' attention. The blurb states the level of the workshop, as well as its venue and length. Students are provided with a brief synopsis of what the session will cover and its key learning outcomes. Making clear the workshop outcomes will be particularly important for adult, often time-poor, students who want to see the benefit they derive from attending an optional session. To improve the blurb, images could be incorporated to increase its visual appeal, and an accessible QR code or link could be integrated to enable students to have a quick and direct way of booking.

Promoting and publicising workshops is only the first step. You will also need to think carefully about the practicalities of the session itself. The next few sections consider questions of location, timing, and structure.

Where should workshops take place?

Workshops can take place in-person, typically in a classroom or lecture room, in an outdoor environment, or online using a video conferencing platform such as Zoom or Teams. It may be that the location of your workshops is prescribed or that you have flexibility and choice on this. Following the COVID-19 pandemic, many LD services successfully pivoted to offer fully online support, including online workshop provision (Key, 2022; Fallin, 2023). For many providers, there has since been a movement back to offering in-person teaching whilst trying to retain the benefits of online and digital learning (Keane et al., 2024).

When making preliminary decisions about location, it can be helpful to think through these initial questions:

- What is the purpose and objective of the workshop?
- Can the activities and tasks I have planned be easily completed online or would they work better in-person?
- Will students be able to access the online platform or physical classroom?

The purpose and objectives of your workshop might not be the deciding factor as to whether it should be best held in-person or online. For instance, a workshop with the aim to develop students' presentation or group work skills could be delivered effectively both online and in-person. A workshop which includes lots of physical tasks might work equally well in an online context or could be better suited to in-person. Thus, decisions as to workshop location might be better informed by the pragmatic question of the likelihood of students attending in-person as opposed to online.

For in-person workshops, think carefully about classroom layout, if you have any control over this. How do you want students working? If you want lots of small group discussion, you could organise the layout in 'café-style' so that tables are grouped together. If you are planning to lead a more didactic session, rows might work well. If you want room for movement, a horseshoe layout would be well suited. Consider how many students are likely to attend your sessions and whether there are enough tables and chairs in the room you have booked. Check that the room has access to the resources you need. If it is an unfamiliar room, it can be helpful to visit it in advance to see that everything is in working order. For instance, is it accessible to students with mobility issues? Are computers and visual display screens working? Does the sound work? Is the room warm or cool enough? Are chairs positioned in a way that students can see you and the whiteboard? If you are using a manual whiteboard, are there pens and a board eraser?

For workshops taking place outdoors, be conscious of the external environment. Is the suggested location easily accessible to all students? Will conditions such as the weather be appropriate for leading an outdoor session? Will you need to do any health or safety checks beforehand and, if so, what is your university's policy on this? How many students will attend the session, and can this be managed safely if it is outdoors?

In terms of online workshops, consider the virtual classroom environment. Which video conferencing platform (e.g. Zoom or Teams) will you use? This might be prescribed by your institution, or you may get to choose. You will need to decide whether students can enter the session automatically or whether you will employ a 'waiting room'. Other practical considerations include whether you will enable student participation in the form of reactions, comments, and microphones and whether 'breakout' rooms will be used. You should also decide in advance if you will record the session and, if so, ensure that students are aware and have given their consent for this. This might be as simple as displaying a visual message on a slide or putting a message in the chat stating that the session will be recorded. Consider the workshop from the students' perspectives. For example, will they have stable internet access to participate in your workshop? Will they know how to use the video conferencing platform, or will you need to provide instructions? If you have included lots of tasks or breakout room activities, will they still be able to engage in the workshop if they are on the move or not in a fixed location?

Another thing to think about when delivering online (and in-person) workshops is your use of slides or technology. Will you be using presentation software such as PowerPoint or Prezi? Are you intending to use an interactive whiteboard? Are you planning to use online interactive or collaborative tools such as Mentimeter, Miro, or Padlet? If so, make sure you do a run-through of the technology or slides beforehand to counter any potential mishaps. If it is the first time you have used the technology or software, it is fine to share this with students in the session as they will tend to be very accommodating. However, always have a backup plan for if the technology fails. For example, in an online session, if a video clip fails to load or to play sound, you could instead provide students with a short pre-prepared transcript or key stills or images from the video with associated captions. Having an alternative plan can help you feel more at ease and in control and will prevent panic setting in for when things do (inevitably) go wrong.

Thinking through these types of practical questions and issues, and potential solutions, prior to your workshop, is good pedagogical practice, can aid with your session being successful, and reduces the likelihood of things going awry.

How long should a workshop last?

In terms of the duration of a workshop, this is not set in stone. My online and in-person workshops range anywhere from 30 minutes (for more didactic sessions) to 90 minutes where the content is complex or where several activities are planned. Factors to take into consideration include the nature of the topic, the number of learning aims, how many activities you wish to include, and whether it is in-person or online. You will also need to think about how much content there is to cover, whether the content is sufficiently engaging for the time you must teach, and whether students (and you) will be able to keep up concentration for the time. Over prepare rather than under prepare, but do not be tempted to pack in too much as otherwise students might perceive that you are rushing through the content, and you will be rushing through. I have been there trying to cram two hours of content into an hour session, and it is not much fun!

It is also important to consider the estimated length of time for tasks and to factor in additional time; for instance, plan in extra time for if things go wrong with the technology and for responding to student questions. Keep in mind that activities or tasks might take longer or shorter than estimated, so build in some 'flexitime' to account for this potential fluctuation and always have backup or extension tasks for students. For longer workshops, particularly those held online, you might wish to factor in time for a short comfort break to help reduce screen fatigue for attendees. In an in-person workshop, you also need to account for students arriving to the venue, making sure you allow flexibility and have a plan to enable late arrivals to catch up with the session content.

How do I structure a workshop?

Task

You are delivering a beginner-level optional skills standalone workshop on essay writing.

- Picture your ideal scenario. How would it start?
- In what ways would the students be interacting with you and one another?
- What activities would students be engaged in?
- What role would you play? Would you be more of a facilitator or a lecturer?
- How much talking would you encourage?
- If online, would you want cameras off or on?
- How would you conclude the workshop?
- How would you know students have learned something from the session?

Similarly to an engaging story, lesson, or performance, a workshop needs to have a clear beginning, middle, and end. This holds true even for more experimental or playful type workshops which might be more free flowing. The mantra for the structure of a workshop should run something like this: 'This is what we are going to learn', 'Here we are learning it', and 'This is what we learned'. This does not mean that you need to stick rigidly to what you have designed or planned as it is crucial to allow for flexibility, where necessary. However, having an idea of the overall or basic structure of your session and its aims and intended outcomes allows you to think clearly about how you will manage the class, activities, and timings. We will consider structure in detail later.

Have clear objectives and outcomes

With workshops, the aim is that students leave the session having learnt something new, having developed a skill, or with a better understanding of a key concept. As such, it is important to have clear learning objectives and outcomes. Share these with students at the start of the session. This might be done verbally or in writing on your slides. If you are confident, you could also get the students to devise their own workshop objectives based on what they know about the upcoming workshop content.

A learning objective should be phrased in relation to the intended learning. For instance, you could use a theoretical model such as Bloom's Taxonomy (Bloom, 1956) to frame your objectives.

Bloom's Taxonomy – named after the educational psychologist Benjamin Bloom who led the group responsible for creating the framework (Harvard University, n.d.) – categorises learning skills progressively from lower order to higher order, that is, from more 'basic' skills such as remembering and understanding to increasingly complex skills such as creating and evaluating (see Figure 5.1). Whilst this classification has been subject to extensive critique and modification (Harvard University, n.d.), it does provide a useful aide memoire when planning workshop objectives. The following examples of learning objectives explicitly incorporate the wording from the taxonomy.

Example learning objectives

- Students will be able to *recognise* the key elements of an academic essay.
- Students will better understand how to *construct* an effective thesis statement.
- Students will be better able to *evaluate* the effectiveness of thesis statements.

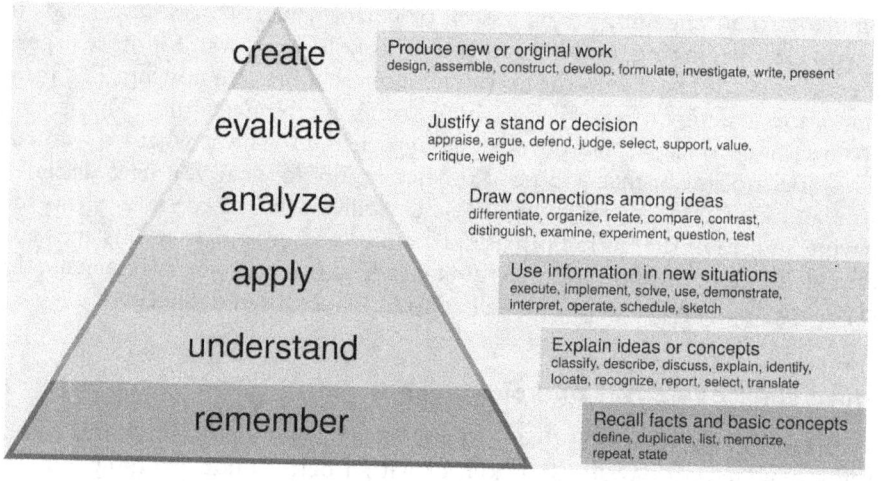

Figure 5.1 Bloom's Taxonomy of learning.

Source: Image by Tidema – Own work. Licensed under CC-BY 4.0 via Wikimedia Commons at https://commons.wikimedia.org/w/index.php?curid=152872571

Learning objectives should be specific and achievable within the time allocated for your session. Try to keep these to a maximum of one or two unless you have sufficient time to address more. It is also important that any tasks that you choose to include in a workshop align with or support the intended objectives. This link between what students do (the activities) and the workshop (or learning) aims is known as the theory of 'constructive alignment' (Biggs, 1996). For instance, take the following intended learning outcomes (ILOs):

ILO: Students will be able to *recognise* the key elements of an argumentative essay.

Relevant tasks that might align with this intended aim include the following:

- Working in pairs to annotate the different elements of an argumentative essay, for example, introduction, thesis statement, main body analysis, and conclusion.
- Piecing together/restructuring an essay that has been cut up into sections, for example, introduction, main body, and conclusion.
- Looking at an extract from a 'poor' argumentative essay to identify what is missing structurally.
- A Mentimeter quiz on the various elements of argumentative essays and their function.

Learning outcomes should focus on the learning and not the activity. For example, note how the outcomes in the 'Example learning objectives' box specify the expected learning rather than the activities or tasks the students will complete. For instance, instead of 'Students will fill out a planning template to structure an academic essay', as an intended learning objective this is better worded as, 'Students will understand how to construct an essay plan for an academic essay'.

> **Task**
>
> Rephrase this ILO so that it focuses on the learning rather than the task.
>
> - Students will annotate an introduction to an essay.

For Task 5.7, you might have written something like 'Students will be able to identify the elements of an effective introduction'. This draws explicitly upon the wording from Bloom's Taxonomy and relates specifically to the learning and not the task. Once you have clear learning objectives and intended outcomes, you can then plan or outline the relevant tasks, activities, timings, and structure using a planning frame. Appendix 2 provides an example of a workshop plan.

Have a clear beginning to the workshop

As we saw earlier, it can be helpful to think of your workshop like an essay – it needs a clear beginning, middle, and end. If, for instance, your workshop is for one hour, you will need to decide how to introduce the session, what you want students doing during the main part of the session, and how to end it.

One way to start is with some practicalities. If you are online, check that students can see you and any slides and that they can hear you. Introduce yourself, state how long the workshop is expected to last, when questions can be asked, and, if online, provide instructions about how students can interact with the platform (e.g. cameras on/off, chat function, and use of 'reactions' such as emojis). Not all learners will be familiar with the functionality of the video conferencing platform (e.g. Teams or Zoom) so a brief run-through of how to use it can be helpful for attendees. This can be done verbally, but it is often helpful, particularly for neurodivergent learners, to provide this information in different modes. For instance, you could provide a verbal explanation accompanied by a slide or visual that explains how to use the raise hand function or reactions. Whether online or in-person, be clear about when questions will be answered.

Would you like students to save questions until the end? Do you want students to ask questions verbally or in the chat? If students can ask questions during the presentation, how will you ensure that you stay on track in terms of timing? How will you deal with questions that go off on a different tangent?

After the initial practicalities, you could then launch straight into the session outlining the goals and objectives. Figures 5.2 and 5.3 are examples of preliminary slides that I use in a workshop about analysing the essay question. I talk through these to introduce the workshop objectives and workshop structure.

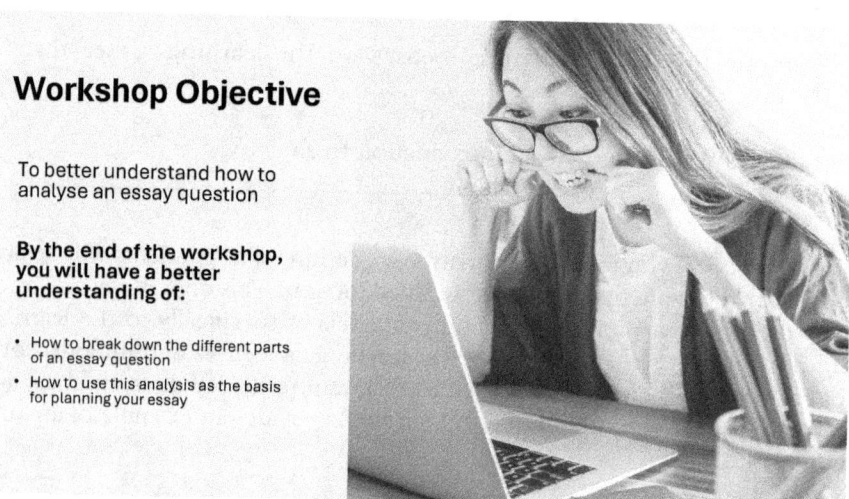

Figure 5.2 Slide with workshop objectives.

Figure 5.3 Slide outlining workshop structure.

Ideally, after these preliminaries, you would then try to get a sense of the students in the workshop. As a reminder, LD practice aims to help students make sense of HE *as the student experiences it* [original emphasis] (Johnson and Bishopp-Martin, 2024, p. 16; ALDinHE, 2024a). This is why it is useful to begin by identifying or assessing students' starting points. What do the students already know about the topic? What is their previous experience, prior knowledge, or confidence level in relation to the topic? For this, you could ask students to complete a task or starter activity to assess their current understanding or confidence levels. This could be revisited at the end of the workshop. For instance, you could start with a poll using an interactive learning platform as in Figures 5.4 and 5.5.

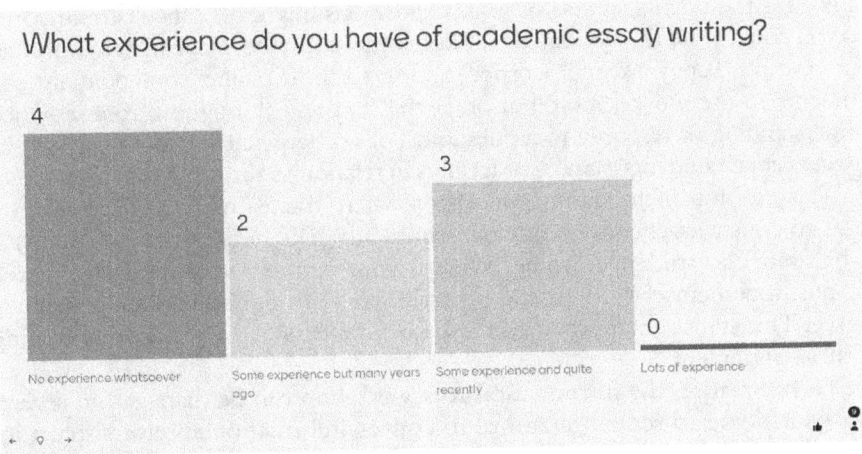

Figure 5.4 Starter activity: an interactive poll.
Source: Created with Mentimeter.com

Figure 5.5 Starter activity: an interactive word shower.
Source: Created with Mentimeter.com

Such activities can provide the basis for initiating dialogue and can be used formatively to assess students' initial confidence and prior knowledge. For example, you could ask students to complete a poll at the beginning of the workshop about how confident they feel about the topic and repeat the same poll towards the end of the workshop to gauge if their perception of their confidence level has shifted.

Incorporating images or short video clips with discussion points or questions as a starter activity is another way to create immediate interest and participation in the session.[2] You could use simple emoji images or smiley faces to assess how students feel about a topic. This could provide a starting point for exploring commonalities or challenges within the group. Note that for some students, particularly autistic students, emojis or facial expressions might be difficult to interpret, so you could write the associated emotion underneath the image to help with this, for example, happy, excited, worried, and so forth. If online, you could also get students to use the 'reaction' button at the start and throughout to assess their understanding or response to a question. Polls or targeted questions can also be used to check students' stances or feelings in relation to the topic as in Figure 5.6.

This poll was included in a workshop where the learning objective was on how to construct effective academic arguments. The heading states, 'GenAI is a hindrance to student learning. What is your opinion?'. Students were asked to position themselves on a sliding scale from strongly disagree to strongly agree. This stance then provided the basis for a later activity involving writing a thesis statement.

To summarise, the introduction to a workshop can be managed in several ways including to set expectations, to convey information about its structure

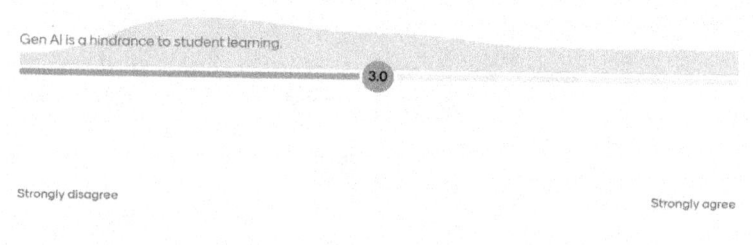

Figure 5.6 Gauging students' stances: an interactive poll.
Source: created with Mentimeter.com

and aims, to manage students' expectations about the content, to get a sense of students' starting points, and to create interest in what is to follow. What other ideas do you have for starting your workshops?

What should I do during the main part of the workshop?

As it is a 'workshop', students should ideally be engaged in doing something at regular stages so aim to intersperse periods of you talking with an activity or task for students to complete. For instance, in an hour workshop, you could divide this into bite-size chunks or mini sessions, for example, for every 10 minutes of explanation and talking (when student attention span starts to decline) students could complete a five-minute task. This would mean that in a workshop of an hour you would have three or four interactive tasks for students to complete. The next section provides examples of tasks used during a workshop.

Include relevant multimodal tasks

Aim to include a variety of tasks that incorporate elements of group and pair work, whole class discussion, and independent work. Remember that according to the theory of constructive alignment tasks should clearly align with and create the conditions for students to meet the learning objectives. If the use is pedagogically sound – that is, if it is relevant to the workshop aims – include multimodal teaching and learning materials such as video, sound, and images. This does not mean that in every single workshop you must include all these modes but, across your entire workshop offering, there should be variation so that students' interest is maintained. Here are some examples of tasks used within an hour workshop.

The ILO of the online workshop in Figure 5.7 was to better understand and be able to apply criteria for assessing the credibility of a source. To align with this objective, students were asked to review three online sources, two of which were unacceptable or acceptable, and one that was deliberately debateable according to the criteria. They were given 10 minutes to complete the task in pairs. Following this, they had to provide reasons and justify their ratings. Students were encouraged to feedback in any way they wanted, via the chat or on the microphone.

The activity in Figure 5.8 was a main body task in an orientation workshop where the aim was for undergraduate students to better understand what learning at university entails. Students were asked to watch a short video of about two minutes with lecturers from different institutions explaining the learning behaviours they value in students. The video incorporated closed captions to make it accessible for all learners. Prior to watching, students had to think about what they expected the lecturers to mention. Students were asked

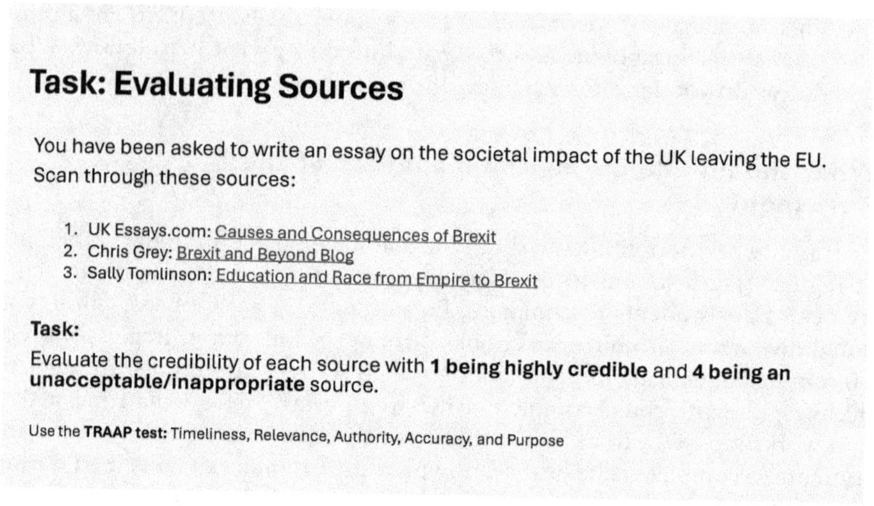

Task: Evaluating Sources

You have been asked to write an essay on the societal impact of the UK leaving the EU. Scan through these sources:

1. UK Essays.com: Causes and Consequences of Brexit
2. Chris Grey: Brexit and Beyond Blog
3. Sally Tomlinson: Education and Race from Empire to Brexit

Task:
Evaluate the credibility of each source with **1 being highly credible** and **4 being an unacceptable/inappropriate** source.

Use the **TRAAP test:** Timeliness, Relevance, Authority, Accuracy, and Purpose

Figure 5.7 Example workshop task (a).
Source: Image by Jan Vašek from Pixabay

What do lecturers value in their students?

We are going to watch a short video featuring lecturers talking about what they value in students

- What do you think the lecturers might mention?
- Write your thoughts in the Menti slide.

Now that you have watched the video

- Were your ideas similar or different to those put forward by the lecturers?

Figure 5.8 Example workshop task (b).
Source: Image by StockSnap from Pixabay

to write their thoughts in a slide, and these ideas were then compared to the ideas mentioned in the video.

Assess students' learning

During the main part of your workshop, aim to routinely assess or check whether students have made any progress or whether the learning objectives are being met. This can be done throughout, and not just as a final review, by asking simple, precise questions. For example, instead of saying, 'Does that all make sense?' or 'Do you understand?' which leaves room for students to simply nod or thumbs up at you even if they have no idea of what you mean, you can ask specific open questions related to the content. For example, you might ask, 'How might you use this approach in your essay?' or 'What is one area that you found difficult to understand?' or 'How would you explain [this concept] in your own words?'. If it is an online class, you can check for understanding using the chat or microphone, or you could gamify assessment by asking poll or quiz questions related to the workshop content as in Figure 5.9.

Here, the slide title was, 'White collar crime is, arguably, one of the most harmful types of crime to society as those with, and in, power'. Students were asked to decide whether this statement was an 'opinion', 'description', or 'argument'. Opinion was selected as the correct answer as there were no reasons or evidence provided to support the stance and no attempt to persuade. This led to further discussion as to how this stance might develop into an effective academic argument.

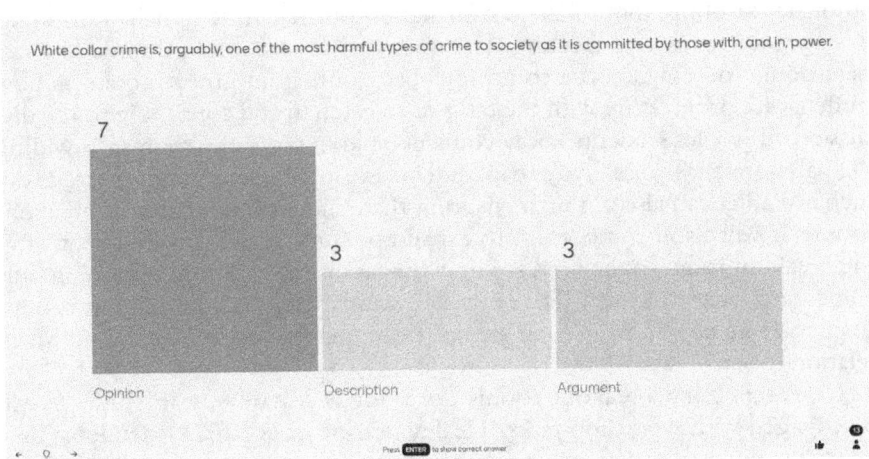

Figure 5.9 Assessing understanding: an interactive poll.

Source: Created with Mentimeter.com

Online teaching: to breakout room or not to breakout room?

Online breakout rooms in video conferencing platforms such as Zoom or Teams are intended to function like small group work in a real live classroom. For many reasons, even though they are designed to replicate in-person group work, breakout rooms often strike fear into the hearts of students, and you may start to notice a gradual drop in numbers as students silently exit the virtual classroom. Breakout rooms can be difficult for students for several reasons; for instance, they may experience it as an 'unexpected interruption' from the 'insulated world afforded by' being on platforms such as Zoom or Teams (Healey-Benson et al., 2024, p. 4) or as enforced conversation with unfamiliar people. However, part of 'workshopping' should be an element of engagement and participation from the students. How might this be encouraged if students are unwilling to go into breakout rooms? Should you use breakout rooms at all?

Structured breakout rooms can be effective for promoting participation and student voice. I emphasise the word 'structured' here. Students should have a clear task to complete when in groups or breakout rooms. Specific tasks or discussion points should be explained verbally, visually, and/or in the chat function prior to opening the breakout room and you should provide a clear time limit for each breakout (for an hour workshop, aim for a breakout room of no more than 10 minutes). You may choose to assign students specific roles such as timekeeper, recorder, and reporter to feedback which might help in terms of ensuring that every student has a role. Taking these steps can help to reduce students' fear of the unknown. Further, doing so might be particularly helpful for neurodivergent learners who may benefit from clear instruction, rationale for doing the task, and explanation of their role, to help with minimising uncertainty and creating structure. Just as you would do in a physical classroom, you may choose to go into breakout room groups to assess how students are progressing with the tasks or to listen in and contribute to the discussions. If so, let students know you will be going into the rooms. Providing a collaborative task or activity that students must complete using a shared tool such as Padlet can also aid with ensuring that students participate in breakout rooms. It will also be important to explain to students what will happen after the breakout room so they can see how the task is relevant to the learning outcomes and what to expect. For example, you may say, 'After breakout rooms, I will ask one person from each group to summarise the three main points in relation to [state task]'.

However, using breakout rooms does not necessarily mean students will be engaged with workshop tasks (Healey-Benson et al., 2024). Students may be sat in the breakout rooms not speaking to one another or speaking about unrelated topics to the activity you have set. This is when you may need to employ other ways to encourage students to converse that do not involve having to rely on breakout rooms. This could include the use of polls, quizzes, use of the chat function, and 'reactions' if online. It is important to give as many options as possible to students about how to engage in your sessions. This can help with them taking ownership over their own learning. For instance, if online, you can give students the alternatives of contributing via the chat, on the microphone, or simply thinking through questions in their heads. Avoid putting students on the spot and give them time to formulate their thoughts regardless of the way they choose to get involved.

Online teaching: cameras on or cameras off?

There are many benefits to having cameras on in an online context. For example, it can aid with fostering a sense of connection, allowing you as the LDer to see students' reactions and to notice visual clues about engagement. However, whilst it can be helpful to you from a pedagogical view to get a sense of 'who is in the room' by asking students to keep their cameras on, this can end up being counter-productive, in that it can deter or put undue pressure on students who may have a number of reasons for not wanting their camera on. For instance, research shows that students may be conscious of their home environment or other people in the household such as children being visible, they may be shy or feel pressure to speak when their camera is on, have anxiety or similar conditions that create difficulty, or feel concerned about their personal appearance (Lin et al., 2021; Jayasundara et al., 2023; Healey-Benson et al., 2024). As such, try not to insist that cameras should be on unless it is essential. Rather, encourage cameras on through a gentle suggestion at the start; for example, 'It would be great to see everyone as this helps with feeling more connected. If you can, please put your cameras on, but don't feel pressure to do so'. You can also encourage camera use by leaving your own camera on, by giving a time limit for cameras to be on (e.g. 'Please turn your camera on for five seconds and wave hello'), or by suggesting students turn on cameras when in smaller breakout rooms, which may feel safer for some students. If the issue is that students do not wish to see themselves on camera as this may evoke self-conscious behaviours, you can show students how to turn off self-view on the video conferencing platform at the start of sessions. Students can also use a virtual 'background' if they are concerned about their home environment being visible.

How do I encourage student engagement during the main part of the workshop?

Use digital interactive tools

Using online interactive tools that allow for anonymity such as Mentimeter or Kahoot can help with increasing engagement and participation. Such digital tools allow students to interact with your presentation or workshop and, if the technology is available, these can be used in both online and in-person contexts. For example, Mentimeter includes different interactive functions such as question and answer, quizzes, text response, word clouds, and many others. It also allows you to integrate video and audio clips directly into your presentation. However, do use such tools sparingly and include a range of activity types so that students do not experience digital overwhelm or fatigue. In an online or in-person workshop, active engagement can also be encouraged through targeted questioning, group and pair work, using scenarios and case studies, and via the use of images, video, or audio clips to explore concepts. We will explore some of these approaches for encouraging student engagement later.

Ask questions

It is important within workshops, to encourage dialogue amongst participants and yourself. Dialogue is a way that students can begin to make sense of their learning, can learn from others, and can be challenged to think deeply about their rationale for their assumptions and beliefs. Remember, dialogue does not necessarily need to be spoken. It is fine to use chat or other interactive tools or, in a classroom situation, to get students to respond in other ways other than speaking (post it notes work well). An effective way to promote dialogue and participation is to ask open-ended questions.

Questions can be either closed or open. Closed questions are questions that can be answered with a simple yes or no or specific response. For example, 'How many examples of signposting language can you see?' Closed questions can be helpful for checking whether students have understood a particular aspect of the learning. Open questions, as the name implies, encourage longer, more detailed responses. For example, you may ask, 'What do you understand by the term criticality?' or 'How would you define an academic argument?' Both forms of questioning have their place in a workshop but the aim for either should be to encourage students to think about their learning. Whilst it is possible to ask good questions spontaneously, in the earlier days of your role aim to plan the types of questions you may ask to ensure that they are relevant to the learning objectives. You could write potential questions in the notes section of your slides or materials, or they could be listed on a sheet of paper or somewhere visible on your computer screen. However, pre-prepared questions should be used as a guide, rather than to be followed slavishly as it is important to be responsive to students' concerns.

Incorporate group, pair, and independent work

Group and pair work can be used effectively in both online and in-person workshops. Positives of group work include developing transferable skills such as collaboration, communication, and leadership skills and potentially increasing engagement (Francis, 2002). However, group work managed poorly can lead to animosity and issues between group members (Francis, 2002). As such it will be important to plan carefully for group or pair work in preparation for your workshop.

Group work can work particularly well when giving students problem-solving scenarios or when posing difficult or challenging questions. For example, in an in-person workshop on essay writing structure, you might set students a task to work in pairs to reconstruct a lengthy essay that has been cut into its constituent parts and then ask them to provide feedback on structure to the larger group. When planning group work, think about the timings, how you want students working, and what you want students to be doing. Plan for how you will introduce the group work and how you will draw it to a close. If you are teaching online, you will need to ensure you know how to move students into the breakout rooms and to practise this before the live session.

There are many group work activities that you could try. As an example, jigsaw-type activities encourage a wide range of interactions and can be highly effective particularly when exploring complex topics. For this, students are given a group number (e.g. 1s, 2s, 3s, and 4s) and initially work with members with the same number (the expert group) to work on a set problem or task. At the next stage, each student from the expert group then rotates to form a 'teaching' group (i.e. the newly formed groups now have a 1, 2, 3, 4). Each student from the expert group then 'teaches' their new group as to what the expert group knows. For the last step, students provide feedback to the whole class. The jigsaw approach is illustrated in Figure 5.10.

The jigsaw approach is just one example so do experiment with several types of interactions and group work tasks. It can also be helpful to assign specific roles within groups (e.g. notetaker, reporter, timekeeper) to aid with encouraging participation from all students.

Remember that students can also be engaged when they are not speaking. Independent tasks and activities can provide time and space for students to apply what they have learned. As with paired or group work, independent

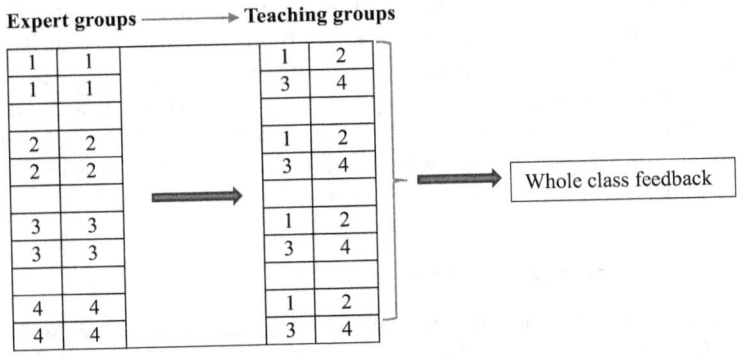

Figure 5.10 The jigsaw approach to group work.

work should be planned, and students should be provided with clear instructions as to what to do and the length of time they will have to complete the activity. To introduce an independent task, you might choose to scaffold or model a particular approach and then ask the students to complete a similar task using a different example. During independent tasks and at intermittent periods in the workshop, do not be afraid to allow for silence. This allows students (and you) time to think and to process the information they have been given. After an independent activity, check in with students by asking questions to find out how they found the task or do a whole class review.

Engagement can occur in different forms. Students might appear disengaged but might be actively thinking or processing what you have said. Silence can provide space and time for reflection and grasping of concepts. Try to ensure that you incorporate a variety of ways for students to interact with your activities to promote inclusivity for all participants.

Use images, video, and audio

Another way of engaging students in workshops is to use short film, documentary, video clips, sound files, or visuals as a discussion point. These can be used in both online and in-person workshop contexts. Chapter 7 provides more examples of how to use visuals. Always have students doing something when they are viewing a video (or listening to audio), so they are not sitting passively watching or listening. Students could have a task or question to think about that relates to the learning aim and content of the video or audio clip. For example, you could give instructions such as, 'We are going to watch a short video about [topic]. As you watch, see if you can identify three key points made about academic writing and decide whether you agree with these points'. This aids the students with taking an active approach to watching and can be applied when listening to audio clips, music, or for other forms of visual and creative media. If you are using video during your workshop, check whether it is accessible for all learners. Make sure closed captions or a transcript is enabled if online, and you might choose to slow down the playback speed if possible. It is also important to watch the video content prior to the session to check for any issues. Try to set up the video in advance of your session so that it is at the point ready to play at its appropriate time stamp and so that you are not having to fumble around trying to find the right section which can make a workshop lose momentum. Videos can be embedded in software like PowerPoint and Mentimeter and can be played within your presentation to save having to change between windows on your desktop.

Use scenarios and case studies

Relatable scenarios and case studies can also provide a useful means for stimulating dialogue amongst students. Scenarios should relate to the learning outcomes and should provide students with a problem or issue that needs to be resolved. Chapter 7 provides specific examples of how scenarios might be created and used in the classroom context.

How do I respond to student questions?

As a new LDer, you may feel worried about how to respond to student questions, particularly when you are not sure of the answer. Your workshops may be open to students from varied disciplines, or you may work with students from one discipline who have specific questions related to their course content and subject.

To deal with this, it can be helpful to remind yourself that students do not want to see you fail (i.e. why they have attended your workshop) and, mostly, they do not expect perfection. Students attending optional workshops will be there voluntarily, so they will tend to be motivated and on your side. In a situation where you do not know, do not try to bluff the answer. You will get yourself into a muddle, and students will sense that you are bluffing. It can be encouraging to students to show that you do not know the answer to everything – it shows that you are human. If you really do not know then say so, with the caveat that you will investigate it and try to get back to them at a later stage, then do your best to follow up, in a post-workshop email explaining your response to the question. Try to avoid feeling that you must present yourself as all-knowing. It is okay – and a strength – to say when you do not know the answer to something. Not knowing the answers can also provide a useful developmental point for you as you can then later do some research and will have a response for next time a similar question is posed.

You will find that students' peers often have good solutions or answers to tricky questions. Therefore, another way around not knowing the answer is to ask the other students in the workshop, that is, 'That's a great question, what do others in the room think?' To manage students' expectations, you can also make it clear at the outset that you are happy to take questions related to the workshop content but that students will need to direct subject-specific questions to their lecturers or module tutors. Usually, after some experience, you will see that student questions, although phrased differently, tend to fall under similar themes or concerns. Therefore, you might also wish to pre-empt the types of questions that students might ask about the workshop topic by creating a frequently asked questions bank plus relevant resources which you can draw upon, if needed. You might choose to answer questions throughout verbally or, if online, by students putting their questions in the chat or typing it into an interactive tool like Mentimeter. To reduce interruptions during the workshop, you might instead have a dedicated question and answer (Q&A) element (usually towards the end) so that you give sufficient time to respond to the workshop content and to clarify any misconceptions.

How do I end a workshop?

At the end of the workshop, it can be helpful to review with the students whether the objectives have been met. This might be as simple as asking whether they feel they have met the objectives via a physical or virtual thumbs up if online. You could 'gamify' the review of objectives by asking them questions or conducting a short quiz to check their understanding. When concluding a workshop, it can also be helpful to summarise what has been covered in the session and then to ask students what they will take away from the session and what they might do differently as a result. This can help bring the workshop to a natural conclusion. You can also end the workshop by signposting students to relevant resources and self-study tools or use it to promote any upcoming workshops. If you wish to capture data about students' experiences of the workshop, you could end by sharing a link to your post-workshop survey.

How do I design my workshops for diversity and inclusivity?

One of LD's core values is the notion of 'embracing and respecting diverse learners through critical pedagogy and practice' (ALDinHE, 2024a). This means that, when you are designing your workshop, it will be important to critique your use of imagery, language, and content to garner whether it appropriately accounts for inclusivity and recognises diversity, so that all students feel adequately represented, respected, and included. To help with this, you can ask yourself questions such as follows:

- Have I included a range of images representative of diverse types of students and situations?
- Are any images I use stereotypical or derogatory in some way to any individuals, particularly those with a protected characteristic? In the UK context, under the Equality Act 2010, these characteristics are age, gender reassignment, disability, race, sex, sexual orientation, religion, pregnancy and maternity, marriage, and civil partnership (see Chapter 3 for a discussion on this).
- What metaphors or imagery am I using in these workshops? Will students understand these? Are they inclusive and do they recognise the diversity of experiences?
- What cultural or linguistic references are being used and will all students in the workshop understand these?
- Have I allowed in my workshop design space for minority or quieter voices to feel included and in what way?

If you are not sure whether the materials you are using are conscious of inclusivity and diversity, then it may be a good idea to start by researching or using existing high-quality tools or materials, such as those on the ALDinHE Learn-Higher resource bank (ALDinHE, 2024b) or its Neurodivergence Resource Bank (ALDinHE, 2024c). These are banks of teaching and learning resources created and developed by LDers that have undergone a process of peer review before publishing.

Words matter. Think carefully, about the language that you use in workshops both verbally and in your materials. Reflecting on the following questions might be helpful as a starting point:

- Are the terms and phrases that you use inclusive of different genders, races, disabilities, and sexualities, for instance?
- Are you using any hackneyed or colloquial phrases that might exclude those who do not share that same cultural reference point?
- Are all voices in the workshop being given equal opportunity to be heard?

Task

You are designing slides for an optional workshop introducing students to effective group work skills. The students attending your workshop are a mix of ages, genders, and cultures. Go online and find three images that illustrate groups working together.

How might students attending your workshops perceive your images?

Similarly to language, visual representation is important in terms of students feeling a sense of belonging and inclusion. Think carefully about how the visual materials you are using in workshops are reflecting and constructing reality for the students who attend.

It is also important that your materials are accessible for learners, meaning that any student should be able to access them, regardless of background or individual learning need or disability. Universal design for learning (UDL) principles can be particularly helpful when thinking about accessibility and inclusivity (CAST, 2024). This approach posits that if you apply inclusive design principles, all students will benefit and be able to access the materials, regardless of disability, neurodivergence, or specific learning difference (SpLD). For instance, this might entail checking that workshop slides are accessible for all, including those with visual disabilities, by incorporating alternative text (alt text) or ensuring that captions are enabled on any workshop recordings for students who are Deaf or hard-of-hearing. Chapter 7 discusses UDL principles in more depth and considers how to develop inclusive and accessible teaching and learning materials.

How do I deal with challenges with class management?

Workshops are usually a very enjoyable part of the LD role and as you gain more experience, you will develop confidence in teaching and managing them. However, infrequently, they can raise challenges in terms of classroom management. These can be difficult to deal with as a new LDer, so the next section provides some ideas for managing certain challenging scenarios.

Part of the challenge of running optional LD workshops is that you will often work with new students in each workshop. This means that there has usually been no development of relationship, and you may have little context about who the students are who attend the sessions. It is important then to establish, from the outset, an environment where students feel safe and willing to contribute, and to carefully manage students' expectations about the content and structure of the workshop. The planning and preparation that you do prior to the session will be integral to aiding with this. For instance, if you have made it clear, when promoting the session, what it involves, and what students should expect, if your workshop materials have been designed for inclusivity and accessibility, and if you have planned for a range of tasks that encourage student participation, this can go a long way to ensuring that students are clear on their roles within the workshop and that they are sufficiently engaged such that classroom management problems should be minimised. However, you may do everything 'right' in terms of preparation and still come across challenging behaviours during the workshop itself.

> **Reflective task**
>
> - What classroom management challenges might you expect, or have you experienced when teaching workshops?
> - How have you dealt with these?

Class management is important. From the outset of your workshop, set the stage. The way you start the workshop – if engaging, encouraging, and positive – can set the tone for how participants will relate to you and each other during it. You should tell the students who you are, how long the workshop will last, when they can ask questions, and so forth. This helps with establishing clear expectations and understanding for how the session will run. Having a clear structure to the workshop can aid with dealing with any challenging behaviours as students will know what to expect. Plan your transitions of tasks and timings in your workshop plan. Practise or run through the session with a colleague or by yourself beforehand and pre-empt questions. During the workshop itself, make sure to provide students with clear time limits for activities, for example, 'You have 5 minutes to [insert task]'. Students know when an LDer is confident and in control of the workshop. Prepare well beforehand, and this will come across and dissuade negative behaviours.

Difficult behaviours might involve students interrupting you or monopolising discussions. This is where good workshop design comes in. If you have planned for a range of tasks and different interactions, this will hopefully encourage engagement and dialogue from a range of students. Also, the more prepared you are, the more confidently you will be able to state expectations about when and how students contribute, for example, 'There will be time for a Q&A at the end of the workshop, but I'm also happy to take questions during if anything pertinent comes up' or 'We'll have to move on because of time but thanks very much for your valuable contribution'. If a student persists in interrupting, pause, let them finish, and then continue exactly where you left off. If they continue, say their name and explain that you will have to stop them there, for example, 'Thanks Jay. I'll have to stop you there so we can continue with the workshop, but I'm happy to discuss this with you further at the end of the workshop'. If they monopolise the conversation, thank them for their contribution and continue to encourage other students' contributions through targeted questioning and your pre-prepared group and pair tasks. As mentioned earlier, you might also wish to give students set roles in any group tasks (e.g. reporter, notetaker, timekeeper, and so forth) to encourage more reticent students to have confidence to contribute.

Another issue that you may find challenging is when students do not contribute or speak (either online or in-person). This can be a tricky situation – how to teach when the students are silent? This can be mitigated by providing different options for interaction, particularly if online and students have cameras off. Incorporate interactive tools such as Padlet or Mentimeter which students can engage with anonymously or encourage participation in the chat for students lacking confidence with speaking in front of others. To foster contribution in in-person workshops, use a range of teaching approaches such as group, pair, and independent work. This encourages students to participate in different interaction types. For both online and in-person workshops, when posing questions, provide students with thinking time, get them to share their ideas with a partner (this can be in breakout rooms if online), and then explain that you will be nominating individual students to share their ideas with the class.

It is rare for students to be hostile or antagonistic (to you or towards other students) because they have usually opted to attend the workshop and will respect the space. If hostility does occur, remind the class that it is a space where everyone should be treated with courtesy. Should a student continue to be overtly hostile, or become physically or verbally abusive, it is best, for the safety of other students and you, to explain that you will need to ask them to leave the session if in a physical location, or remove them from the Zoom or Teams' classroom if online. If it is an online workshop and the hostile comments have occurred in the chat, you can disable the reactions or chat function through the settings on the video conferencing platform. You should then subsequently make a record of the incident with date, time, and details of what happened and arrange to discuss this with your line manager or a senior LDer. Thankfully, such incidents or challenges during workshops are uncommon as students are usually 'on your side' and respectful of the value that you provide.

How do I measure and evaluate the impact of my workshops?

In your role as an LDer, you will need to think about the 'impact' of your provision. As we saw in Chapter 3, the HE sector is highly regulated. Universities are places where the stakes are high and, therefore, where provision is increasingly measured and quantified and where data gathering and evaluation are expected. This means that it is necessary to provide evidence of what you do, who you reach, and how this impacts their university experience. Such data might also be used to inform wider college priorities, such as your institution's access and engagement plan, or priorities around student engagement and continuation.

At the end of Chapter 4, we saw that measuring impact is not always straightforward; first, because it is hard to conceptualise what exactly we mean by impact and, second, because it can be difficult to prove causation between your LD provision and whatever the 'impact' has been. For instance, if you notice that a student's assessment marks improve after attending your workshops for a term, you might assume that there is a direct link. However, there could be myriad other factors interacting with and impacting their performance, such as improved study habits, increased understanding of the subject content, additional study support from other sources, and so forth. Nevertheless, depending on the rigour of your analysis, it might still be possible to draw tentative assertions about potential impact even though you may not be able to prove direct correlation (see Loddick and Coulson, 2020).

It may be that your institution prescribes the way in which you collect data or measure impact. However, if this is not the case, as a starting point, you will need to consider why you are capturing the data, what you hope to find, and how the data will inform your practice or answer the question. For instance, do you wish to understand students' experience of your workshops to think about areas of improvement? If so, you may send a survey to student attendees post workshop with questions including whether the workshop met their expectations, whether the workshop was relevant to their needs, and a rating of their experience (e.g. from poor to excellent). If you wish to evaluate the impact of attending workshops on assessment, you might gather data on who has attended your workshops and track their assessment results over a period. If you were seeking qualitative data about students' perceptions of

LD workshops, you might approach this through a student focus group. It is a good idea to keep a log or tracking table of attendance at workshops, linking these data to specific students, where possible. For instance, your tracker might record student identification number, workshop attended, contact details, programme, mode of study, year of study, and so forth. A log can be helpful when you wish to carry out evaluations about your workshops. For instance, you could use simple analytical tools in Microsoft Excel or a similar programme to analyse workshop data by specific criteria such as student programme or year of study. Do ensure that you follow any data collection protocols as prescribed by your institution and keep the data secure.

Any data gathering or evaluative work you do should be for a purpose. This might be to improve your LD offering, to demonstrate impact, or to share with colleagues across other teams to inform them of whom your service is reaching. You might collate this information in the form of a report or newsletter to disseminate to colleagues in your institution or to share with the wider LD community.

What now?

> **Task**
>
> - List three specific actions that you will take to develop further your understanding of workshops. Write these down as specific, measurable, achievable, realistic, timebound (SMART) goals.
>
> Here is an example of a SMART goal: I will find three inclusive images and write three discussion questions based on these to use as a starter activity for my upcoming workshop in two weeks on critical thinking.

Now that you have read this chapter, you should hopefully feel more confident in terms of understanding what workshops are for and how you might structure them. We thought about the importance of promoting workshops so that students attend. We saw that workshops should have clear ILOs and that tasks and activities should be clearly aligned to these. We considered the types of materials that might be used in sessions, how to encourage engagement, and how to deal with challenges that may arise. Finally, we looked at the importance of evaluating the impact of your workshops and how you might go about doing so. However, this is just the start. The more workshops you teach, the more your confidence should grow and then you may decide to share your good practice with the wider LD community, for instance, at conferences or on the Learning Development in Higher Education Network (LDHEN).

There is also much scope for creativity when developing workshops so do not be afraid to take risks or to try novel approaches as this is where much of the fun and enjoyment of your work as an LDer will emerge. Good luck!

> **Summary**
>
> - In this chapter, we looked at what optional or extra-curricular workshops are.
> - The chapter provided guidance on different approaches to running an online or in-person workshop, tips for timing of workshops, developing resources, ways of encouraging attendance, engagement, and participation from students, what to do when technology goes awry, and how to respond to student questions.
> - We thought about ways to structure both online and in-person workshops, and how to deal with difficulties that may arise.
> - You had the opportunity to reflect on your next steps in terms of developing your understanding of running effective workshops.

Notes

1 Chapter 6 covers embedded provision in depth.
2 See Chapter 7 'Developing Teaching and Learning Materials' for detailed discussion on how to create, adapt, and find materials.

References

ALDinHE (2024a) *About ALDinHE*. Available at: https://aldinhe.ac.uk/about-aldinhe/ (Accessed: 9 April 2024).

ALDinHE (2024b) *LearnHigher*. Available at: https://aldinhe.ac.uk/learnhigher/ (Accessed: 12 December 2024).

ALDinHE (2024c) *Neurodivergence Resource Bank*. Available at: https://aldinhe.ac.uk/resource-bank/neurodivergence/ (Accessed: 12 December 2024).

Biggs, J. (1996) 'Enhancing teaching through constructive alignment', *Higher Education*, 32, 347–364. https://doi.org/10.1007/BF00138871

Bloom, B. S. (1956) *Taxonomy of Educational Objectives, Handbook 1: The Cognitive Domain*. New York: David McKay.

Burns, T., Brazant, K., Davenport, E., Huda, N., Sinfield, S. and Smith, J. (2024) 'A day in the life: What the learning developer does', in A. Syska and C. Buckley (eds) *How to be a Learning Developer in Higher Education: Critical Perspectives, Community and Practice*. Abingdon: Routledge, 53–61.

CAST (2024) *Universal Design for Learning Guidelines Version 3.0*. Available at: http://udl-guidelines.cast.org (Accessed: 17 March 2025).

Fallin, L. (2023) 'Learning development in a time of disruption', *Journal of Learning Development in Higher Education [Preprint]*, 29. https://doi.org/10.47408/jldhe.vi29.1078

Francis, N. (2002) *"I Love Group Work"... Said No Student Ever!* Available at: https://www.advance-he.ac.uk/news-and-views/i-love-group-worksaid-no-student-ever (Accessed: 30 April 2025).

Harvard University (n.d.) *Taxonomies of Learning*. Available at: https://bokcenter.harvard.edu/taxonomies-learning#:~:text=In%20the%201950s%2C%20Benjamin%20Bloom,framework%20for%20levels%20of%20understanding (Accessed: 29 April 2025).

Healey-Benson, F., Johnson, M. R., Adams, C. and Turville, J. (2024) 'What is it like for a learner to participate in a Zoom breakout room session?', in M. Johnson, F. Healey-Benson, C. Adams and N. Bonderup Dohn (eds) *Phenomenology in Action for Researching Networked Learning. Research in Networked Learning*. Cham: Springer. https://doi.org/10.1007/978-3-031-62780-4_7

Jayasundara, J. M. P. V. K., Gilbert, T., Kersten, S. and Meng, L. (2023) 'Why should I switch on my camera? Developing the cognitive skills of compassionate communications for online group/teamwork management', *Frontiers in Psychology*, 14. https://doi.org/10.3389/fpsyg.2023.1113098

Keane, A., McFerran, K., Acton, B., Taylor, S. and McLaughlin, D. (2024) 'Exploring the changing modes of learning and teaching in campus-based curricula during and post- Covid-19', *Journal of Learning Development in Higher Education [Preprint]*, 30. https://doi.org/10.47408/jldhe.vi30.1062

Key, L. (2022) '"Beyond the crisis": Accepting and adapting to the virtual academic skills workshop', *Journal of Learning Development in Higher Education [Preprint]*, 25. https://doi.org/10.47408/jldhe.vi25.974

Lin, C. G. S., Tan, K. Y. and Müller, A. M. (2021) 'Exploring students' experience with and perceptions towards elearning in an online public health module', ASCILITE-2021-Proceedings-Goh-Tan-Muller. Available at: https://2021conference.ascilite.org/wp-content/uploads/2021/11/ASCILITE-2021-Proceedings-Goh-Tan-Muller.pdf (Accessed: 29 April 2025).

Loddick, A. and Coulson, K. (2020) 'The impact of learning development tutorials on student attainment', *Journal of Learning Development in Higher Education [Preprint]*, 17. https://doi.org/10.47408/jldhe.vi17.558

Ideas for further reading

Effective group work

Corradi, H. R. (2021) 'Does Zoom allow for efficient and meaningful group work? Translating staff development for online delivery during Covid-19', *Journal of Learning Development in Higher Education [Preprint]*, 22. https://doi.org/10.47408/jldhe.vi22.697

Elston, C. (2009) 'Making groupwork work', *Journal of Learning Development in Higher Education [Preprint]*, 1. https://doi.org/10.47408/jldhe.v0i1.36

Active learning

Race, P. (2014) *Making Learning Happen: A Guide for Post-Compulsory Education*, 3rd edn. London: Sage.

Chapter 6

Embedding Learning Development

> **This chapter provides an overview of**
> - What embedded Learning Development (LD) provision is.
> - Why embedded provision is promoted as good practice in LD.
>
> **You will be guided on**
> - The different forms of embedded provision.
> - How to articulate the need for embedded practice in your institution.
> - How to plan for and structure embedded sessions.
> - How to deal with challenges when providing embedded support.

What is embedded provision?

Embedded provision is an important aspect of LD work. As well as working with students in the form of extra-curricular or optional workshops and tutorials, you will also provide support to students within their subject-based sessions. This is referred to as embedded provision – the teaching or activities that you undertake that are situated within students' disciplinary or curriculum-based sessions (Burns et al., 2024; Chin and Sum, 2024).

> **Task**
>
> 1. In your own words, what do you understand by the term embedded provision?
> 2. How do you think embedded provision differs from optional or extra-curricular workshops and teaching?
> 3. In what ways have you seen LD being embedded in your institution?

Embedded or integrated?

Embedded practice can occur in various forms. For instance, a lecturer might ask you to provide a one-off workshop during students' subject-based seminars or lectures (Burns et al., 2024). An example might be where you teach a standalone general essay planning workshop in a seminar or disciplinary class. The fact that the skills session takes place within subject time can, arguably, help students to find more value and meaning from such sessions, as opposed to a standard optional or extra-curricular skills workshop (Hill and Tinker, 2013; Burns et al., 2024). However, some in the field have suggested that one-off LD lectures or classes provided in this way are not embedded in the true sense of the word.

Going one step further than embedding then is the idea of integrating LD provision. Advocates of integration propose that skills sessions and subject sessions should be taught in conjunction with one another; that is, skills and LD provision should be seen as integral and not aside from the disciplinary subject itself (Johnson, 2022). Moreover, they argue that integrated provision can be highly influential on a strategic level in terms of highlighting the benefits of LD (Hill and Tinker, 2013). An example of integrated provision might be where you work with a lecturer to design and co-teach a series of skills sessions as a required part of a module that are explicitly linked to and draw upon students' disciplinary content and that are tailored to students' assessments.[1] Thus, the material that you use in these sessions, rather than being generic, will be subject-specific and linked to disciplinary materials and content.

Embedded or integrated provision can also occur in other ways, such as through the production of subject-specific resources that are embedded into students' virtual learning environment (VLE). For example, you might develop a suite of interactive skills videos and associated online tasks or workbooks that are tailored to students' assessments which they are required to watch or complete asynchronously as part of their weekly pre-sessional or post-sessional activities for their module.

Why is embedded provision so common in LD practice?

As a reminder, LD takes as its principle a 'developmental' model to student learning rather than a deficit or remedial view (see Chapter 2 and Hill et al., 2010; Hilsdon, 2011). Rather than rooting 'problems' within individual students, this approach to LD advocates that the practices and institution of higher education (HE) should instead be the object of scrutiny and problematisation (Chin and Sum, 2024, citing Lillis, 2001). Thus, as Learning Developers (LDers), we do not focus on fixing or correcting the students' individual 'ails'. Instead, we aim to meet students where they are, and through conversation, teaching, and tutoring, promote their autonomy and self-agency such that they can better make sense of an HE environment that might otherwise be alienating, unfamiliar, or even 'hostile' towards them (Abegglen et al., 2019, p. 3). This approach recognises that students bring their existing knowledge and skills to their learning which are capable of being developed and enhanced.

Proponents of embedded provision advocate that skills development, teaching, and support should be integral to rather than detached from students' disciplinary learning (Wingate, 2006; Johnson, 2022). This means that rather than LD being an add-on or 'bolt-on' element (Wingate, 2006, p. 457; Johnson, 2022, p. 3), it ideally becomes an essential component, intertwined with, and critical to students' developing understanding of their disciplinary content. Embedded provision then, ideally, is valued and viewed as a core feature of students' learning. Whilst this is the ideal, this is not always reflective of the reality and, instead, LD provision is still often seen as tangential to students' 'real' learning. Indeed, amongst some in the HE sector, LD cannot escape from its associations with a deficit or 'study skills' remedial model (Johnson and Bishopp-Martin, 2024, p. 18).

However, research has shown that embedded provision has benefits for students and for aiding to alter the deficit perception of LD as remedial 'study skills' (see Johnson, 2022; Wingate, 2006). First, unlike optional or extra-curricular academic skills workshops, embedded sessions take place during students' class time and therefore, in theory, you will have a 'captive audience', if attendance at such sessions is mandatory. This means that there is the ability to promote LD to students who may not already be aware of or ordinarily choose to use the service (Hill et al., 2010). This, of course, might put pressure on you as an LDer to deliver or teach engaging embedded sessions so that students are drawn to use LD services outside the scheduled classes. We will look at suggestions for how to structure embedded sessions later in this chapter.

Embedding LD provision also has benefits in terms of working with colleagues and staff. It can help to highlight LD as an essential part of students' learning. This is important because as stated earlier, in the HE sector, LD is often misunderstood or seen as 'marginal' (Verity and Trowler, 2011, p. 243), so providing opportunities to work collaboratively with academic and subject lecturers to integrate LD can aid with demystifying and positively promoting your practice to those who are not LDers. Embedded provision can also help to promote good working relationships between you and academic subject lecturers and tutors as it often entails working alongside staff to decide and co-design what such provision should look like. Thus, working in an embedded way relates explicitly to two of the core guiding values as stated on the Association for Learning Development in Higher Education (ALDinHE) website, that is: 'working in partnership with students and staff to make sense and get the most out of HE' and 'adapting, sharing and advocating effective learning development practice to promote student learning' (ALDinHE, 2024a). In theory this all sounds positive; however, in practice, you might find that within your institution you need to advocate for and articulate quite strongly the need for embedded provision.

How do I get 'buy-in' for embedded sessions?

The success of embedded provision will rely partly on the existing relationships that you have with academic and teaching staff and will also depend on how LD is viewed within your institution. It might be that your LD team or unit has an established relationship with subject lecturers, such that you might not need to do much in the way of advocating for embedded support. If it is the case that LD provision is highly valued, established, and visible, you will encounter little opposition or 'push-back' from subject lecturers, senior education managers, and other relevant staff and they should welcome ideas for such provision and collaboration. This is the ideal scenario where embedded work is viewed as important, is supported at the institutional level, and is designed and planned collaboratively with academic or teaching staff. However, if this is not the case in your institution, given its benefits, it will be important to identify opportunities within the curriculum where you might seek to articulate the need for embedded provision.

One issue is that universities are time-poor institutions. Academics, in UK higher education institutions (HEIs) and internationally, are subject to significant demands on their time managed through a workload allocation model which provides a framework for the time dedicated to their administrative, research, teaching, and other responsibilities. Subject lecturers might, therefore, at times, be unwilling to 'sacrifice' valuable subject teaching time for what they perceive as 'non-integral' skills sessions. As a new LDer, this can be hard to navigate and challenge and, in such cases, it is helpful to seek support for advocating for embedded provision from senior or more experienced LDers in your team.

It can help, when trying to promote embedded provision to 'reluctant' colleagues and senior education staff, to arrange a meeting to discuss how and why embedded provision will be beneficial and impactful for the students. When having such discussions, try to incorporate language that lecturers and managerial colleagues might find value in, for example, by referring to the potential impact on retention and continuation (see Chapter 3). Such discussions are best supported by evidence of the impact of LD provision. This could be context-specific data you have gathered from optional skills workshops and tutorials, or in reference to the wider body of LD research or institutional case studies about the positive impact of embedded provision.

Another way to gain subject lecturer and senior management support for embedded sessions is to make the profile of LD in your institution more visible. As a new LDer, it might feel daunting to be a highly visible member of the university community. However, it is an essential part of the role as, to be able to 'work in partnership with students and staff to make sense and get the most out of HE' (ALDinHE, 2024a); that is, to demonstrate a core guiding value of LD, students and staff need to be aware of what LD offers and how to access your services. One way to make LD more visible in your institution is to participate in wider staff and university-wide meetings, particularly if you request an item on the agenda that enables you to feedback on LD provision. This can be a useful space to promote any LD initiatives that you are undertaking and to get wider staff feedback on the services you provide. You might choose to produce a written report for such meetings using data collected from workshops and tutorials as well as student feedback. Making LD more visible in this way can help to create a sense of reassurance amongst 'time-poor' lecturers and other relevant staff that any embedded sessions you provide will be impactful and of high quality. Having a visible presence at induction and during your institution's open days or student events can also help. If you are an LDer based in a specific faculty or department, you might also wish to send out regular communications to teaching staff in the faculty or department to remind them of LD services and to suggest, tactfully, ways you can support their courses. It is not always the case that academics will take you up on your offer, but it can help with promoting the value of LD and may be a fruitful way of developing stronger relationships outside your immediate LD team.

How might I plan for and structure embedded sessions?

As mentioned earlier, embedded sessions can occur in several forms. If you are 'delivering' or teaching an embedded class as a one-off skills session, this could be framed very similarly to a standard generic extra-curricular or optional skills workshop (see Chapter 5), except that you will include content and tasks that relate and draw explicitly on the students' discipline. The specific structure of an embedded session of this nature would be dependent on the learning aims and outcomes but, as in the case of an optional skills workshop, there should be a clear introduction where you set out the aims and session outcomes, a main body, with students 'doing' something by engaging in relevant tasks and activities, and conclusion where you summarise or review the learning.

As examples of relevant activities, in a one-off embedded session on improving referencing skills for psychology students, you might include a task whereby students have to identify specific errors in an American Psychological Association (APA) formatted bibliography that you have generated. For law students, you might provide them with a case, a legal journal article, and a statute, and have students research how to cite each source using an online Oxford Standard for the Citation of Legal Authorities (OSCOLA) referencing guide which is the system used widely across law schools in the UK and common law jurisdictions. In a one-off embedded session for education students to develop reflection skills, you might have them annotate a sample of reflective writing from student teachers to identify its key elements and structure.

In a session for literature students on developing analytical and close reading skills, you might model a close reading of a literary text and then ask students to do their own close reading of another extract. The point here is that whatever tasks and activities you include in one-off embedded sessions should be meaningful and relevant to the students' disciplinary studies.

For embedded sessions that are 'integrated' or provided as a series of sessions, you will need to think about planning over a longer period. Having a discussion with the relevant module or subject lecturer should enable you to ascertain the number of sessions that are needed, their duration, and the relevant content that will need to be covered. Once you have established this, you might find it helpful to create a detailed plan, including the intended aims and outcomes, pre- or post-session tasks, in-session tasks and activities, and any necessary resources, using a planning template like Table 6.1.

Planning embedded sessions in this detailed way can provide you with a 'roadmap' or overview. That is not to say that your plans will not change and this is fine but, preferably, any changes should be made in agreement and consultation with the subject or module lecturer. Ideally, planning would be completed collaboratively with the relevant module lecturer or tutor, but, if this is not possible, you could plan the sessions independently (or with your LDer colleagues) and then consult with the lecturer to get feedback and discuss any necessary modifications.

Similarly to optional skills workshops, try to allow for some flexibility in the session itself as you might find that, when teaching, the students' comments lead you along other tangents. As long as these relate to the aims of the session, there is no need to stick rigidly to your session plan but do bear in mind that if students are attending embedded sessions as part of their module, they will have certain expectations about what will be covered based on yours (and the lecturers') prior communications regarding the sessions. Completing a reflection after each session by considering questions such as 'What went well?' 'What could have gone better?' 'What would I do differently next time?' can be a helpful way of thinking through the effectiveness of each session, considering what might need adjusting for upcoming sessions, and should aid with planning and improving future iterations.

Because such embedded or integrated sessions occur over time, there is also the scope to apply a flipped learning approach where students complete asynchronous activities at 'home' and then class time is used to address questions and comments related to the homework tasks (see, e.g. Mansfield, 2020). Flipped learning can work well for both online and in-person teaching. As an example, you might provide students with tasks to complete in the virtual learning environment (VLE) related to developing their referencing skills and then discuss and clarify misconceptions in the seminar or class context itself. For a session on academic integrity, you might ask students to, for homework, read a sample disciplinary essay produced by ChatGPT and get them to critically analyse its strengths and weaknesses, ready for a discussion or debate

Table 6.1 Planning template for embedded teaching.

Session Aims and Objectives (What are the aims for the session? How do they relate to the module requirements and assessments?)	Session Outcomes (What should students be able to do by the end of the session?)	Pre-session Tasks (What tasks should students complete prior to the session, including by when)	In-session Tasks (What tasks should students complete in the session itself, including timings)	Post-session Tasks (What tasks should students complete after the session?)	Resources (What resources are required, e.g. handouts, slides, digital tools, etc.?)	Reflection on Session (What worked well? What could have gone better? What have you learned? What would you do differently next time?)

Session 1
Date:
Time:
Session 2
Date:
Time:
Session 3
Date:
Time:

in class about the ethics of using ChatGPT for assignments. The success of a flipped approach relies on students having completed the set tasks (Syska, 2021), so it might be the case that you initially trial such an approach in modules that are weighted – that is, where the stakes are higher – or where you know that student attendance and engagement tend to be high. You could also provide ethical 'incentives' for doing the asynchronous work (e.g. students could earn a digital badge for completing set tasks). It is also good to have backup activities related to the session aims and outcomes in case students have not completed the tasks.

Whichever approach you take, students need to see the value of embedded sessions and not experience them as something they could have accessed optionally in their own time elsewhere. In this regard, it is critical to make the content of embedded sessions subject-specific and relevant to the students' discipline.

What are pre-session and post-session tasks?

Depending on the module aims, students could be asked to complete work prior to (pre-session) and after (post-session) to prepare them for the embedded classes and to consolidate their learning. The scope for pre-session activities is wide, but they should be directly relevant and prepare students for what will be covered in the 'live' session (whether this is held online or in-person). Activities might include a diagnostic quiz, preparatory readings and associated comprehension questions or tasks, watching recorded lectures or introductory videos to the topic, or asking students to engage in online class forum discussions. As an example, if you were teaching embedded classes to develop students' essay writing skills, you might ask students to prepare for a particular session by skim reading a selection of disciplinary-specific sample essays to identify elements of typical essay structure, as in the following example:

Example pre-session task for embedded teaching

Read the two sample literature essays by undergraduate students.
Make notes on the following questions and be prepared to discuss them during the seminar:

1. Can you identify a clear overall structure?

    a. Can you find an introduction?
    b. How is the main body structured?
    c. Does it go back and forth between sides, or does it look at one side first then the other side?
    d. How are the paragraphs structured?
    e. Is there a counterargument?
    f. Have they included a conclusion?

2. What do you like/dislike about the writing style?

Post-session tasks can also be used to consolidate learning covered in class. These could include, for instance, an assessed or unassessed multiple-choice quiz, a video summary, or a post-session handout with consolidating activities. Using post-session tasks can aid with students taking ownership of their learning, particularly if such activities are an optional element of the module. Students can be made aware in advance of any necessary pre-session or post-session tasks through the medium of communication by which they are regularly contacted such as your institution's VLE pages for their module or in email notifications.

How else might I embed LD support?

There is significant scope to embed LD provision in ways that do not necessarily involve synchronous or live teaching in a classroom or online. For embedded provision in asynchronous ways (i.e. not 'live' teaching), you could, for instance, develop a suite of explanatory assessment-specific skills videos which are then embedded in the students' VLE for a particular module. You could develop a resource that enables students on a specific module to understand a particular skill or process, for instance, an online interactive guide to dissertation writing for final year undergraduate students. You might embed provision using standalone online formative quizzes or tasks set in students' module VLE pages. You could produce physical handouts and guides about a specific skill that could be distributed by subject lecturers during seminar time. The key thing with such provision is to aim to develop such resources in coordination and collaboration with the subject tutors' or lecturers' input so that it is relevant, timely, and specific to the student' needs for their module or a particular assignment or subject.

When developing embedded asynchronous resources, you will also need to think carefully about how to ensure that they are accessible and inclusive. For instance, although digital education has become the norm in many countries, there are still large numbers of students who experience 'digital poverty'; that is, they do not have equal access to or understanding of the online technologies that will enable them to work on equal footing with their peers (Allmann, 2022). An asynchronous embedded video resource presumes that students have reliable internet access and that they know how to view the video resource on their device, whereas this might not be the case. Your institution should provide guidance or a baseline standard for producing such materials and it is a good idea, if available, to make use of support and training services from your digital or IT team when designing and producing such resources to ensure that they are accessible (see also Chapter 7 for discussion on universal design for learning (UDL) principles).

A case study

A case study

You have been asked to run an embedded session on critical reflection for first-year UG education students. The session is part of their module on 'Becoming a critically reflective teacher'. The module is not weighted, but students must attend and complete the assessments to progress to their next year. The first module assessment is to write a 1,000-word critically reflective blog post about their experience of education and how this might impact their future teaching style. This is weighted at 80%. They also must produce an individual video or podcast presentation critically reflecting on an educator that they are aware of in popular culture (e.g. in a film or in literature) and why they like or dislike their approach. This is weighted at 20%. Both assessments are due in 12 weeks.

1. What further information would you need from the lecturer?
2. How might you plan and approach the preparation for this session?
3. What might your aims for the session be?
4. What activities and tasks might you ask the students to do during the session?

Suggested response to the case study

In terms of further information, you would clearly need to understand the module aims and outcomes. You would need to find out practical considerations such as how many students are expected to be on the module, specific details about the students' assessments, and, if possible, information about any students with a study support plan or requiring reasonable adjustments.

In terms of planning, you could start by looking at current (and previous) iterations of the module content on the students' VLE or speak to the subject lecturer to get an idea of how and if skills teaching has previously been incorporated. You could look at the data related to the cohort and module. This contextual understanding would provide the basis for starting to plan materials for your sessions.

> You might identify one or two specific aims and outcome for the session. For instance, one aim might be to understand what is meant by critical reflection and an outcome might be that students will be able to apply a critical reflection model to their assignment writing (or presentation).
>
> There are many potential tasks and activities that you could include during the session. The key thing to consider is to make sure that the tasks and activities align or allow students to meet the intended session outcome, also referred to as 'constructive alignment' (Biggs and Tang, 2011). For instance, if the aim is to understand what is meant by critical reflection, you might look at an example of a critical reflective model such as Gibbs' reflective cycle (see Chapter 4, Figure 4.3) and then ask students to apply the model to a specific educational or personal experience. You might ask the students to read sample pieces of writing to identify typical phrases used when writing a critical reflection. An outcome might then be that students better understand how to apply a critically reflective model to an educational experience or better understand the language of critical reflection.

Where might I find materials for embedded sessions?

A good starting point is to look at what has been done on the module by LDers in previous years to see if there is scope to use existing materials to suit the specific cohort you will be working with. If the materials are outdated or no longer relevant, you could adapt or develop them to meet the aims and objectives of the sessions you are teaching. The subject lecturer will also likely be able to signpost you to relevant subject-specific readings and text extracts that could be used within your sessions. Starting with pre-existing materials, even if outdated and needing modification, can aid with reducing the feeling that you are having to start 'from scratch'.

If there are no pre-existing embedded materials, it is not always the case that you will need to start designing completely new materials as the generic materials that you use for optional skills workshops might work well if they are repurposed and adapted to suit the needs of the cohort. For instance, a general workshop that you have developed on essays could be adapted to include subject-specific examples and content when talking about, for instance, essay writing structure or argumentation. If you have no suitable materials that could be repurposed, you could follow a similar approach to developing LD materials and workshop content more generally (see Chapters 5 and 7). For instance, you might look at resources available on the LearnHigher resource website which is a peer-reviewed resource site developed by ALDinHE (ALDinHE,

2024b). These resources are categorised according to different 'study skills' and could be adapted and developed to suit the purposes of your sessions, of course paying credit to the creator of the resource. You might also look to other university websites for materials they have used for embedded provision or seek advice via the ALDinHE networking and expertise directory (ALDinHE, 2024c) – a directory through which you can contact and ask questions of experienced LDers with different specialisms – or ask LD colleagues within your immediate institution.

What should I do if I run into problems in an embedded session?

Embedded sessions are typically led individually or in a co-teaching situation with another LDer (or colleagues that you are collaborating with to deliver the session such as an academic librarian or digital advisor). They are not subject teaching and so it will be important to make sure that you do not stray into disciplinary teaching unless you have expertise and remit for this. In some cases, you might find that subject lecturers are willing to co-teach sessions with you. This can be helpful for reasons we will consider shortly.

We have seen that there are many benefits to embedded provision. However, there are times when you may run into challenges. A common situation that occurs is where students expect you to answer subject-specific questions as they may not understand that the remit of your role is to teach the skills related to their subject. Ideally, students should already be aware of your purpose from any pre-session communications that you have had with them. However, if this is not the case, to manage student expectations, it can be helpful at the start of the embedded session to provide a brief verbal explanation of your role, what your remit is, and what the objectives of the sessions(s) are. Accompany any such verbal explanation with a visual or slide (whether online or in-person) that conveys the same information. Another solution for this issue is to ask if it is possible for the subject lecturer or module tutor to be present (or to co-teach) during your sessions to answer disciplinary-related questions. Having the lecturer present can also aid with modelling the integrated nature of embedded LD provision as you work, collaboratively, to respond to students' disciplinary and skills-based questions.

Another issue that you may encounter with embedded LD sessions is students not attending. This might happen for several reasons. First, if such classes are not compulsory or weighted towards their degree classification, students may see little value in making the effort to attend the sessions. Another reason might be that students may lack interest in attending sessions that they perceive are not related to their disciplinary studies, particularly if such sessions involve travelling to a physical classroom. One way of dealing with this issue is to promote the sessions in such a way that students do see the value in attending. This might be by linking the session outcomes explicitly to the assessments that students must undertake for the module. For example, you might explain that your session on referencing skills and avoiding plagiarism links directly to their upcoming assessment due on 'x' date. You can also emphasise the value of such sessions in a more developmental way, explaining that what they learn in the sessions will be valuable as they progress through the course of their studies and beyond. You might also wish to ask the module lecturer to support you in encouraging students to attend embedded sessions. Another thing that you might consider is the location in which such embedded teaching takes place. Might students be more likely to attend if these are held in an online format? Is the physical classroom environment suitable and easily accessible to all students?

If you are running an embedded session in-person, you may be unfamiliar with the classroom where your session is taking place which may pose a challenge. If so, it can help to feel more at ease to do a practice run. Visit the classroom beforehand and, just as you would with an in-person extra-curricular workshop, familiarise yourself with the room layout and functionality. Are the computers and devices that you will need working? Are there whiteboard pens if you need to use a whiteboard? How are the desks set up? Is there room to change the layout of the classroom to suit your session? Can students easily access the room? Do you know whom to contact if you run into issues with the technology? If it is an online class, through video conferencing platforms like Zoom or Teams, for instance, ensure that you are familiar with the technology and its functionality and that you have the right 'permissions' for hosting the class and enabling participants to enter the online room.

Classroom management can also present a challenge as a new LDer. Again, this might be for a myriad of reasons, for instance, students not perceiving 'value' in the session, students not seeing you as the 'real' lecturer or tutor, students feeling 'tired' as they have had to attend classes all day and this is an 'unnecessary' session, and students lacking confidence that you are able to answer their questions. Research has highlighted that students are also more likely to undermine and dispute the 'authority and expertise' of teaching staff, including LDers, who are 'women, people of colour, young and/or queer, transgender, or nonbinary' (Rickard, 2024, p. 9, in reference to Chesler and Young (2013)). Challenging classroom behaviour can be overt such as inappropriate comments, laughing at or mimicking you, or interrupting and talking over you. However, difficult behaviours can also be less overt, such as displaying general passivity, showing reluctance to respond and answer questions, choosing to not engage in tasks that you have planned, or playing on mobile devices and disregarding what you are saying. It can be difficult in such situations particularly as, unless it is a cohort you have previously worked with, you will not have established a relationship with the class. However, there are ways to deal with such behaviours that might be helpful.

One approach is to find out as much about the students before the sessions as you can. Prior to delivering the embedded session, see if you can locate details about their chosen programme (remember that just because they are in your session, they might not all be studying the same degree programme). Try to identify students who may have student support plans, disabilities, or specific learning differences (SpLDs) so that you are aware of any reasonable adjustments that may be needed during your session. If you can, meet with the subject lecturer prior to teaching the session to get a sense of their experience of the class. A well-planned session, with clear learning objectives, and interactivity can also go a long way to reducing the likelihood of poor classroom behaviour.

It can also be helpful to establish an agreement as to how you will work together in the first session with the students. Spend a few minutes eliciting some 'ground rules' for working well together. This might be things like, 'listening to others', 'being constructive with comments', 'being respectful', and so forth. Emphasise the importance in a university context to treat everyone with respect and dignity. If online, this might include making it clear when and how students should ask questions, whether microphones should be kept muted, and general online etiquette. You might choose, because of limited time, to set out the expectations yourself in a slide that you display and talk through. Spending a few minutes in this way at the start of an embedded session can pay dividends as you can refer to the 'rules' if challenging behaviours do arise. Try to take a register of the class that you can refer to and, if you can, remember and use students' names. If the behaviours are overt or very problematic, note down any comments about specific individuals that you would like to follow up with the subject lecturer or your line manager. If the lecturer is willing to be there during the session, this should also aid with reducing or dispelling poor classroom behaviours.

Not all behaviours need to be addressed in the moment, particularly if they are not overtly disruptive to the other students and to you leading the session. Indeed, certain behaviours might have nothing to do with you or the way in which you are teaching. For instance, as mentioned, there might be external factors affecting the students' mood (such as feeling cold, feeling tired, feeling hungry) or students might have things going on in their private lives that are impacting the way they behave in class. So, if the behaviour is not visibly disruptive and is not interrupting the session per se, then you may choose to tactfully ignore it, making a quiet note of the issue or student's name if you have this information. You could then follow up more discreetly by checking-in with the student afterwards or speak to the subject lecturer or an LDer colleague following the session with your concerns.

All this being said, embedded work is usually a very enjoyable aspect of doing LD. Students tend to be appreciative of embedded teaching and respectful of the space particularly when sessions are well planned, discipline specific and engaging.

How do I evaluate and show the impact of embedded provision?

Chapter 4 highlighted the point that 'impact' in relation to LD work can be difficult to measure. For instance, how do we know that what we have done has directly affected an individual student or cohort of students? How can we 'prove' causality or even correlation between our embedded provision (or tutorials or optional workshops) and the effect? If we take impact as meaning that our practice has had some form of effect on students or their learning, then to measure impact will clearly necessitate collecting data to inform us as to what that effect has been.

When gathering data, it can be helpful to ask what, why, and how questions such as follows:

- Why am I gathering the data? What am I trying to find out? (e.g. are you trying to find out about students' experiences of sessions, students' learning, about the effectiveness of your teaching, about the impact of your sessions on students or something else?)
- How can I find the answer to my questions?
- What data will I need to gather?
- What will I do with the data?

If, for instance, you are gathering data to find out about students' experiences of your embedded sessions, the impact on their learning, or the effectiveness of your teaching, then a sensible starting point might be to gather feedback from students about the embedded sessions. If the sessions are integrated into a module, it is likely that there will be some form of institutional-level module evaluation where the students are able to provide feedback on the module content and teaching. Where students are not required to complete a module evaluation, you could create a simple survey. The following box provides an example of the type of questions you might include in a survey:

Example survey questions to capture data about embedded sessions

1. How would you rate the sessions you attended on 'essay writing'?
   a. Very good
   b. Good
   c. Adequate
   d. Poor

2. Did you find the essay writing sessions helpful?
   a. Very helpful
   b. Helpful
   c. Quite helpful
   d. Unhelpful

3. What would help to improve the sessions? (Tick all that apply)
   a. More subject-specific materials
   b. More time to complete tasks and activities
   c. More time for questions and answers
   d. A greater variety of tasks
   e. Other (please specify) _____

4. What were the main things that you learned from attending the sessions on essay writing?

5. Do you have any other comments about the essay writing sessions that you would like to make?

Capturing data in this way can provide rich insights into student experience and can also aid you with improving and developing the quality of your embedded sessions. This data could be gathered immediately after the embedded sessions, or you could ask students to complete an initial survey and then a later comparative survey to see if students perceive that there has been any effect on their understanding. For instance, your initial survey might ask students about how confident they feel in relation to a stated skill and then at a later point you might ask them to assess how confident they feel about these skills after attending the embedded sessions. It can be affirming to receive positive comments and feedback about your sessions from students. This can encourage you to build on the strengths of your existing provision. On the other hand, negative feedback can be difficult, particularly when you have invested a significant amount of time and effort into producing materials and content for the sessions. However, try to think of such feedback as a means to gain insight into the student experience and use it to hone and improve your future offering.

You might also wish to look at the impact of your embedded sessions on factors such as attainment. This might involve collating data about who attended your sessions and investigating whether there is any correlation between pass rates and attendance at the embedded sessions. Remember though that causality can be difficult to establish, so such data analysis might be indicative rather than conclusive. Data could also be evaluated for any emerging themes or trends (if gathered over time) as evidence of the potential impact of embedded teaching. This is important for when thinking about wider institutional and regulatory concerns such as continuation, progression, and engagement. Collating and evaluating data can also aid with planning for future iterations and with gauging their overall success.

Data can be evaluated using simple analytical tools such as Microsoft Excel or Access. Such tools allow you to gather and to assess or evaluate the data. Whichever tool you use for data collection and evaluation, it will be important to think about the purposes of the data collection, any ethical concerns that might arise, and how the data will be used and stored. For instance, if you collate survey data about embedded sessions, will the data be anonymised or linked to student identification information? If so, how will students be made aware of this? How long will the survey remain open? Can students withdraw their survey responses if they wish? If you are analysing data according to demographic information such as sex or ethnicity, are there any ethical implications that will need to be considered? Data used well can be illuminating in terms of providing information about how students are experiencing your service, but it will be important to scrutinise the data for any quality or other issues. This might be as simple as ensuring that the data are reviewed by more than one member of your team, or by cross-checking the data for accuracy.

Gathering and evaluating data should not be the last step. It will also be important to think about how this information might be disseminated or shared with relevant colleagues, staff, and students. For instance, you could produce a simple report that outlines the impact of your service, including embedded provision. This might include survey data represented in tabular or graphic form. Key findings or data could also be shared verbally in meetings with wider staff members or via a bulletin summarising the key findings. If you work with a larger LD team, it is likely that there will be processes or established ways of gathering, evaluating, and disseminating information about embedded LD provision. However, a significant aspect of effective LD practice is communicating its merits and impact to those who might be able to influence the perception and visibility of LD in your institution. To aid with this, it can be helpful to participate in university-wide meetings which are attended by cross-university staff and ask for space to be allocated on the agenda to speak about LD provision. Expressing the impact of LD support in such a context can mean that academics and senior management involved in decision-making get to hear of the benefits of your service. By referring to reliable data in such contexts, you also aid with, 'adapting, sharing and advocating effective learning development practice to promote student learning' a core guiding value of LD (ALDinHE, 2024a).

How might I further develop my understanding of embedded support?

This chapter is a starting point for considering how to run embedded sessions. However, it is important to consider how this guidance might apply to your specific context.

> **Reflective task**
>
> 1. What are your next steps in developing your understanding of embedded provision?
> 2. Who might you need to speak to as a starting point for developing embedded provision in your context?
> 3. What is one thing that you will now do to aid with developing embedded provision in your practice?

One thing that you might do is to speak with an experienced LDer about different approaches to embedded LD that have worked successfully in their practice. You might then identify gaps in a particular cohort that you work with where skills provision might be helpful and arrange to speak with or email the relevant lecturer. Taking initial and small steps in this way can be a starting point to developing your confidence in providing embedded support. Remember, though, that as a new LDer establishing yourself in your role, you may find it more difficult or lack the confidence to advocate for such provision, particularly if LD is not visible or supported within your institution. This is where it is advisable to seek support from more established team members or from LDers further afield – for instance, via the Learning Development in Higher Education Network (LDHEN) professional communications JiscMail, or from an expert on the ALDinHE networking and expertise directory (ALDinHE, 2024b). LDers and the LD community are very willing to help, and you will find that any challenges with embedded provision that you are having, someone in the field will be able to advise and provide guidance.

You should now have a clearer sense of what embedded provision entails and its importance in LD practice. With embedding, there is much scope, if carefully planned, and collaborative in nature, to promote LD as an integral and valuable part of students' learning.

> **Summary**
>
> - This chapter defined embedded LD provision as the teaching or activities that are undertaken within students' disciplinary or curriculum-based sessions.
> - The chapter highlighted the significance of embedded provision for LD practice, particularly in terms of shifting away from a deficit or remedial view of LD.
> - The chapter also considered alternative ways of embedding support via use of asynchronous materials.
> - It provided guidance on advocating for embedded provision, planning for and structuring embedded sessions, developing materials, and evaluating the impact of embedded teaching.
> - You had the opportunity to reflect on next steps in terms of developing your understanding and provision of embedded support.

Note

1 For an example of the challenges of integrating academic skills into an undergraduate (UG) primary education programme, see Bishopp-Martin (2023).

References

Abegglen, S., Burns, T. and Sinfield, S. (2019) 'It's learning development, Jim – but not as we know it: Academic literacies in third space', *Journal of Learning Development in Higher Education [Preprint]*, 15. https://doi.org/10.47408/jldhe.v0i15.500

ALDinHE (2024a) *About ALDinHE*. Available at: https://aldinhe.ac.uk/about-aldinhe/ (Accessed: 9 April 2024).

ALDinHE (2024b) *LearnHigher*. Available at: https://aldinhe.ac.uk/learnhigher/ (Accessed: 9 April 2024).

ALDinHE (2024c) *Networking & Expertise Directory*. Available at: https://aldinhe.ac.uk/support/expertise-directory/ (Accessed: 23 December 2024).

Allmann, K. (2022) *UK Digital Poverty Evidence Review 2022*. Available at: https://digitalpovertyalliance.org/wp-content/uploads/2022/06/UK-Digital-Poverty-Evidence-Review-2022-v1.0-compressed.pdf (Accessed: 23 December 2024).

Biggs, J. and Tang, C. (2011). *Teaching for Quality Learning at University*. Maidenhead, UK: Open University Press.

Bishopp-Martin, S. (2023) 'Tales of a three-year journey to integrating academic and information literacy skills in an education course', *Journal of Learning Development in Higher Education [Preprint]*, 29. https://doi.org/10.47408/jldhe.vi29.1124

Burns, T., Brazant, K., Davenport, E., Huda, N., Sinfield, S. and Smith, J. (2024) 'A day in the life: What the learning developer does', in A. Syska and C. Buckley (eds) *How to be a Learning Developer in Higher Education: Critical Perspectives, Community and Practice*. Abingdon: Routledge, 53–61.

Chin, P. and Sum, K. (2024) 'Academic literacies as a theoretical underpinning for learning development support', *Journal of Learning Development in Higher Education [Preprint]*, 32. https://doi.org/10.47408/jldhe.vi32.1392

Hill, P. and Tinker, A. (2013) 'Integrating learning development into the student experience', *Journal of Learning Development in Higher Education [Preprint]*, 5, 1–18. https://doi.org/10.47408/

Hill, P., Tinker, A. and Catterall, S. (2010). 'From deficiency to development: The evolution of academic skills provision at one UK university', *Journal of Learning Development in Higher Education [Preprint]*, 2. https://doi.org/10.47408/jldhe.v0i2.54

Hilsdon, J. (2011) 'What is learning development?', in P. Hartley, J. Hilsdon, C. Keenan, S. Sinfield and M. Verity (eds) *Learning Development in Higher Education*. Basingstoke: Palgrave Macmillan (Red Globe Press), 13–27.

Johnson, I. (2022) 'To embed, not to embed, how to embed', *Journal of Learning Development in Higher Education [Preprint]*, 25. https://doi.org/10.47408/jldhe.vi25.966

Johnson, I. and Bishopp-Martin, S. (2024) 'Conceptual foundations in learning development', in A. Syska and C. Buckley (eds) *How to be a Learning Developer in Higher Education: Critical Perspectives, Community and Practice*. Abingdon: Routledge, 15–24.

Mansfield, S. (2020) 'Changing the face of academic skills workshops', *Journal of Learning Development in Higher Education [Preprint]*, 17. https://doi.org/10.47408/jldhe.vi17.508

Rickard, L. (2024, June) 'Teaching and WOKE – suggested handrails for educators in HE', *Educational Developments*, 25(2), 8–11. Available at: https://www.seda.ac.uk/wp-content/uploads/2024/05/Ed-Devs-25.2_JUNE_2024-1.pdf (Accessed: 1 August 2024).

Syska, A. (2021) 'When the flipped classroom disappoints: Engaging students with asynchronous learning', *Journal of Learning Development in Higher Education [Preprint]*, 22. https://doi.org/10.47408/jldhe.vi22.771

Verity, M. and Trowler, P. (2011) 'Looking back and looking into the future', in P. Hartley, J. Hilsdon, C. Keenan, S. Sinfield and M. Verity (eds) *Learning Development in Higher Education*. Basingstoke: Palgrave Macmillan (Red Globe Press), 241–252.

Wingate, U. (2006) 'Doing away with "study skills"', *Teaching in Higher Education*, 11(4), 457–469. https://doi.org/10.1080/13562510600874268

Ideas for further reading

Embedding Learning Development

Maldoni, A. and Lear, E. (2016) 'A decade of embedding: Where are we now?', *Journal of University Teaching and Learning Practice*, 13(3), 1–22. https://doi.org/10.53761/1.13.3.2

Chapter 7

Developing teaching and learning materials

This chapter provides

- A description of the types of teaching and learning materials you might use in your role.
- An explanation of universal design for learning (UDL) principles and why they are important when designing materials and resources.
- An example toolkit of resources and materials.

You will be guided on

- How to find, adapt, and create teaching and learning materials.
- Ways to make materials inclusive and accessible.

What are teaching and learning materials?

Teaching and learning materials are the resources that you find, develop (create), or adapt for use in Learning Development (LD) workshops, tutorials, and embedded teaching. Materials can be teaching-focused, that is, used by you in the classroom context (e.g. workshop slides) or they can be learning materials that are developed for students' use (e.g. worksheets and online interactive tutorials). Materials can be physical such as paper handouts and study guides, or online, for example, audiovisual resources or interactive online guides. Teaching and learning materials also encompass digital materials that students can access in their own time without the need to attend 'live' sessions (i.e. asynchronous material) which might be housed on your LD website or student virtual learning environment (VLE) or learning management system such as Moodle or Google Classroom. Materials also refer to the resources that you create for use in embedded teaching, perhaps in conjunction with subject lecturers. As well as this, they include any resources that are produced for sharing with the wider LD or higher education (HE) community

DOI: 10.4324/9781003604266-7

at conferences, through writing, or for specific resource repositories like the LearnHigher resource bank (more on this shortly). Teaching and learning materials can be developed by you (i.e. created from scratch), adapted (i.e. where an existing resource is modified), or found and used in their original form. In this chapter, we will consider how to find, create, and adapt existing materials for use in your LD practice. Given the diversity of students you will work with, we also consider ways to make materials accessible and inclusive. It will be important to be adaptable when creating and curating your own resources as digital tools and platforms rapidly evolve.

Where can I find teaching and learning materials?

In your early days as a Learning Developer (LDer), it can save time to use materials that are already available and to adapt them to suit the needs of the students you work with. This can help relieve the pressure of having to develop new materials when you are still trying to get to grips with the job. Your university or LD team may have established teaching and learning resources available so do make use of them rather than feeling obliged to replicate what is already out there.

If your LD department or team does not have an extensive range of existing materials, you might choose to use or adapt what is available in the wider LD community. A good starting point is the LearnHigher site (ALDinHE, 2024b). LearnHigher is a resource bank/online materials library published through the ALDinHE website that contains resources submitted by LDers. A benefit of the materials on the site is that they have been through a process of peer-review to check and verify their quality. The resources are available for free use, download, and adaptation under a Creative Commons (CC) licence (ALDinHE, 2024b) which grants individuals the right to use others' creative work under certain conditions. They cover a wide range of topics including assessment, AI, academic writing, digital literacy, diversity and inclusion, and critical thinking and reflection (ALDinHE, 2024b). Knowing that these resources have been created and verified by members of the LD community can help to ease the worry of whether your workshop material is 'good enough'. ALDinHE also hosts a small but growing Neurodivergence Resource Bank that contains materials specifically developed to be inclusive and to meet the needs of neurodivergent learners (ALDinHE, 2024c). Similarly to the LearnHigher resource bank, these materials have been peer-reviewed and scrutinised for quality, thus providing reassurance for your own use.

Another source of materials is to ask experienced LD colleagues for ideas and pointers. Speak to colleagues in your immediate team or widen the scope by asking colleagues in other institutions. For instance, you could put out a call asking for ideas for teaching and learning materials on a professional mailing list like the Learning Development in Higher Education Network (LDHEN) JiscMail,[1] or contact an experienced LDer for guidance, via the ALDinHE networking and expertise directory (ALDinHE, 2024d). This has the same benefits as the peer-reviewed materials on LearnHigher in that you will have reassurance that experienced LDers have successfully used the resource. Any recommended materials can then be adapted to suit your learning objectives and the types of students you work with.

Failing this, you could run an internet search for materials produced by other universities and colleges. When doing so, specify the academic or education domain extension (e.g. ac.uk, ac.za,.edu) to aid with refining your search. There are excellent LD-related materials available in educational institutions worldwide. When searching, it can be helpful to use broad search terms; for instance, rather than specifying 'learning development resources.ac' you could search under 'study OR academic skills.ac'. University writing centres often have very comprehensive online resources that are suitable for use in LD practice. For instance, colleagues at the Writing Center: University of North Carolina at Chapel Hill (n.d.) have created an excellent range of freely available 'Tips and Tools' handouts (under a CC licence) for essay and assignment writing.

Online guides, commonly referred to as 'libguides', are produced by librarian colleagues working in academic institutions. These tend to be well designed and accessible, and contain information and resources related to study skills, research, and referencing. They can be a useful starting point for finding, adapting, or incorporating teaching and learning materials into your own practice. Online 'skills' or 'subject' guides often provide a treasure trove of materials or ideas for resources. For instance, colleagues at the University of York have created comprehensive and interactive online skills guides covering academic writing, critical thinking, and other skills (University of York, 2025a).

The internet, more generally, is a useful source to find materials that you can adapt and use to fit your purpose. You could start from a general skills-related search (e.g. 'resources for teaching study skills') or a specific topic (e.g. 'lesson ideas for teaching critical thinking'). If you find it a distraction and do not wish to have an artificial intelligence (AI) generated overview of your search results, you can type –AI after your search term to exclude it. Of course, if you are not against the use of GenAI, you could use tools such as ChatGPT to generate ideas for resources and teaching – more on this later. Be careful to check for the quality and accuracy of any materials that you find online. A critical point to remember is to verify that any images or resources you intend to use that are found online have a CC licence. As mentioned earlier, this licence grants permission under copyright law to use others' creative work. If you are using others' material, as you would encourage students, good practice is to give credit to the original author, unless this is not required under the licence.

Resources and materials can also be found in your immediate environment. For example, if you are running an outdoor-based workshop, you could use the natural environment as a resource to prompt discussion and engagement. For instance, outdoor 'walk and talk' sessions where students are encouraged to interact with nature are used increasingly in LD, often engendering feelings of belonging and wellbeing amongst student participants (Gregory, 2023). If you are running a workshop, say on critical thinking, you could use materials found in everyday life (realia) such as a topical newspaper or magazine article, advertisement, board game, or subject-relevant podcast or vlog to prompt debate and discussion.

Students themselves can be a source of teaching and learning material. For instance, they often produce their own teaching and learning resources. I have worked with students who have produced essay writing guides and their own academic phrase banks. With their permission, and after reviewing them for quality, such resources could be shared or promoted on your VLE, for instance, 'By you, for you: This week's top resource from the student community'. With students' permission and after discussion and agreement with relevant subject lecturers, past assignments can also be used as exemplars or models within taught workshops or embedded sessions, or to place on your VLE for other students to access asynchronously. You could also ask students for their input when creating materials. For instance, I developed a series of one-minute skills videos answering frequently asked questions, for example, 'What is critical thinking?' 'What is referencing and how do I do it?' Prior to developing these, I sought students' ideas via a survey as to what they would find helpful for the videos to cover. This fed into the development of the video content. These videos were recorded and edited in our university recording suite with the support of a digital education colleague to provide a professional finish. They were then closed-captioned and housed in an online video library (Panopto) for students to access asynchronously. You could of course also work alongside students as partners to co-create materials if time and funding allow for this. Chapter 8 discusses working in partnership with students in more depth.

A further source of ideas for materials is in the scholarship of LD. Papers, academic articles, and opinion pieces in the *Journal of Learning Development in Higher Education* or similar might inspire and provide creative prompts as to the type of resources that you could develop. For instance, you might be interested in the literature on how to 'gamify' LD through activities such as role play scenarios or escape rooms (see, e.g. Hahn et al., 2025) or in the use of digital technologies and GenAI materials (see, e.g. Cirstea, 2024; Koromila, 2024). Thinking broadly in this way about what is meant by 'materials' can create exciting possibilities for your own practice. There is a vast range of literature demonstrating innovative and inclusive approaches to LD teaching and learning materials and I signpost to some of these under further reading at the end of the chapter.

In the next section, we will consider how to create and develop your own materials for aspects of the role such as workshops and embedded sessions and online or digital materials. These are ideas, so enjoy the process of searching and investigating for resources to adapt and use for your own purposes.

How do I create teaching and learning materials?

Creating materials for workshops and embedded teaching

When creating teaching and learning materials and resources for workshops and embedded sessions, start from the learning or skills that you wish the students to develop. What do you hope students will learn or be able to better do (the intended learning outcomes (ILOs))? You can then think about how these ILOs or objectives align with the tasks that you have devised (see the principle of 'constructive alignment' as discussed in Chapter 5). This can provide the basis for considering which materials or resources will aid with meeting these objectives. Table 7.1 provides an example of the types of materials that might be used for an in-person workshop where the aim was for students to develop a clearer understanding of argumentative essay structure.

ILOs can provide the basis for incorporating relevant materials. However, you could also flip this and use the material or resource itself as inspiration for developing your learning outcomes. For instance, LDers have developed a whole series of workshops using Lego, the toy brand of plastic interconnecting bricks, as a prompt to promote skills and subject understanding with fashion students (James, 2013). Be creative with your approach to developing materials and open to how they might work in the context of your practice.

Table 7.1 Materials and resources for a specific intended learning outcome.

Intended Learning Outcome	Activity	Materials and Resources
Students will be better able to identify the key elements of effective argumentative essay structure.	Identify what students already know about essay structure.	Slide with starter quiz to gauge students' current understanding of argumentative essay structure
	In groups, students will reconstruct a short sample essay that has been cut up to identify its introduction, main body, and conclusion.	Short sample essay cut into paragraphs (one per group) Blu-tac Poster paper
	In pairs, students will annotate a main body paragraph that uses the PEEL approach (point, evidence, explain, link) for argumentation.	Main body paragraph of same sample essay (one per pair) Coloured pens/ highlighters

Creating slides for online or in-person teaching

You may use slides or a presentation when teaching workshops or embedded sessions. Slides might incorporate visuals, images, and audiovisual content. Slide design is important for ensuring that information is communicated to students in a clear and comprehensible manner (see Figures 7.1 and 7.2 and Table 7.2 for an evaluation of their effectiveness).

Task

Compare these two slides. They are for use in a workshop on the essay writing process.

Essay writing as a process
Prepare and analyse the question
Put together a reading list
Plan your time
Read and take notes
Draw up an essay plan
Write the first draft
Edit your draft as many times as possible
Proofread the final draft

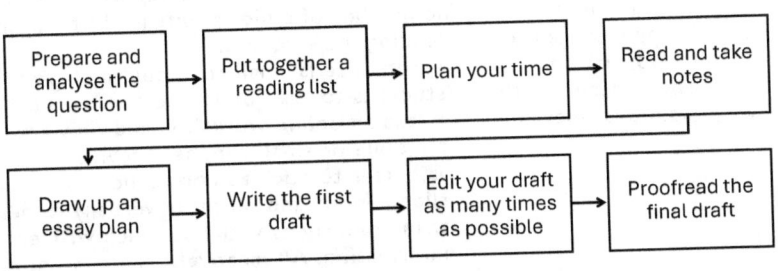

Figure 7.1 Slide one.

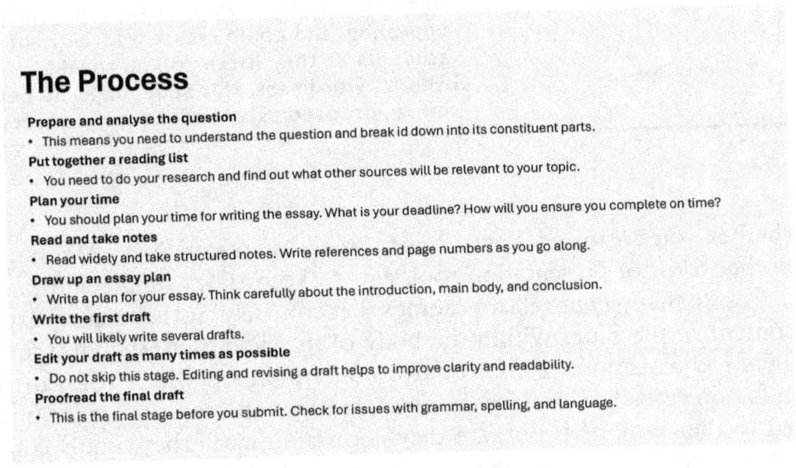

The Process
Prepare and analyse the question
• This means you need to understand the question and break id down into its constituent parts.
Put together a reading list
• You need to do your research and find out what other sources will be relevant to your topic.
Plan your time
• You should plan your time for writing the essay. What is your deadline? How will you ensure you complete on time?
Read and take notes
• Read widely and take structured notes. Write references and page numbers as you go along.
Draw up an essay plan
• Write a plan for your essay. Think carefully about the introduction, main body, and conclusion.
Write the first draft
• You will likely write several drafts.
Edit your draft as many times as possible
• Do not skip this stage. Editing and revising a draft helps to improve clarity and readability.
Proofread the final draft
• This is the final stage before you submit. Check for issues with grammar, spelling, and language.

Figure 7.2 Slide two.

- Are the headings relevant? Do they relate to the slide content?
- Which of the slides might students find clearer?
- What strengths and weaknesses can you identify in each slide?

Table 7.2 Response to task.

	Strengths	Weaknesses
Slide one	Slide one uses a graphic with boxes and arrows to show the progression of the various stages of the essay writing process. The heading used is clear, and the content is relevant.	An issue with slide one is that it presents essay writing as quite straightforward when it can be a much messier process with back and forth between the stages. The linear nature of the diagram does not really account for this. This could be a talking point within your workshop. For instance, you could ask students how they typically approach essay writing and what they find 'messy' about the process.
Slide two	Uses bullet points to present the same information which can be a helpful way to organise information. The content on the slide is relevant.	There are several issues with the slide. It is unclear what the heading 'The process' refers to and this might be better expanded upon a little, e.g. 'The essay writing process'. The number of bullet points might be overloading for students. The font size is small and could be hard for students to read on the screen, particularly if it is an online workshop and they are using a mobile or small handheld device. It is better to stick to core concepts on the slide and expand on these verbally rather than cram slides with too much written information. Alternatively, the content could be split over two or three separate slides. Use of an image on the slide could help reinforce the content, would be more visually appealing, and could create a focal point for students as they listen to you speak. Given its wordiness, this slide might be better off repurposed as a handout for students.

Whether you are using PowerPoint, Prezi, Microsoft Sway, Mentimeter, or another form of presentation tool, aim to keep slides simple and uncluttered. Ensure that you use clear headings that concisely and adequately express the content of the slide. Within the body of the slide itself, stick to the core concepts – a maximum of four or five bullet points – which you can then expand upon verbally. Consider your use of images and colour. Are the images related to the content? If not, are they necessary or will they simply confuse students? Is the font size large enough that students will be able to read it? Remember that if it is an online workshop some students will be accessing the session through a mobile device with a small screen. Optimal font size for text on a slide should be at least size 24 and for headings at least size 36 (Association of Research Libraries, 2025). Have you chosen an accessible font? For instance, have you used a non-serif font such as Arial, Aptos, or Calibri? Have you thought about and checked your slides for accessibility in terms of colour contrast, readability of text, and reading order? Do any substantive images or graphics include alternative text (alt text) that convey what the image shows to aid those with visual impairments to access the slide content? For PowerPoint presentations, you can use the 'check accessibility' function under the 'review' tab to address these questions. Other presentation tools will have similar built-in accessibility checkers, or you can check your slides manually.

It can be tempting to cram slides with content to ensure that you are covering all bases. Even now, as an experienced LDer, I sometimes fall foul of creating far too much content in far too many slides. However, try to avoid this as it can be overwhelming for the students participating in your workshops or embedded sessions. Instead, use slides as a prompt and stick to the core concepts that you wish to cover. Part of the beauty of LD work is in that letting go of sticking rigidly to teaching to the content and, instead, allowing space for questioning, reflection, and discussion. This is necessary if we are to work successfully alongside students 'to make sense out of HE', a core LD value (ALDinHE, 2024a). By creating fewer slides, you allow space and flexibility for conversation and discussion. For instance, in an hour workshop, 60 slides would mean having to dedicate no more than one minute per slide, whereas 20 or so slides, whilst still high in number, would allow you much more wriggle room. Whilst 'letting go' in this way can be especially scary for the new LDer, it is a confidence that will develop over time the more you apply the 'less is more' approach to slide usage.

Slides can be made dynamic by incorporating audiovisual content such as videos or sound/audio clips. For instance, PowerPoint has the function to embed video and audiovisual material directly into slides (under 'insert' then 'media') such that they can be played during the presentation without needing to jump between your slides and the video resource. Other presentation tools have similar functionality. When using slides in this way, always do a run-through beforehand to ensure that the audiovisual material works. When presenting on an online video conferencing platform such as Zoom or Teams, remember to 'share' sound such that the students or attendees can hear the content. As is good practice with workshops, always have a backup in case the technology fails; for instance, you could have a text or written version of the media content to hand.

Creating digital teaching and learning materials

Digital teaching and learning materials are any materials that students (and staff) can interact with online or electronically, through technology. This includes resources such as videos, interactive online tutorials, presentations, virtual reality, and simulations, and so forth. If you are creating asynchronous digital materials, consider carefully how the students might interact with the platform, what might best serve the development of their skills, and what form these materials might take. Like any other teaching materials, the use of digital materials should be based on sound pedagogical principles. For instance, you might consider the following questions:

- What are the ILOs? What do I hope students will learn by interacting with or engaging with this material?
- Do the digital materials allow for students to meet the ILOs (the principle of constructive alignment)?
- Are the digital materials inclusive?
- Do the materials allow for all students to access them, regardless of any identified disability, specific learning difference, or neurodivergence?
- What other pedagogical principles are important when designing the materials? For instance, are you aiming to encourage critical thinking, collaborative, or independent learning, experiential, or immersive learning, and so forth?

Typically, digital materials are housed within a website or a VLE such as Blackboard Learn, Moodle, or Canvas, that students can easily access, usually with an institutional login. Like the LearnHigher resource bank (ALDinHE, 2024b), aim to categorise such materials on your VLE according to specific skills; for instance, you could create sections specifically related to critical thinking, essay and assignment writing, or time management and organisation. This enables students to easily navigate the VLE to find materials that are relevant to their needs. You could also include tags or keywords so that students can search for appropriate resources.

You do not need to be aware of every new digital tool or technology that comes out, but it is a good idea to have a handful of tried and tested resources that you are confident with using. Start from the technologies and digital tools to which your university subscribes. For instance, what possibilities for creating materials are available on your VLE? What software platforms are available? What presentation software is used? Experiment with these. Such tools will already have been checked by your institutions' digital or information technology team for quality and issues with accessibility and inclusivity. For instance, I have developed many simple interactive study skills tutorials using Panopto, a platform used for sharing video content. I use this platform as my institution subscribes to it, because all students can easily access it, and because it is intuitive to navigate. For similar reasons, I also use Mentimeter which is software that can be used to create interactive slides for use during workshops.

When creating digital materials, work alongside colleagues from your digital education team, if you have one, or colleagues with expertise in use of technology for teaching purposes. They can advise on good practice, accessibility issues, and the most appropriate technologies to use for your specific purpose. If you are not digitally inclined, consider upskilling through online platforms such as the Microsoft Learn Educator Centre or LinkedIn Learning or attend any internal staff training provided by your digital education or information technology team. Digital tools will usually have how-to guides or sections so make use of these (there are also many excellent channels on platforms such as YouTube teaching digital skills). With rapid advancements in digital technologies, including GenAI, and software being updated, becoming obsolete, or being discontinued by companies, it is a good idea to not place complete reliance on the use of one tool. The potential for incorporating digital materials is vast so do not be afraid to experiment. However, always carefully consider the pedagogic reasons for why you wish to use the tool and whether it will aid students' learning.

Using generative artificial intelligence to create materials

Generative artificial intelligence (GenAI) such as ChatGPT, Claude, and others can provide a convenient and quick means to formulate initial ideas, create plans and resources, and get feedback for your LD practice. GenAIs are large machine learning models that take instructions (also known as prompts) which are subsequently used to create (or generate) content (King's College London, 2023). The content generated is based on applying a 'statistical model' to the material that the GenAI has been trained on (King's College London, 2023). In the case of ChatGPT, for instance, content generated is based on the huge dataset it has been trained on, that is, textual data from the internet, including books, articles, and webpages (King's College London, 2023).

Reflection task

- What GenAI technologies are you aware of?
- Have you used GenAI in your teaching practice or to develop materials?
- What do you think are the advantages and disadvantages of using GenAI?
- Can you think of any ethical implications of using GenAI to develop materials?

GenAI can be used to generate a range of material. For instance, you could create workshop plans and outlines, case studies, scenarios, problem-solving activities, quiz or multiple-choice questions, tables and figures, example assignment questions, worksheets, visuals and images, video simulations, examples of subject-specific writing, audio resources, and video materials – namely, any form of teaching and learning resource. As a basic example of a resource, in Appendix 3, I prompted ChatGPT to generate a set of quiz questions for use in a workshop. The prompt was to 'Write five multiple choice quiz questions about structuring an argumentative essay. The questions should be targeted at first year undergraduate students who are new to essay writing. Include answers'.

If you use ChatGPT or alike to create such materials, it is important to check the accuracy of the information as it can be prone to misleading and inaccurate information, commonly referred to as 'hallucinations' (University of Leeds, 2025). The specificity of the prompt is important. The clearer and more specific, the more likely it will be able to provide you with a relevant answer. ChatGPT and similar GenAI models are dynamic in that you can provide feedback on the quality of the response which feeds into subsequent refining (increasingly relevant responses) (King's College London, 2023). Do be aware that as GenAI material draws on online content, the material generated by it may be in breach of the intellectual property rights of the original creator, so you should check for issues with copyright if you are using it for educational purposes. Your academic librarian or library service will be able to provide advice on this.

Many students (and staff) are choosing to engage with GenAI. If you are sceptical about such technology, you might use this as a driver to explore its drawbacks and advantages with students through a critical lens. For instance, in a workshop on essay writing, you could create a sample essay generated by a GenAI tool and ask students to analyse it according to marking criteria, discussing, for instance, its readability, use of sources, and quality. GenAI imagery and written content also provides a source of material for discussing issues around bias, representation, and credibility of sources (see Hosseini, 2023).

There are many benefits to using GenAI for developing materials: it can be helpful for initial idea generation and can be used to create and refine content quickly for workshops or teaching. GenAI can also be used in a dialogic way to ask questions and get feedback on your teaching practice. However, there are also ethical implications. These include concerns around how GenAI replicates and reinforces existing societal stereotypes and prejudices, issues with how such technologies use and appropriate human intellectual property, concerns about the carbon footprint produced when training and using GenAI, implications for personal and sensitive data, and concerns around the exploitation of workers in its creation (University of Leeds, 2025). It will be important to consider your ethical stance on such issues and to be aware of and follow your university policies and procedures around its use. Remember that part of the joy of being an LDer is in 'developing' so, if you wish to use GenAI tools, aim to make these supplementary to rather than a replacement for your own thinking. When using GenAI to create or develop materials, it is also good practice, and ethical, to acknowledge this, in a simple declaration; for example, 'The scenarios on slides four and five were generated using a prompt on ChatGPT' or 'Images on this handout were generated with Microsoft's AI image generator'. This also serves as a model to students of how to use GenAI in a way that is transparent and honest.

How do I make teaching and learning materials inclusive?

As LDers, we work with and support diverse student cohorts (see Chapter 8). If we are to work in 'partnership and with respect' for diversity as advocated by the ALDinHE values (ALDinHE, 2024a), then we need to ensure that the materials that we use are inclusive and accessible for learners. Universal design for learning (UDL) principles can be helpful for this.

UDL principles were developed in the 1990s by researchers at the Harvard Graduate School of Education and the Centre for Applied Special Technology (CAST) (CAST, 2024; Newcastle University, 2025). UDL principles advocate for designing for inclusive learning from the outset (Fovet, 2020). They recognise that learners are diverse and that by providing students with multiple ways to engage with the curriculum, all students, regardless of disability or neurodivergence, gain (CAST, 2024). The rationale is that removing barriers to learning through purposeful design reduces the need for individual adjustments or accommodations (CAST, 2024; Newcastle University, 2025). The principles apply not only to materials but also to wider systems such as module and programme design and educational structures. The UDL framework is dynamic. It suggests three overarching approaches to design for universal learning, these being multiple means of 'engagement', 'representation', and 'action and expression' (CAST, 2024). These three means are further subdivided into options for design related to access, support, and executive function (CAST, 2024).

> **Task**
> - Go to the UDL Guidelines 3.0 at https://udlguidelines.cast.org/.
> - Find examples of each type of multiple means to design, that is, 'engagement', 'representation', and 'action and expression'.
> - Can you see how the ideas might apply to your practice?

As illustrative examples, 'multiple means of engagement' might involve including activities in a workshop that enable students to take part actively through exploring and experimenting (CAST, 2024). Designing a workshop that allows for 'multiple means of representation' might necessitate expressing concepts through a range of modes beyond just text; for instance, incorporating an explanatory video, diagram, or photograph alongside written definitions (CAST, 2024). Enabling 'multiple means of action and expression' could entail using examples and checklists as models or frameworks in a taught session or providing individualised and carefully differentiated feedback to students (CAST, 2024).

Keeping UDL guidelines at the forefront and adopting a critical approach when designing or adapting your materials is good practice and helps to ensure that you are 'working with respect for diverse learners' (ALDinHE, 2024a).

Can I see some examples of teaching and learning materials?

> **Task: searching for materials**
>
> - Go to the LearnHigher website at www.learnhigher.ac.uk and click on 'view resources'. Look through this section to familiarise yourself with the site.
> - Browse the 20 most popular resources by going to https://aldinhe.ac.uk/learnhigher/20-most-popular-resources/.
> - Are there any materials that you think look useful for a workshop that you are intending to teach?
> - How might you adapt the material to suit your ILOs?

Whilst this chapter is not intended as a resource bank, the following section provides a few examples of quick and simple ideas for materials for workshops or tutorials as a starting point. At the end of the chapter, there are further links to aid with developing resources.

Using images and visuals

Using images and visual resources is an excellent way to prompt debate and discussion during workshops and embedded teaching. Visuals can be found in many places including online, as stock images in tools like PowerPoint or Microsoft Word, under a CC License, on royalty-free websites like Pixabay, Shutterstock or Unsplash, or via a general Google Images search, though do check for any copyright or permissions needed. Images can also be generated using GenAI tools like Canva, Midjourney, or Microsoft Designer's image creator but, again, consider the ethics of using such tools and note that some of these tools require a subscription. If using GenAI images, remember that these are based on existing datasets and can be prone to reinforce existing societal biases and stereotypes (University of Leeds, 2025). GenAI images may also produce strange distortions. When selecting and using any type of image, it is important to be conscious of UDL principles, particularly in terms of inclusivity, diversity, and accessibility, for instance, by including alt text to describe the image on slides for students with visual impairments.

Task

Figure 7.3 Using images: a rollercoaster.
Source: Image by Connor Johnson from Pixabay used under a CC0 licence

Can you think of ways this image might be used to represent an issue, theory, or concept that you wish to explore in an upcoming workshop?

As an example, in an optional induction workshop for new students, you could display the image in Figure 7.3 accompanied by a question such as 'What might this image tell us about learning at university?' Students could be encouraged to respond either verbally or, if online, in the chat or using an interactive learning platform such as Mentimeter. Students might mention things like studying having unexpected 'twists and turns', or having 'highs and lows', or of it being 'fun but scary'. You could then move onto exploring shared challenges students might face and ways to manage these. Note that this type of question and image is quite abstract and some students, such as those who identify as neurodivergent, might prefer more literal representations. However, the point is that images can often capture or inspire meaning and prompt discussion without having to use written or verbal content.

Simple images can also be used to represent different elements or concepts that you are trying to teach. For instance, in a workshop on essay writing, you could display the image of a burger, as in Figure 7.4, to illustrate and act as a reminder of the different elements of the common PEEL (point, evidence, explain/evaluate, link) paragraph structure:

The point (or topic/controlling sentence) is represented by the top bun. The evidence is represented by the fillings. The meat or vegetable main represents the evaluation or explanation, and the linking sentence is the bottom bun. The PEEL structure could be further illustrated by annotating an example main body paragraph or you could incorporate a subsequent slide with a written explanation, as in Figure 7.5:

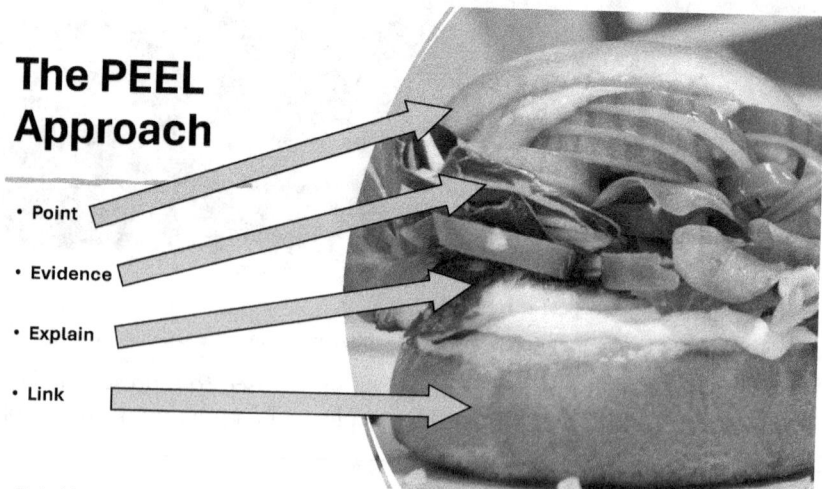

Figure 7.4 Using images: a veggie burger to illustrate the PEEL approach to paragraph structure.

Source: Adapted burger image by Nici Keil from Pixabay used under a CC0 licence

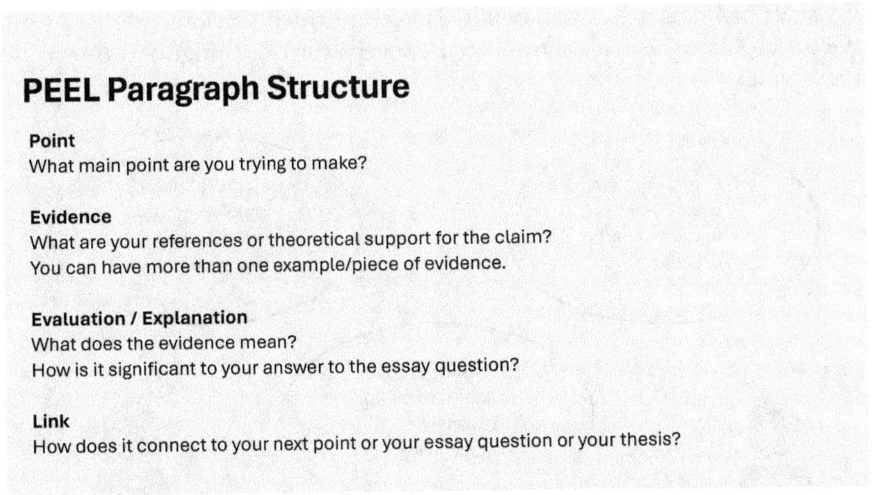

PEEL Paragraph Structure

Point
What main point are you trying to make?

Evidence
What are your references or theoretical support for the claim?
You can have more than one example/piece of evidence.

Evaluation / Explanation
What does the evidence mean?
How is it significant to your answer to the essay question?

Link
How does it connect to your next point or your essay question or your thesis?

Figure 7.5 Slide explaining the PEEL approach to paragraph structure.
Source: Image by Nici Keil from Pixabay

Task

- Think of a topic or skill that you will be teaching in an upcoming workshop.
- Find an image online, generate an image, or draw your own image that relates to that topic.
- Write at least five questions related to the image that you could ask students.
- How could you use the image to illustrate a learning point?

Using concept cartoons

Concept cartoons are a useful way of encouraging higher-level questioning and thinking (see Bloom's Taxonomy (Bloom, 1956) in Chapter 5). They are typically used in schools for introducing new scientific concepts but are also used across other subject areas. Students are presented with a scenario where various viewpoints are posited by different characters. This encourages students to think about which (if any) viewpoint they agree with and leads to further, deeper questioning. Using concept cartoons is a helpful and engaging way to check for and clarify any misconceptions. Concept cartoons can be visuals or images, but you could also create video versions (perhaps using a GenAI tool) or search for animated concept cartoons. Figure 7.6 provides an example:

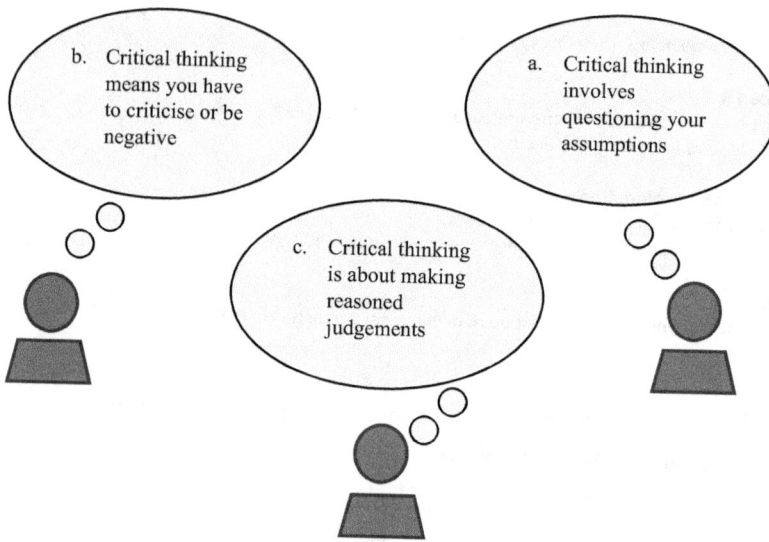

Figure 7.6 A concept cartoon.

Concept cartoons can be easily adapted for teaching university students across any discipline. You present students with a scenario, for example, 'Ideas about academic argument' and put a few perspectives in a concept cartoon format. For example, 'academic argument is the same as opinion', 'academic argument needs to be a critique', 'academic argument involves making judgements', and so forth. Ask students to think of which stance they take (if any), then allow the students to discuss (using breakout rooms or in small table groups if they are in a classroom) around the concept. Such discussions tend to lead to fruitful conversations, and you can then work to clarify any misconceptions. As a follow-up or additional activity, you could ask students to create their own concept cartoons around a key theory or idea.

Using case studies and scenarios

Case studies or scenarios can be great material for encouraging engagement in workshops and embedded teaching. They can also be created for asynchronous use. Case studies can be presented in a written format, through images or in an audiovisual format, for instance, in a video recording. They can involve students in thinking through relatable and relevant scenarios and asking them to present their thoughts or solutions to the issues highlighted.

They are an excellent way of encouraging dialogue and allow for students to participate in many ways, both verbally and in writing, for instance, in the chat if online.

You can find example case studies and scenarios in books such as Stella Cottrell's *Study Skills Handbook* (a brilliant book for students and for those new to LD) where she presents scenarios to stimulate thought. You could also write your own scenarios or generate them using prompts in a GenAI tool such as ChatGPT or Claude. For instance, in an online optional workshop on developing essay writing skills, you could present the students with the following scenario on a slide, accompanied by an image of a fictional student, 'Maryam':

> 'I'm a first-year undergraduate studying English and I'm finding it impossible to motivate myself. I am really struggling with my essays. I just keep putting them off because I'm worried that I'm not up to studies at this level, but this means I end up not bothering to write at all. I usually don't bother planning as I stress that I'll run out of time. When I do eventually write, I tend to keep stopping to check what I have written is perfect. I feel stuck and like I just can't hack it at university to be honest. I love English, but I just feel like I'm really slipping behind. If anyone has any advice, especially for essay writing, I would be immensely grateful!

Give students thinking time and then ask them to give advice to Maryam in the chat or verbally. From this simple activity, you can have a group discussion that may generate a whole host of suggestions and advice for Maryam including the following:

- Just get started, however little.
- Use an online Assignment Survival Kit to plan your time.
- Make mini-deadlines and work towards these.
- Create a simple outline for your essay.
- Get your ideas down first. You can revise and clarify once you have the ideas down.
- View each paragraph as a mini-essay and write in bite-sized chunks.
- Remember, first drafts do not need to be perfect.
- Deal with smaller-level concerns such as spelling and grammar at the proofreading stage.
- Speak to an LD tutor if you would like further guidance or support.
- Go to a writing skills workshop to improve your confidence with essay writing.

Case studies or scenarios are a simple resource that are not time intensive or arduous to create, and they can stimulate much discussion and interest. For embedded teaching, you could create case studies that are specific to the students' disciplinary content. You could also draw on real-life scenarios from newspapers, films, podcasts, and other types of media. Be creative.

Creating a 'toolkit' of resources

You will teach similar skills-related content over the years and, as such, aim to create your own personalised 'toolkit', a repository or resource bank, like that available at LearnHigher, of go-to resources and materials.

Task

- Note down your top two or three resources for developing the following skills:
  - Essay and assignment writing skills;
  - Language and grammar skills;
  - Critical thinking, reading, and writing;
  - Reading and note-making skills;
  - Time management and organisational skills;
  - Revision and exam skills;
  - Academic integrity and avoiding plagiarism skills;
  - Dissertation and research project skills; and
  - GenAI and digital literacy skills.
- How do/will you organise these materials? (e.g. Online bookmarks, Padlet).

An example of a personalised toolkit

Here, I provide a (non-exhaustive) list of websites or resources that make up my own LD teaching toolkit. These are some of my go-to teaching and learning materials which I often use as a starting point or foundation to create new or adapted material. The list is illustrative of materials that I have used in my LD practice and is not intended as endorsement for any particular resource. It is organised around key study skills.

Essay and assignment writing skills

There are many resources available that can be used or repurposed for teaching academic writing skills. The following are two that I use frequently:

- The University of York's online practical guide to academic writing (University of York, 2025b). This is an excellent and comprehensive

resource containing advice, videos, writing templates, and much more. This guide can be used in many ways, for instance, using the content in generic workshops or drawing on the examples of subject-specific material for embedded teaching.
- The Writing Center at the University of North Carolina at Chapel Hill has produced a range of online handouts covering the essay and academic writing process (Writing Center: University of North Carolina at Chapel Hill, n.d.). These are available under a CC licence. I have used, with acknowledgement, material from this site in workshops and regularly signpost students to the content.

Critical thinking, reading, and writing skills

- The critical writing online guide is another resource from the University of York (University of York, 2025c). This is a comprehensive guide for students (and staff) wishing to improve their general critical thinking skills. It contains videos, exemplars, and guidance on all aspects of being critical in the academic context. The website can be used in many ways, for instance, to aid with workshop planning or to signpost to students who need guidance on developing critical writing skills.
- *Critical Thinking Skills* by Stella Cottrell (Cottrell, 2017). This book is a rigorous and comprehensive introduction to critical thinking. I have adapted material from this book to use in workshop slides and often suggest its use to students.

Reading and note-making skills

- The SQ3R method is a helpful and well-known approach for teaching effective note-making and reading skills. SQ3R stands for survey, query, (and three Rs) read, recall, and review. It is an active reading method that involves students identifying the purpose of their reading, reading with that purpose in mind with a questioning approach, and recalling and reviewing that information. For teaching about SQ3R, there are many excellent video explanations on YouTube that can be used within teaching or as a resource to refer students to access in their own time. Do always check any online videos for accuracy of information and quality of content before sharing them with students.
- The Cornell note-making method is an active approach to taking notes, developed by Walter Pauk, a professor at Cornell University. Templates for Cornell are available for free download via an internet search, but many organisational and note-making apps including OneNote and Notion also now incorporate Cornell planning templates. I use the templates in workshops and within tutorials when modelling and discussing effective note-making strategies.

Time management and organisation skills

- The Learning Corner website by colleagues at Oregon State University hosts a comprehensive range of teaching and learning materials on academic skills including the topics of time management, dealing with procrastination, and managing stress (Oregon State University, 2025). Their site includes handouts, videos, and worksheets for students.
- You will find that student concerns tend to centre around assignments including not only essay writing but also other genres such as reports and reflective writing. Useful resources for planning a schedule for writing assignments include the Assignment Survival Kit by colleagues at the University of Kent (University of Kent, 2024). This can be used in workshops and as a student resource to help them manage their time and essay writing schedules. It is a scheduler that helps students to plan backwards from the deadline for when certain tasks (such as analysing the question, writing the first draft, editing, and revising) need to be done and by when. I refer students who are struggling with time management and planning to this website during tutorials and in workshops.

Revising and taking exams

- The Learning Scientists website contains evidence-based videos and explanations on effective learning strategies (Learning Scientists, n.d.). This website is particularly helpful for developing good revision and memorisation strategies.

Language and grammar

In my context, English is the predominant language of instruction in which students are expected to write, read, and communicate for academic purposes. However, many students come from different linguistic backgrounds or have questions about how to improve their academic language competency. These are my three go-to resources I use to aid with developing English language and grammatical skills:

- The Manchester Academic Phrasebank (University of Manchester, 2023) provides a corpus of useful academic phrases which can be used for different purposes such as signalling transition or showing evidence of criticality.
- English for Academic Purposes (EAP) Foundation is another useful site (Smith, 2025). Whilst it is targeted at students and teachers of EAP, the resources are relevant to LD and can be adapted for use in teaching or shared with students to access independently.
- Grammar-Monster.com (Shrives, 1999) is a helpful site for students (and LDers) wishing to improve their general English and grammar skills. It contains lessons, quizzes, games, and word lists. It is interactive and makes learning and understanding English grammar fun rather than arduous.

Whilst LDers are not language tutors or lecturers, many have EAP or language teaching experience so do seek guidance about developing or finding materials for developing language skills from such colleagues if needed.

Referencing, citing, and avoiding plagiarism

- For referencing and avoiding plagiarism resources, I make use of existing online referencing guides such as the excellent OSCOLA guide produced by Swansea University for law students. These are intuitive to navigate and allow students to understand how to cite the key source types they will use in their studies. It is possible to produce your own referencing or online study guides. If you are interested in producing a referencing guide, contact your academic librarian for guidance on how to create and set one up for students to access.
- Selected YouTube videos can be helpful when teaching about academic integrity. For instance, I have used videos showing side-by-side similar speeches by famous political public figures to provide a useful visual and humorous stimulus for discussion about the ethics of 'copying' others. Make sure to check the content of any such videos before their use for any issues with accuracy of information and copyright.

Digital literacy and information technology skills

- For teaching digital skills, I refer as a starting point to the peer-reviewed resources on 'digital literacy' from the ALDinHE LearnHigher resource bank.
- A new addition to my toolkit is the Open University's detailed framework for developing critical GenAI literacy skills (Open University, 2025). This framework can be used to plan workshops and embedded sessions that challenge students to think critically about their use of GenAI technologies.

Dissertation and research project skills

- The *Planning Your PhD* and *Completing Your PhD* books from the Pocket Study Skills book series provide a handy overview of how to prepare for a dissertation and PhD. I signpost students to these books and have used them, with acknowledgement, to design teaching content.

As you develop in your role, you will start to curate your own materials and build up a bank of key resources. There are many ways you might choose to organise your personal resource bank. For example, you could create a digital or physical folder according to specific skills such as essay writing, critical thinking, and so forth, or categorise resources into sub-folders by the types of students you will be working with, for instance, undergraduate or postgraduate, by module, or by level. You could create bookmarks on your browser of useful websites, which you can then further subdivide and arrange them into relevant categories, or you could use an online visual organiser such as Padlet or Pinterest. For example, given the rapid developments in GenAI, you might bookmark and collate academic articles and online links to GenAI-related topics in a visual organiser for quick retrieval or to read later.

It is important to emphasise that whilst having a toolkit of useful materials is helpful, it is also crucial to stay responsive to the needs of the students you work with. For instance, a generic handout on essay writing that you find online will be better received in an embedded workshop for history students if it is tailored to their disciplinary requirements and is based on an exemplar from their discipline.

Where next?

You should now have a clearer understanding of what LD materials are and how to find, adapt, and create them. In this chapter, we have seen that materials and ideas for resources can be sourced from many places, so do be creative about the available possibilities. We thought about the need for inclusive and accessible design and looked at the UDL principles as a guide for good practice. We also considered the importance of developing and curating your own bank of resources that you can draw upon. As you gain confidence in developing your own materials, you could also look to submit these to the ALDinHE LearnHigher website (ALDinHE, 2024b) to share with colleagues external to your institution. You might also choose to specialise in the design and creation of teaching and learning materials. This chapter should have given you some initial ideas on how to get started. What will you now do to further develop your understanding of creating materials?

Summary

- This chapter provided an explanation of the types of materials you may use in your role. Materials are the resources that you find, adapt, or create for the purposes of teaching and learning.
- The chapter provided suggestions on where to find teaching and learning materials including making use of the ALDinHE LearnHigher and Neurodivergence Resource Banks, peer-reviewed bank of materials created by LDers.
- We considered how to create your own materials including exploring how GenAI might be used for this purpose whilst acknowledging the ethical issues related to its use.

- We looked at designing materials for inclusivity and accessibility by considering universal design for learning (UDL) principles and what this might look like on a practical level.
- We thought about the benefits of creating a toolkit of go-to resources whilst being mindful of being responsive to students' specific needs.

Note

1 JiscMail lists can be accessed at https://www.jiscmail.ac.uk/. These are professional email discussion lists for practitioners in the education and research community. It is a UK-based site but has many subscribers worldwide. The lists cover a range of professional interests including the Learning Development in Higher Education Network (LDHEN). You can sign up to as many JiscMail email lists as you wish.

References

ALDinHE (2024a) *About ALDinHE*. Available at: https://aldinhe.ac.uk/about-aldinhe/ (Accessed: 9 April 2024).

ALDinHE (2024b) *LearnHigher*. Available at: https://aldinhe.ac.uk/learnhigher/ (Accessed: 12 December 2024).

ALDinHE (2024c) *Neurodivergence Resource Bank*. Available at: https://aldinhe.ac.uk/resource-bank/neurodivergence/ (Accessed: 12 December 2024).

ALDinHE (2024d) *Networking & Expertise Directory*. Available at: https://aldinhe.ac.uk/support/expertise-directory/ (Accessed: 12 December 2024).

Association of Research Libraries (2025) *PowerPoint Guidelines for Presenters*. Available at: https://www.arl.org/accessibility-guidelines-for-powerpoint-presentations/ (Accessed: 17 March 2025).

Bloom, B. S. (1956) *Taxonomy of Educational Objectives, Handbook 1: The Cognitive Domain*. New York: David McKay.

CAST (2024) *Universal Design for Learning Guidelines Version 3.0*. Available at: https://udlguidelines.cast.org/ (Accessed: 17 March 2025).

Cirstea, A. (2024) 'Pedagogical uses of AI tools: Reflection on a case study', *Journal of Learning Development in Higher Education* [Preprint], 32. https://doi.org/10.47408/jldhe.vi32.1402

Cottrell, S. (2017) *Critical Thinking Skills: Effective Analysis, Argument and Reflection*, 3rd edn. London: Red Globe Press.

Fovet, F. (2020) 'Universal design for learning as a tool for inclusion in the higher education classroom: Tips for the next decade of implementation', *Education Journal*, 9(6), 163–172. https://doi.org/10.11648/j.edu.20200906.13

Gregory, J. (2023) 'How can we incorporate nature connection into our work as learning developers?', *Journal of Learning Development in Higher Education* [Preprint], 29. https://doi.org/10.47408/jldhe.vi29.1098

Hahn, S., Springmann, M.-L., Denninger, T. and Kiegelmann, M. (2025) 'Extension of escape rooms with roleplays: Promoting a sense of belonging and fostering communication skills among first-year university students', *Journal of Learning Development in Higher Education* [Preprint], 34. https://doi.org/10.47408/jldhe.vi34.1292

Hosseini, D. (2023, 8 August) 'Generative AI: A problematic illustration of the intersections of racialized gender, race, ethnicity', *Dustin Hosseini Blog*. Available at: https://www.dustinhosseini.com/blog/2023/08/08/generative-ai-a-problematic-illustration-of-the-intersections-of-racialized-gender-race-ethnicity (Accessed: 17 February 2025).

James, A. R. (2013) 'Lego serious play: A three-dimensional approach to learning development', *Journal of Learning Development in Higher Education [Preprint]*, 6. https://doi.org/10.47408/jldhe.v0i6.208

King's College London (2023) *Activity 1.3: What is Generative AI? Generative AI in Higher Education* [Online]. Available from: https://www.futurelearn.com/courses/ai-in-education/2/steps/2034149 (Accessed: 8 May 2024).

Koromila, G. (2024) 'Generative artificial intelligence and university study: A guide for students by the study advice team at the University of Reading', *Journal of Learning Development in Higher Education [Preprint]*, 32. https://doi.org/10.47408/jldhe.vi32.1474

Learning Scientists (n.d.) *Videos for Teaching and Learning*. Available at: https://www.learningscientists.org/videos (Accessed: 9 January 2025).

Newcastle University (2025) *Universal Design for Learning*. Available at: https://www.ncl.ac.uk/learning-and-teaching/effective-practice/universal-design/ (Accessed: 17 March 2025).

Open University (2025) *A Framework for the Learning and Teaching of Critical AI Literacy Skills*. Available at: https://www.open.ac.uk/blogs/learning-design/wp-content/uploads/2025/01/OU-Critical-AI-Literacy-framework-2025-external-sharing.pdf (Accessed: 30 June 2025).

Oregon State University (2025) *The Learning Corner*. Available at: https://success.oregonstate.edu/learning-corner (Accessed: 30 June 2025).

Shrives, C. (1999) *Grammar-Monster.com*. Available at: https://www.grammar-monster.com (Accessed: 30 June 2025).

Smith, S. (2025) *EAPFoundation.com*. Available at: https://www.eapfoundation.com/ (Accessed: 17 March 2025).

University of Kent (2024) *Assignment Survival Kit*. Available at: https://student.kent.ac.uk/studies/written-assignments/assignment-survival-kit (Accessed: 9 January 2025).

University of Leeds (2025) *Strengths and Weaknesses of Gen AI*. Available at: https://generative-ai.leeds.ac.uk/intro-gen-ai/strengths-and-weaknesses/ (Accessed: 16 April 2025).

University of Manchester (2023) *Academic Phrasebank*. Available at: http://www.phrasebank.manchester.ac.uk/ (Accessed: 30 June 2025).

University of York (2025a) *Skills Guides*. Available at: https://subjectguides.york.ac.uk/skills (Accessed: 9 January 2025).

University of York (2025b) *Academic Writing: A Practical Guide*. Available at: https://subjectguides.york.ac.uk/academic-writing/home (Accessed: 9 January 2025).

University of York (2025c) *Being Critical: Critical Writing*. Available at: https://subjectguides.york.ac.uk/critical/writing (Accessed: 9 January 2025).

Writing Center: University of North Carolina at Chapel Hill (n.d.) *Tips & Tools*. Available at: https://writingcenter.unc.edu/tips-and-tools/ (Accessed: 9 January 2025).

Ideas for further reading

Inclusive Learning and Teaching

Brown, S. (2024) 'Review of inclusive learning design in higher education: A practical guide to creating equitable learning experiences by V. Rossi', *Journal of Learning*

Development in Higher Education [Preprint], 30. https://doi.org/10.47408/jldhe. vi30.1186

CAST (2024) *Universal Design for Learning Guidelines Version 3.0*. Available at: https://udlguidelines.cast.org/ (Accessed: 17 March 2025).

Tobin, T. and Behling, K. (2018) *Reach Everyone, Teach Everyone. Universal Design for Learning in Higher Education*. Morgantown: West Virginia University Press.

Developing materials

ALDinHE (2024a) *LearnHigher*. Available at: https://aldinhe.ac.uk/learnhigher/ (Accessed: 12 December 2024).

ALDinHE (2024b) *Neurodivergence Resource Bank*. Available at: https://aldinhe.ac.uk/resource-bank/neurodivergence/ (Accessed: 12 December 2024).

ALDinHE (2024c) *ALDinHE Book Sharing*. Available at: https://padlet.com/ALDinHEcommunity/aldinhe-book-sharing-i9ts12gndp8istjh (Accessed: 4 June 2025).

Creative Commons (n.d.) *About CC Licenses*. Available at: https://creativecommons.org/share-your-work/cclicenses/ (Accessed: 15 April 2025).

Intellectual Property Office (2014) *Exceptions to Copyright: Education and Teaching*. Available at: https://assets.publishing.service.gov.uk/government/uploads/system/uploads/attachment_data/file/375951/Education_and_Teaching.pdf (Accessed: 15 April 2025).

Chapter 8

Working with students and colleagues

This chapter provides an overview of

- The types of students and staff you may work with as a Learning Developer (LDer).
- The wider statutory context and how it applies to your work.
- What is meant by equality, equity, diversity, and inclusivity.
- Ways to work with diverse students, including partnership and co-creation.

You will be guided on

- Pragmatic ways to work effectively with students and staff.
- Managing imposter syndrome.
- How to 'embrace and respect diverse learners' (ALDinHE, 2024).
- Ways to promote inclusive teaching and learning practices.
- How to articulate the need for Learning Development (LD) in your institution and beyond.
- Ways to care for yourself in your professional role.

Working with students and staff

Most of your work as an LDer (i.e. workshops, tutorials, embedded provision) will be student-facing. However, LD practice also involves working collaboratively with staff including other LDers, academic, and professional services staff. You will interact with colleagues with different but, complementary, remits who have their own professional protocols, priorities, and principles. This will include subject lecturers and coworkers such as Educational or Academic Developers,[1] academic librarians, and digital education staff. Given that LD work is often misunderstood and undervalued by some in the wider higher

DOI: 10.4324/9781003604266-8

education (HE) sector, you may need to articulate the value and impact of your service to those with direct influence at an institutional level such as senior managers and educational leads. Navigating this range of professional dynamics can be difficult as a new LDer and you may have questions about ways to work effectively with students and staff.

As a starting point, we will begin with a reminder of the community-driven values that underpin how LDers may approach their practice. These five values are stated on the Association for Learning Development in Higher Education (ALDinHE) website, which is the UK-based, though international in reach, professional association for LDers:

1. Working in partnership with students and staff to make sense and get the most out of HE.
2. Embracing and respecting diverse learners through critical pedagogy and practice.
3. Adapting, sharing, and advocating effective LD practice to promote student learning.
4. Commitment to a scholarly approach and research related to LD.
5. Critical self-reflection, ongoing learning, and a commitment to professional development.

(ALDinHE, 2024)

The first three values refer specifically to interactions with students; that is, 'working in partnership with students', 'embracing and respecting diverse learners', and 'promoting student learning'. The final two values do not mention students (or staff) directly but are implicit in recognising that through 'a scholarly approach', 'critical self-reflection', and 'ongoing learning', we aim to improve students' experience of HE. An initial question that you might ask is: do my own values align with these community values? This might then raise another question: if my personal values do align, how do I ensure that I am working with students and staff with these values in mind?

This chapter will consider practical ways in which you can 'work in partnership with students and staff' (ALDinHE, 2024). It will also provide guidance on what 'embracing and respecting diverse learners' might look like in practice (2024). Given that LD work is collaborative in nature, it considers participatory ways of working with students such as co-creation and partnership, approaches that can promote student agency and engagement with LD. It outlines the types of staff you are likely to work with and provides guidance on developing professional relationships, including how to articulate the value of LD to colleagues working outside the field. The chapter concludes by providing pragmatic suggestions for how to look after yourself in your professional role, emphasising the importance of setting clear boundaries. Before we think about how we might practicably 'work in partnership with students and staff' and 'embrace and respect diverse learners' (ALDinHE, 2024), we will take a brief segue on the topic of imposter syndrome.

I feel like an imposter! What should I do?

On my first day as an LDer, after a helpful, but exhausting, induction, I returned to my new office on campus, sank into my chair, and buried my head in my hands. Even though I was a qualified teacher with years of practice in different contexts, I experienced an overwhelming sense of dread that I was completely unqualified to support the adult students that I would imminently have to meet and teach. How would I manage when I had 'only' taught in schools or on short-term university summer programmes? What would the students be like? How would I be able to work with staff when I was a nervous wreck? Would I be able to offer anything of value? These self-preoccupying questions were very much at the forefront of my mind on that first day and remained so for several years into the role as I struggled with questions of professional identity about my efficacy and who I was 'being' and 'becoming' as an LDer.

You may have experienced similar feelings of being a fraud or somehow inadequate. You may at times doubt yourself and even question your professional competence. It is common for those teaching (and learning) in HE to feel imposter syndrome (Parkman, 2016), particularly so if you are new to a role, or if you are progressing and taking on new responsibilities. Imposter syndrome can arise at any stage of an individual's career (Faulkner, 2015). If you are willing to have an honest conversation about it, you will find that many of your more experienced LD and (non-LD) colleagues have felt it at some point.

Imposter syndrome often afflicts those who are highly qualified and competent but who lack confidence in their own abilities and therefore attribute their success to 'external factors' (Faulkner, 2015; Parkman, 2016). As a starting point, remind yourself that you were employed because your employer had reasonable faith in your qualifications and competence to fulfil the responsibilities of the job. Part of the process of developing as an LDer is establishing professional, respectful relationships with students and staff, and most will be appreciative of what you offer. But professional relationships can also be messy, complex, and unpredictable. As such, things will not always go smoothly, and you will naturally make 'mistakes' and sometimes feel a fraud. This is okay and is part of the nature of the role: making mistakes, reflecting on them, and considering what you might do differently next time – that is, becoming a critically reflective practitioner.[2] The idea that mistakes can be a professional learning tool can help to free you from the need to chase perfectionism, a trait linked to imposter syndrome (Parkman, 2016). The following are thoughts from experienced practitioners on making mistakes and managing feelings of being an imposter.

> **Thoughts from experienced LDers**
>
> Stand up, shoulders back, and keep going. Do not relinquish your happiness to other people. Imposter syndrome only exists if you think you're an imposter and you are not. Claim your space. Claim your place. Throughout your career store positive things that people say and read them to feel better.
>
> Dr Katharine Jewitt, Associate Lecturer,
Open University
>
> Making mistakes is normal. We want to encourage students to feel OK with it, so must be OK with it ourselves. Just explain and laugh it off. Don't be constrained by where your institution's structure places you – be brave and feel OK with trying to break down walls.
>
> Dr Ian Johnson, Teaching Fellow in Learning
Development, University of Portsmouth

To build a secure professional confidence such that you feel empowered to try to 'break down walls', you need to understand your role and how it fits into your institutions' overall aims. This includes being aware of your university's mission, its objectives, and the composition of the student population that you work with. It also entails being clear about the structure of the programmes and modules that you support, assessment types, and deadlines, and where to locate pertinent data relevant to your role. This might include data about enrolment figures, access and participation data, and data regarding continuation, completion, and progression rates.[3] This knowledge will aid with you in contributing meaningfully and in an informed manner to discussions about LD input.

> **Task**
>
> Find the answers to the following questions.
>
> Tip: You should be able to find the answers to these questions by talking to colleagues or by looking on your university website or intranet/internal data management system. If you are based in the UK, you can also look at the Higher Education Statistics Agency (HESA) website for data on your institution:
>
> - What type of institution do you work in? When was it established? Is it an older/newer university/college? Is it a research-intensive or teaching-focused institution?

- What is its mission statement? What are its short- to long-term priorities?
- How many students are enrolled in your institution? What is the breakdown between those studying part- or full-time? What is the breakdown of undergraduates to postgraduates? What is the proportion of 'home' and 'international' students?
- Can you find any demographic data (e.g. on ethnicity, gender, and age) about the students at your institution? How many students at your institution identify as having a disability or specific learning difference?
- What types of students does your LD service support? At what stage of their programme/degree are most of the students you work with? Are the students you work with based in a specific faculty or do you support students across the university/college?
- Does your institution have an access and participation plan? What are its key priorities?
- What types of assessments do the students you work with undertake on their programme? When are the deadlines for these assessments and for any reassessments?
- What are the most recent overall continuation, completion, and progression rates for the department/faculty/university you work with?
- What else is important to know about your institution? How will you find the answers?

With such insight, you can begin to appreciate the significance of your work in relation to wider institutional and regulatory priorities. This knowledge can provide the foundation for building credence and should aid with increasing your professional confidence, and reducing feelings of imposter syndrome, when working with students and staff.

What type of students might I work with as a Learning Developer?

As an LDer, you will work with students of diverse demographic, cultural, and social characteristics. For instance, recent data from the HESA website for 2021 to 2022 indicate that in the UK context:

- The total number of HE students stood at 2,862,620 in 2021/22, an increase of 4% from 2020/21. Including HE students registered at FE providers throughout the UK, the total number of HE students was 3,007,545.
- Of all HE students in 2021/22, 57% were female. This has been the same since 2016/17.

- Between 2020/21 and 2021/22, the number of students with a known disability increased by 34,190 or 1 percentage point.
- Since 2015/16, the proportion of students from a state-funded school or college has remained constant at 91%.

This data analysis is published on the www.hesa.ac.uk website and is licensed under CC-BY 4.0.

(HESA, 2023)

The HESA data illustrate some of the diversity of students attending higher education institutions (HEIs) in the UK context. Regardless of your specific cultural context, your role will involve working with diverse students.

In addition to working with a diverse student population, LDers work in varied contexts.[4] You might work in a large institution, supporting a substantial number of students, or a smaller one providing more bespoke style support. Students might be primarily 'traditional' 18-year-old entrants (or younger) who have applied (in the UK) through the Universities and Colleges Admissions Service (UCAS) straight from sixth form or college-level studies. Or maybe the majority of students you work with are career changers, mature students over the age of 21, or those returning to HE after a long break. Students in your institution might be campus based, distance learners, or regularly commute in for classes. Students may be majority 'home' students, or you may have a significant international student presence. The student population may be comprised mostly of full-time students or there could be a considerable proportion of part-time students. Lectures and classes might take place online, in-person, or in a hybrid form. Students may study primarily during daytime hours or in the evenings. Depending on the scope of your role and the way in which LD operates in your institution, you may be based in a particular faculty, department, or 'School', working exclusively with students from specific disciplines; or you may have a wider remit, providing LD support across the university or college. Your provision may be targeted at a specific cohort. For example, you might work solely with undergraduate students in the first year of their study, or you may provide a breadth of support working with students across a range of levels from foundation year to postgraduate level including doctoral students.

These examples are not exhaustive. The point is to highlight the diversity of students and contexts within which LDers must carry out their work. Whatever your specific situation, we will look later in the chapter at the practical implications of such diversity on your work.

What should I be aware of when working with students and staff?

Your primary responsibilities will entail running tutorials, delivering optional or extra-curricular skills workshops and embedded sessions, and creating teaching and learning materials. However, LD practice is not disconnected from its wider external environment. Wherever you are based, your institution will be subject to laws, regulatory frameworks and standards, and institutional polices which enact these. For instance, we have already seen in Chapter 3 that most universities are regulated by independent bodies like the Office for Students (OfS). To work effectively with diverse students and staff, you will need to be aware of statutory provisions that are relevant to your work as an LDer so that you work with consideration for these.

Table 8.1 highlights several laws that are relevant to working 'with respect for diverse learners' (ALDinHE, 2024) in the UK context. If you are based outside the UK, then you should try to identify any such laws that impact your role as an LDer so that you work with these in mind.

What do we mean by equality, equity, and diversity?

> **Activity**
>
> - What do you understand by the terms, 'equality', 'equity', and 'diversity'?
> - How do you think these might impact your LD practice?
> - What might you expect 'respect for diverse learners', 'equality', and 'inclusion' to look like in practice?

It is helpful to try to conceptualise what we mean by equality, equity, and diversity. Equality is about ensuring that everyone is treated alike regardless of their background, starting points, or needs (UCL, 2025). Related to equality is the idea of equity which is interconnected but distinct in meaning. Equity recognises that people have different starting points and that achieving equality, or equal outcomes, necessitates providing resources to 'even the playing field' (UCL, 2025; United Nations, n.d.). Diversity relates to the varied backgrounds, experiences, and characteristics of students. As shown in Table 8.1, some characteristics such as age and disability are protected in the UK context under the Equality Act 2010.

As an LDer, you will work in institutions that reflect the diversity of wider society including those who have historically been marginalised or discriminated against. This might include students identified with disabilities and specific learning differences (SpLDs) such as dyslexia or dyspraxia, students from global majority or Black and (the contentiously termed) minority ethnic (BAME) backgrounds, mature learners, students who identify as LGBTQIA+, students from asylum seeking and refugee backgrounds, carers, and care-experienced students. Whilst you should take individual action in your

Table 8.1 Three UK statutory provisions relevant to 'working with respect for diverse learners' in the HE context.

What Is It?	Where Does It Apply?	What Does It Concern?	How Does It Apply to LD Practice? Why Is It Important?
Equality Act 2010 (Replaces the Disability Discrimination Act 1995)	Applies to England, Scotland, and Wales (in Northern Ireland, some provisions apply)	Under the Act, people should not be discriminated, harassed or victimised in the workplace, public services like education or healthcare, businesses, and other areas. The Act protects people based on nine protected characteristics. These are age, gender, gender reassignment, sex, sexual orientation, race, disability, religion or belief, marriage and civil partnership, and pregnancy and maternity. The legislation exists to prevent such individuals being unduly disadvantaged as compared to those individuals who do not have any protected characteristics.	Most universities in the UK are charities and are treated as public bodies for the purposes of the Act. As such, they must act in accordance with the Equality Act 2010. You will need to be aware of university policies that deal with and are intended to enact this legislation such as student codes of conduct, complaints policies, dignity at work policies, anti-discrimination and harassment guidance and policies, and reasonable adjustments support. Your university will also provide functions such as wellbeing and mental health services, disability and dyslexia services, student services, and so forth to support students which you should be aware of as you may need to refer students to such services. It is important to be aware of the provisions of the Act and ensure you act in accordance with it in your everyday practice as an LDer. Your university will provide equality and diversity training which it is advisable (and often mandatory) to complete.

(Continued)

Table 8.1 (Continued)

What Is It?	Where Does It Apply?	What Does It Concern?	How Does It Apply to LD Practice? Why Is It Important?
Special Educational Needs and Disability Act (SENDA) 2001	Applies to England and Wales, with some provisions relevant to educational bodies in Scotland.	This Act puts a duty on 'responsible bodies' not to discriminate or 'substantially disadvantage' (in terms of access to education and services) disabled students or prospective students in comparison to other students.	The Equality Act 2010 has superseded certain provisions of SENDA 2001. However, it is important to be aware of sections that set out the duties of educational providers in relation to students with disabilities and how this might impact your practice. How do you ensure that disabled students can access your LD service?
The Special Educational Needs and Disabilities (SEND) Code of Practice 2014	Provides statutory guidance for education providers. It came into force via Part 3 of the Children and Families Act 2014. Applies to England.	Education providers providing services for children and young people (up to 25 years old) with disabilities or special educational needs are required to follow the statutory guidance set out in the Code. The aim is to ensure good outcomes for education and adult life for such students.	Whilst the duty is placed on the education provider (your university), it is good practice to be aware of the statutory guidance in the Code when working with young people up to the age of 25.

role to ensure that you are working with respect for equality and diversity (see ideas later on *How do I work with respect for diverse learners?*), your institution is responsible for ensuring that this is embedded and promoted at the systemic level.

What do we mean by inclusive teaching and learning practices?

HEIs are legally obligated to ensure that their provision is inclusive (Hubbard and Gawthorpe, 2023). Inclusive practice recognises the diversity of backgrounds, experiences, and characteristics of each learner such that they feel a valued part of the institution (Hubbard and Gawthorpe, 2023). This includes, for instance, ensuring that the curriculum is accessible for all learners, working to ensure that all students feel a sense of belonging and community, and making sure that assessment processes are transparent and equitable for all learners (Hubbard and Gawthorpe, 2023). However, inclusion is 'relational' (United Nations, n.d.). It depends on the student's perception of their relationships between them and their peers, academics, and other staff. If students feel that they belong, then they will also feel a sense of inclusion. As LDers, we can play a key role by recognising and showing authentic respect for diversity, and by ensuring our provision is accessible and inclusive for all, thereby aiding learners to 'make the most' of their studies. We will look at practical ways of doing so shortly.

Working with 'respect for diverse learners' as an LDer (ALDinHE, 2024) involves being aware of practices that promote inclusion. For example, there have been ongoing calls to decolonise the curriculum to make it more reflective and inclusive of the experiences and knowledge of those from Black and minoritised backgrounds or those who have historically been marginalised and oppressed (Bhambra et al., 2018; Bhopal, 2018; University of Hull, n.d.). Decolonial practice is the process of dismantling existing historical power structures that promote inequalities (Bhambra et al., 2018; Bhopal, 2018; University of Hull, n.d.). For instance, in the UK (and Western) context, it is recognised that many HEIs have actively benefitted from colonialism and colonialist practices and the power disparities that this has created (Dhillon, 2020; Tikly, 2025). Decoloniality interrogates the question of power and whose and what knowledge is viewed as legitimate (Bhopal, 2018; Tikly, 2025). Traditionally, research on decoloniality has focused on the histories of those from Black and minoritised backgrounds but increasingly it also explores the experiences of other historically marginalised groups such as those identified with disabilities or from the LGBTQIA+ community (see, i.e. Dirth and Adams, 2019; Day, 2023). Moreover, there is an increased emphasis on how different identities, such as race, age, class, and gender, intersect or interact to reinforce an individual's experience of discrimination. Proponents of diversifying and decolonising the curriculum argue that it is not enough to simply include texts or materials by diverse authors or from diverse voices (Felix and Friedberg, 2019; University of Hull, n.d.). Instead, they argue that it requires a complete overhaul of the educational system to tackle and undo long-established existing structural inequalities (Tikly, 2025; University of Hull, n.d.).

In relation to 'race' and racism, Arthur (2024) asserts that the scholarship of LD has remained rather silent on this matter. He points to several potential reasons for this. First, LD's relative newness as a field and profession[5] means that scholarship in this area has not had the time to become established (Arthur, 2024). Second, he suggests that LDers might wish to adopt a 'neutral' approach to the development of students' academic skills and literacies, not wishing to engage in uncomfortable conversations around 'race talk' (2024, p. 127). Third, he argues that the '"whiteness" of the LD field' itself may mean that colleagues without 'lived experience' of racism may choose 'not to engage' in these issues (2024, p. 127). Finally, he posits that scholarship and debate that explicitly highlight race and racism might be less 'palatable' than framing this in relation to 'umbrella issues' such as 'inclusion, diversity, and equality' or 'the attainment gap' which encapsulate but do not directly address issues of race (2024, p. 128). We saw in earlier chapters that our personal and professional values guide our decision-making in relation to our practice. Given this, can LD practice and scholarship ever be completely neutral if we are 'to work *authentically* with respect for diverse learners'? Should the spaces we inhabit as LDers be reimagined as forums where we enable difficult conversations around students' experiences of race, racism, ableism, and discrimination, or is this better cloaked in terms such as inequalities, diversity, and inclusion?

What do we mean by critical pedagogy and practice?

A community-driven LD value is to 'embrace and respect diverse learners through critical pedagogy and practice' (ALDinHE, 2024). We have considered what 'diverse learners' means but what is meant by 'critical pedagogy and practice'?

Pedagogy relates to the study of how and why we teach in the way we do. For instance, this might mean thinking about which educational theories (i.e. constructivist or cognitive approaches) inform or guide our teaching practice and why. Practice relates to what we do or our actions. Critical pedagogy involves adopting a questioning or critical approach to our teaching philosophy and practice. This might be through regular self-reflection, discussion with the LD community, or engagement with the scholarly literature. However, critical pedagogy is also about critiquing assumptions about the nature of teaching and learning itself; that is, examining what and whose knowledge is constituted as valid in HE and why (Tikly, 2025). It involves thinking about the issue of power – who has it in HE and who does not – as well as examining how structural and systemic inequalities are unwittingly or wittingly reinforced in our everyday pedagogical practice (Tikly, 2025). For instance, for many students, the language, processes, and culture of HE may be 'alien', intimidating or 'exclusionary' (Abegglen et al., 2019, p. 3). By adopting a critical stance to your practice and pedagogy through questioning your own biases and assumptions, you can develop a more nuanced appreciation of such issues which should further inform your work with diverse students and staff.

How do I work with respect for diverse learners?

The following are some initial ideas for how, as a new LDer, you might work with students and staff in a way that promotes equality, recognises and respects diversity, and enables inclusivity.

Pragmatic ideas for working with respect for equality, diversity, and inclusivity

Promoting equality

- Be aware of and understand your institutions' policies as relevant to your work with students and staff and ensure that you are working within the scope of these. Pertinent polices might be a staff and student code of conduct, harassment and bullying policies, dignity policies, and any other polices related to equality, diversity, and inclusion.
- Complete any training on equality, diversity, and inclusion (EDI) that your university provides. Seek out external continuing professional development (CPD) opportunities for training in this area. Keep a log of what you have learned.
- Seek CPD in relation to working with neurodivergent students such as those with dyslexia, attention-deficit/hyperactivity disorder, or autistic students. Work together with your disability and dyslexia service to identify means to best support such students.
- Be self-reflective about your own professional and personal identity, experiences, and beliefs. Keep a reflective journal.
- Question your own assumptions, biases, and beliefs, and think about how your personal values and experiences influence your work with students and staff.

Recognising and respecting diversity

- The way we use language both reflects and constructs reality (Fairclough, 2001). Or, simply put, what we say matters. Be conscious of your use of language when working with students and staff, both written and verbal. Are you using any stereotypical, discriminatory, or demeaning terms unwittingly? Is your language inclusive in terms of gender, race, sexual orientation, and so forth? Are you using 'in-jokes' that may exclude certain people?

- Be respectful of and use staff and students' gender pronouns and titles.
- Check with students that you are correctly pronouncing their names.
- In tutorials, workshops, and embedded teaching, listen and allow space for students to make sense of their experience in their own words.
- Consider your choice of images and content for teaching and learning. Are visuals and images representative and inclusive of the student body? Are any stereotypical or demeaning?
- Get to know the individual and avoid homogenising students (and staff).
- If you feel secure to do so, challenge stereotypical and discriminatory behaviours as they arise. Seek support from a more experienced LDer or colleague with this if needed.

Enabling inclusivity

- Encourage a range of interactions in your teaching such that different – and marginalised – voices can be heard. For instance, in online teaching, give options for how students can engage, for instance, in the chat, on the microphone, or through an online interactive learning tool.
- Use a multimodal approach to teach content. Incorporate materials beyond text or written content. For instance, try to include a mix of verbal explanation, visual materials such as video or images, colour, and diagrams, as well as written content in every teaching session.
- Students may be unfamiliar with the language, practices, and customs of HE. You can aid with this by discussing and providing explanations of key aspects of learning (e.g. What is a tutorial? What happens in a seminar? What is a module tutor? and so forth) so that they can access the 'hidden curriculum'. This is the 'implicit knowledge, norms and behaviours that are required for success at university' (Hubbard and Gawthorpe, 2023. p. 10).
- When teaching online (and in-person), give clear, simple instructions for group activities and breakout rooms so that all students know what to do and how to do it.
- Read and research strategies, literature, and practical ideas or resources for inclusive teaching such as those available in the ALDinHE

LearnHigher (ALDinHE, 2025a) or neurodivergence resource banks (ALDinHE, 2025b).

Checking for accessibility

- Ensure that your teaching materials and resources are accessible to all students. Review slides and visual resources with an accessibility checker such as that built into Microsoft PowerPoint or Microsoft Word.
- Use an appropriate font size and type on slides, handouts, and worksheets. Sans-serif fonts such as Arial or Calibri may be easier to read on devices for some individuals.
- Upload captions for audiovisual resources.
- Enable automated transcripts for online teaching sessions.
- Ask students for feedback on your materials and teaching resources to improve them and to check for any issues with accessibility.
- Check whether students can easily access your tutorials or workshops. Are there students with mobility issues that might find in-person tutorials problematic? Could you adapt these to online or offer an alternative, accessible, physical location?
- For online teaching, ensure that issues with digital poverty are not limiting participation. For instance, could you offer both online and in-person sessions? Could workshops offered solely online be recorded for participants who cannot attend at the time? Could you turn off or ask students to keep cameras off if bandwidth might be an issue for certain students?

These ideas are a starting point. However, rather than being viewed as a checklist to work through, they might instead serve as a means whereby you begin to reflect on your existing practices in relation to EDI, and to consider areas in which you may need to develop your awareness. There is much ongoing work in HE and LD regarding EDI, and it will be for you to continually review your practice in relation to these issues. At the end of this chapter, there are suggested further readings and resources to aid with developing your understanding of this critical area.

How else might I work 'in partnership' with students?

You may also work alongside students to co-create, teach, and deliver skills or curriculum work. For instance, the University of Exeter has worked in partnership with students to employ recent graduates as 'Digital Learning Developers' and current students as 'Digital Learning Advisers' to assist in online module reform (Harris and Dyer, 2021). Such approaches very much engender the idea of student agency and empowerment that underlies LD practice. There are also many tangible benefits to students from involvement in participatory work such as developing confidence levels, teamwork, presentation, communication, and employability skills.

If you choose to use such an approach, you will need to consider practical questions of how to recruit students to the project and how to manage and support their involvement during it. It can be helpful when working in partnership with students in this way to seek support at the institutional level. You will need to bear in mind questions around accessibility, inclusivity, and representation – Do all students have equal access to the opportunity? Who are the students involved? Do they represent a diversity of voices? You will also need to consider whether students should be incentivised or paid for their involvement and how you will get funding for this, if needed. A key ethical concern will be about managing the power dynamics between you and the students participating. For instance, if students are co-designing materials or planning with you, this changes the nature of the relationship between you and the student. For this, you might consider having a written document that outlines students' (and your) roles and responsibilities and regular check-in meetings with the students to discuss any challenges or successes they are experiencing.

Another idea for working in partnership with students is to collaborate with existing student structures to promote and design LD services. For instance, you could ask for input about what might be helpful in terms of LD provision from your student union or student representatives, or work alongside students to facilitate peer-learning or peer support groups such as skills-focused writing or academic reading groups.

How do I work effectively with students when I am not a specialist in their subject?

It is important to highlight that, as an LDer, you do not need to be a specialist or expert in students' disciplinary subject content to support them effectively. Unless your remit is a hybrid LD role working as both subject lecturer and LDer (see Grayson and Syska, 2024, pp. 43–50) you should avoid straying into teaching disciplinary content itself even in the case of embedded provision (see Chapter 6). This is because LD practice focuses on developing students' academic literacies and skills such that they can 'make sense of and get the most out of HE' (ALDinHE, 2024). For instance, if you work with biological science undergraduates and are asked to teach a series of workshops on the topic of academic integrity, you will need to know the academic expectations around referencing and incorporating sources as well as common writing genres and how these are typically structured for their subject, as there will be different requirements depending on the discipline. You will not be expected to teach science. Rather, your work is complementary to and embedded within students' disciplinary work.

As an LDer, you are well placed to work meaningfully with students to aid them with managing the challenges of academia (Johnson et al., 2024). Whilst it is helpful to have knowledge of the content that students will cover during their degree programme or course, your focus should be on aiding them to develop the literacies, skills, and understanding of required academic conventions necessary to engage successfully in their studies. However, this does not mean that you should underplay your professionalism by saying things like, 'I'm just an LDer' or 'Sorry, I'm not an expert in your subject'. As a new LD practitioner, you are developing expertise and professional skills in helping students to navigate academia and succeed on their course, and it is important to articulate the value of what you provide (White and Webster, 2023). For instance, if a student asks you in a tutorial whether they have 'got the answer right' in their essay you might say,

> I'm not able to provide feedback on the accuracy of the subject content as that is outside the scope of my role. However, I'd be happy to work together to look at the structure of your essay and think about whether you are responding clearly to the question.

It is crucial to understand the remit of your role – what you can and cannot do – and to communicate the value of what you offer clearly to students and staff.

What types of staff might I work with?

> **Reflective task**
> - Are you part of a wider LD team? How many LDers work in your institution? Do they all have similar remits?
> - In what ways do you work with academics and subject lecturers, management, and professional services staff such as administrators or student advisors?
> - Do you work with other teaching staff such as academic librarians, wellbeing staff, or digital education colleagues?

You will work with a range of staff with distinct functions, remits, and their own professional norms and practices. Most obviously, you will work alongside other LDers and academics and subject teaching staff to decide what type of LD provision is necessary to support students. You will also work with professional services staff such as administrative staff, and with teaching-related staff who might identify as 'third space' practitioners (Whitchurch, 2008) such as digital education colleagues and academic librarians. It will be important to work sensitively and with respect for different colleagues' roles as they may have conflicting priorities. The next section looks at ways to do so.

How might I work effectively with colleagues?

Effective LD practice aims to 'work in partnership with students and staff to make sense and get the most out of HE' and does so partly by 'adapting, sharing and advocating effective learning development practice to promote student learning' (ALDinHE, 2024). One practical way to 'work in partnership' and engage with colleagues is to participate in wider staff and departmental meetings to promote LD provision. Such meetings can provide a space where you can update, report on, and 'advocate' for LD provision as well as seek opportunities about ways of working together. If you are not already involved in relevant wider staff meetings, request to attend with the Chair of the meeting or organise this with your line or a senior manager.

When attending meetings with staff members, prepare. Make sure you understand the purpose of the meeting and the nature of the other attendees' roles and their remit. Usually, larger meetings will start with an introductory round where each participant states their name and function so do listen carefully. If it is a larger, formal, meeting that you are attending, an agenda will usually be sent in advance which is a guide as to what will be covered in the meeting. You can use the agenda to prepare questions or comments that you wish to raise so it is important to request one if it is a formal meeting. However, allow such preparation to guide you rather than be a rigid plan or structure that you stick to as, similarly to our work with students, discussion with colleagues may move you on to interesting and unexpected avenues in terms of your work together. In formal meetings, minutes (detailed written notes) are usually taken as to what was covered in the meeting. As such, particularly if it is an online meeting that is being recorded, try to stay present and focus on what is being said rather than taking copious notes yourself as you can always review the meeting minutes or recording at a later stage. If there is anything that is unclear, this can be raised as a question either during the meeting itself or to the Chair or colleagues post-meeting. After the meeting, follow up on any 'action points' as needed.

One positive outcome of attending meetings where you have space to talk about LD provision is that more staff will be aware of your offering. This can be a starting point for developing professional, respectful, relationships such that non-LD colleagues are willing to 'work in partnership' with you to promote and support LD provision. For instance, subject lecturers or academic librarians may be willing to plan, design, and co-teach embedded sessions with you. Educational leads and academics might seek your input on assessment matters or pedagogical processes. Subject lecturers might actively promote your workshops in their taught sessions. When working with colleagues, try to ensure that you keep communications clear, consistent, and regular and that you follow through with what you have offered to provide. You could, for instance, organise planning meetings or check-in/update meetings when co-planning embedded sessions with subject lecturers.

> **Case study**
>
> You are attending a whole School staff meeting. The meeting includes discussion about support for undergraduates on a first-year module. A subject lecturer mentions that students are worried about their initial assessment and about how to avoid plagiarism. How might you respond? What might you offer in terms of support?

> **A response to the case study**
>
> You could explain the types of LD input that might be helpful such as one-to-one tutorials, an embedded session, or specific resources on completing assignments and avoiding plagiarism. You might also say that you are happy to meet with the lecturer one to one to discuss their concerns in more detail and to organise relevant support.

You might also have informal meetings, chats, or conversations with individual members of staff to discuss ways to collaborate. Such conversations can be fruitful in terms of getting to know individual staff on a friendly basis and can also be used to discuss LD provision or to negotiate time on the curriculum for embedded LD work. It also provides a means for you to learn about colleagues' work and their priorities and opens space for dialogue about ways you might be able to support. Remember to approach such conversations sensitively as other colleagues might have different priorities than you.

With further experience and growing confidence, you could also get involved with working with subject teaching staff in an advisory or consultative role, similarly to an Educational or Academic Developer. This might involve advising on effective pedagogical practice in relation to, for instance, assessments or classroom management, as well as being a sounding board for how to support students. This might also entail running bespoke staff development sessions. For these types of sessions, much of the guidance in this book about running workshops for students applies, though it will be for a staff-facing audience. For instance, ensure any staff development sessions have a clear structure, include multimodal activities that align to the learning objectives, tailor the sessions to the needs of the staff you are working with, and draw upon and be respectful of staffs' previous experiences such that you allow space and time for mutually respectful discussions. You might also choose to work alongside staff to develop the content for such developmental sessions, actively seeking their input through discussions, surveys, or focus groups.

Building trusting, professional relationships with staff will aid with promoting your service to students. Seeking out a critical friend or trusted colleague who can act as a sounding board can build your confidence. You may also find influential academics and senior management in your institution who are supportive and 'champion' your LD service which can be helpful for promoting LD provision at a more strategic level. Aim to work in a reciprocal way and think about what you can also offer colleagues in terms of help and guidance.

How might I articulate the need for Learning Development?

At times, you may need to advocate for LD provision with colleagues who may not understand your role or 'do not get' what it is you do. You can advocate verbally, in writing, through student word-of-mouth and feedback, and in actions that are taken to improve the profile of LD in your institution such as advertising and promotion of sessions. Having a visible presence and opportunity to present at student induction days/evenings or 'open days' for new or incoming applicants can also be a helpful way of reaching students and making staff more aware of your service. Your institution may also hold internal teaching and learning conferences which provide a good forum to present and disseminate any research, practices, or insights you would like to share with colleagues and to advocate for the value of LD. For instance, you could share research in progress or run a workshop for staff demonstrating something that has worked well in your teaching practice. We have discussed how meetings and informal conversations also offer a convenient way of sharing LD practice to a wide range of colleagues. However, advocating for LD can also be done on a micro scale; that is, through your day-to-day interactions with individual staff members and students. It can also be articulated through your professionalism, your reliability, and the way you approach your work.

As a new LDer, having to articulate the need for LD can seem very intimidating, particularly as you are still acclimatising to the role. This is where data and evaluation that you have undertaken in relation to your workshops, tutorials, and embedded provision can aid to demonstrate why your work is impactful. Another approach is to look to not only the scholarly literature both within the field of LD (such as in the *Journal of Learning Development in Higher Education*) but also educational literature more generally to provide evidence for the benefits of LD provision. If you are struggling with communicating the need for LD, ask for support from a senior LDer or your line manager. It can also be helpful to seek the views of the wider LD community outside your institution for suggestions as to practical steps that might be helpful in terms of advocating for LD. As White and Webster (2023, p. 5) assert, 'We need to build time into our work to demonstrate our relevance, value and purpose in ways that speak beyond ourselves'. However, they also go on to posit that '[c]hanging mindsets [about LD] cannot be achieved by individuals working in isolation: ALDinHE's role in bringing us together and curating a united identity and strong communal voice will be critical' (White and Webster, 2023, p. 5). As such, remember that it is not down to you as an individual and new LDer to shoulder all the responsibility of promoting the value of LD – it requires a community response.

How do I care for myself in my professional role?

An important aspect of LD work, which is often overlooked, is to ensure you care for and prioritise your professional wellbeing. Teaching and supporting students and working with staff in the way LDers do, whilst interesting and often fulfilling, can be physically and emotionally demanding. This means that it will be important to carefully manage your time, wellbeing, and workload so that you do not end up burnt out. Some pragmatic guidance here will hopefully be of help.

First, it is crucial to have clear boundaries. You must understand and work within the scope of your remit and communicate that clearly to students. Part of working as a professional is to recognise when student or staff requests falls outside your area of responsibility. This book provides guidance on dealing with challenges in tutorials, workshops, and embedded teaching[6] and emphasises the importance of carefully managing student expectations as to what you can and cannot provide. For instance, this might be where a student asks you for specific guidance related to their mental health needs or for advice on housing or financial issues. It might be a situation where a current student suggests you connect outside work on a social media account to discuss a personal issue they are facing. Whilst LD values promote 'embracing' and working with 'respect' for all learners (ALDinHE, 2024), this does not mean stepping outside the limits of your role. It is important to show empathy and consideration for the student's matter, but it is also essential to be clear when you need to put professional boundaries in place to keep the student and yourself safe.

What if you are faced with a situation where a student asks for advice outside your remit? First, recognise and validate the student's concern by repeating back your understanding of what they have said. Then explain that, with their consent, you will refer the student to the relevant professional service to aid with getting the correct support they need. Do not feel pressured into providing guidance to the student that is not within your expertise. Overstepping your remit in this way can lead to a situation where you provide wrong, misleading, and potentially damaging advice. If you are someone who struggles with setting boundaries assertively, you might take this as a developmental goal to work on in terms of your CPD or ongoing learning.[7] The end of this chapter signposts to further reading about the importance of professional boundaries.

It can help to take an objective stance from dealing with students' worries and concerns so that you do not internalise and take these concerns with you into your personal life. This can be difficult in practice. Some practical strategies to help with this include ensuring that you manage your time so that you stop working at a set time each day, particularly if you sometimes work from home. Have a clear cut-off point and try to maintain your interests, recreational activities, and connections outside of work. If you find that you are feeling overwhelmed or troubled with students' concerns, this is when talking to your network can be helpful. It may be that you speak with a critical friend, line manager, or trusted colleague to debrief. Having supportive colleagues can go a long way to aiding with you feeling well and safe to share concerns in the workplace. If there is not anyone in your place of work that you are comfortable talking to in this way, you could seek guidance and advice from friends and family or from experienced LDers through the ALDinHE networking and expertise directory, or via the LDHEN JiscMail. If things are becoming very difficult or impacting your emotional health, you might also seek professional support through your institutions' wellbeing, counselling, or chaplaincy service or through external support organisations such as, in the UK context, the Employee Assistance Programme or the Education Support Partnership.

In your early years as a new LDer, there can be a tendency to overstretch or overwork yourself by saying yes to too many demands. This is normal as you are establishing yourself in your role and trying to build a credible and reliable professional image and identity. However, whilst it is important to be helpful, flexible, and receptive to working with students and staff, it is also important to not overwhelm yourself in the process. Being an LDer entails giving a lot of yourself and so it is important to recognise when you do not have capacity for tasks and need to decline politely. Prioritise what is essential – keep a diary or planner – and do not be afraid to say no to what is not, for example, 'That sounds like an interesting initiative and thanks for inviting me to contribute to it. However, I need to prioritise . . ., so I will have to say no at this time'. If you struggle with saying no, consider seeking out assertiveness or confidence-building skills courses provided by your institution or externally to aid with this.

For additional support, you might also choose to join available staff or informal networks in your institution that relate to your personal or professional identity such as, for instance, a disability, LGBTQIA+, or

Black staff network. Such networks can provide a safe community to share professional experiences with other staff of a similar background. If you are an LDer that identifies as disabled or neurodivergent, it will be for you to decide whether to disclose this to your employer and colleagues. If you choose to declare your condition, you will, in the UK context, be protected under the Equality Act 2010 and, for instance, will be able to request reasonable adjustments from your employer to aid with performing your duties.

Concluding thoughts on working with students and colleagues

Our work as LDers hinges on the effectiveness of our relationships with students and staff. We saw in this chapter that the HE context is increasingly diverse and complex and that you will work with students from varied backgrounds and staff with varied remits. As an LDer, this requires you to practise in a way that is mindful of diversity and that demonstrates genuine respect for students' and colleagues' priorities and starting points. This chapter has provided initial ideas for how to 'work in partnership with students and staff to make the most out of HE' and how to 'embrace and respect diverse learners' (ALDinHE, 2024). However, it will be to you to continue to adopt a critical stance to your pedagogy and practice, through self-reflection, research, discussion with others, and ongoing learning, both to aid your developing professionalism and for the benefit of the students and staff you work alongside.

Summary
- This chapter outlined the types of students and staff that you might work with as an LDer, highlighting its diversity.
- It discussed the importance of working within your contexts' regulatory and statutory framework and ways this might impact your work as an LDer.
- It considered how to work effectively with diverse learners to promote equality, diversity, and inclusivity in practice.
- The chapter looked at how to work collaboratively with staff and considered ways to articulate the need for LD to those working outside the field.
- It finished by providing pragmatic tips on how to care for yourself in your professional role highlighting the importance of maintaining professional boundaries.

Notes

1 Educational or Academic Developers focus on developing the teaching and educational practices of academics (lecturers and teaching staff) as opposed to students (see Chapter 1, *Introduction*).
2 See Chapter 4, 'Teaching Tutorials' and Chapter 9 'Professional Development' for practical ideas on how to reflect on your practice.
3 See Chapter 3 for detailed discussion of these terms.
4 For exposition on this, see Chapter 3.
5 See Chapter 2, 'What does it mean to 'do' Learning Development?' for an overview of the historical foundations of LD work.
6 See Chapters 4, 5, and 6.
7 See Chapter 9, 'Professional Development'.

References

Abegglen, S., Burns, T. and Sinfield, S. (2019) 'It's learning development, Jim – but not as we know it: Academic literacies in third space', *Journal of Learning Development in Higher Education [Preprint]*, 15. https://doi.org/10.47408/jldhe.v0i15.500

ALDinHE (2024) *About ALDinHE*. Available at: https://aldinhe.ac.uk/about-aldinhe/ (Accessed: 9 April 2024).

ALDinHE (2025a) *LearnHigher*. Available at: https://aldinhe.ac.uk/learnhigher/ (Accessed: 20 January 2025).

ALDinHE (2025b) *Neurodivergence Resource Bank*. Available at: https://aldinhe.ac.uk/resource-bank/neurodivergence/ (Accessed: 20 January 2025).

Arthur, R. (2024) 'Closing the gap: Learning development and race', in A. Syska and C. Buckley (eds) *How to be a Learning Developer in Higher Education: Critical Perspectives, Community and Practice*. Abingdon: Routledge, 126–134.

Bhambra, G. K., Nisancioglu, K. and Dalia, G. (eds) (2018) *Decolonizing the University*. London: Pluto Press.

Bhopal, K. 2018. *White Privilege: The Myth of a Post-Racial Society*. Bristol: Policy Press.

Day, C. M. (2023) 'Decolonial homophobia: Is decolonisation incompatible with LGBT+ affirmation in Christian Ethics?' *Studies in Christian Ethics*, 37(1), 71–92. https://doi.org/10.1177/09539468231215304

Dhillon, S. (2020, 21 February) *Decolonisation Isn't as Simple as Plenty of People Suggest*. WonkHE. Available at: https://wonkhe.com/blogs/decolonisation-isnt-as-simple-as-plenty-of-people-suggest/ (Accessed: 19 July 2025).

Dirth, T. P. and Adams, G. A. (2019) 'Decolonial theory and disability studies: On the modernity/coloniality of ability', *Journal of Social and Political Psychology*, 7(1), 260–289. https://doi.org/10.5964/jspp.v7i1.762

Fairclough, N. (2001) *Language and Power*, 2nd edn. Harlow: Longman.

Faulkner, A. E. (2015) 'Reflections on the impostor phenomenon as a newly qualified academic librarian', *New Review of Academic Librarianship*, 21(3), 265–268. https://doi.org/10.1080/13614533.2015.1070185

Felix, M. and Friedberg, J. (2019, 9 April) *To Decolonise the Curriculum We have to Decolonise Ourselves*. WonkHE. Available at: https://wonkhe.com/blogs/to-decolonise-the-curriculum-we-have-to-decolonise-ourselves/ (Accessed: 13 June 2025).

Grayson, N. and Syska, A. (2024) 'Hybrid learning developers: Between the discipline and the third space', in A. Syska and C. Buckley (eds) *How to be a Learning Developer in Higher Education: Critical Perspectives, Community and Practice*. Abingdon: Routledge, 43–50.

Harris, L. and Dyer, S. (2021) 'Co-creating quality: Moving HE forwards in partnership with students', *Journal of Learning Development in Higher Education [Preprint]*, 22. https://doi.org/10.47408/jldhe.vi22.756

HESA (2023) 'Higher education student statistics: UK, 2021/22 – student numbers and characteristics', *Statistical Bulletin SB265*. Available at: https://www.hesa.ac.uk/news/19-01-2023/sb265-higher-education-student-statistics/numbers (Accessed: 20 January 2025).

Hubbard, K. and Gawthorpe, P. (2023) *Inclusive higher education framework*. Available at: https://www.qaa.ac.uk/docs/qaa/members/inclusive-higher-education-framework.pdf?sfvrsn=209aaa81_6 (Accessed: 9 January 2025).

Johnson, I., Bickle, E. and White, S. (2024, 6 December) *Learning Development should be at the Heart of Conversations about Academic Support*. WonkHE. Available at: https://wonkhe.com/blogs/learning-development-should-be-at-the-heart-of-conversations-about-academic-support/ (Accessed: 21 January 2025).

Parkman, A. (2016) 'The imposter phenomenon in higher education: Incidence and impact', *Journal of Higher Education Theory and Practice*, 16(1). Available at: https://articlegateway.com/index.php/JHETP/article/view/1936

Tikly, L. (2025, 16 January) *Supporting Learning in a Multicultural Environment: The Richness and Challenge of Diverse Universities [Lecture] Inspiring Learning New Year Lecture*. Heriot Watt University [Online].

UCL (2025) *Our Understanding of Equity, Diversity and Inclusion*. Available at: https://www.ucl.ac.uk/mathematical-physical-sciences/equity-edi/our-understanding-equity-diversity-and-inclusion (Accessed: 9 February 2025).

United Nations (n.d.) *Diversity, Equity and Inclusion*. Available at: https://unglobalcompact.org/take-action/action/dei (Accessed: 9 February 2025).

University of Hull (n.d.) *Decolonising the Curriculum*. Available at: https://www.hull.ac.uk/choose-hull/university-and-region/key-documents/docs/quality/programme-development-and-management/decolonising-the-curriculum.pdf (Accessed: 13 May 2025).

Whitchurch, C. (2008) 'Shifting identities and blurring boundaries: The emergence of third space professionals in UK higher education', *Higher Education Quarterly*, 62(4), 377–396. https://doi.org/10.1111/j.1468-2273.2008.00387.x

White, S. and Webster, H. (2023) 'Hey you! They're calling you Tinkerbell! What are you going to do about it?', *Journal of Learning Development in Higher Education [Preprint]*, 29. https://doi.org/10.47408/jldhe.vi29.1120

Ideas for further reading

Equality, Diversity, and Inclusion

AdvanceHE (2025) *Case Studies Related to Disability*. Available at: https://www.advance-he.ac.uk/guidance/equality-diversity-and-inclusion/creating-inclusive-environment/case-studies (Accessed: 9 February 2025).

Arthur, R. (2023) '"Conscious" learning development: Towards a pedagogy of race-consciousness', *Journal of Learning Development in Higher Education [Preprint]*, 26. https://doi.org/10.47408/jldhe.vi26.928

Behari-Leak, K., Mesehela, L., Marhaya, L., Tjabane, M. and Merckel, T (2017, 9 March) 'Decolonising the curriculum: It's in the detail, not just in the definition', *The Conversation*. Available at: https://theconversation.com/decolonising-the-curriculum-its-in-the-detail-not-just-in-the-definition-73772 (Accessed: 13 June 2025).

Bhopal, K. 2018. *White Privilege: The Myth of a Post-Racial Society*. Bristol: Policy Press.

Dhillon, S. (2020, 21 February) *Decolonisation Isn't as Simple as Plenty of People Suggest*. WonkHE. Available at: https://wonkhe.com/blogs/decolonisation-isnt-as-simple-as-plenty-of-people-suggest/ (Accessed: 19 July 2025).

Dhillon, S. (2021) 'An immanent critique of decolonization discourse', *Philosophical Inquiry in Education*, 28(3), 251–258. https://doi.org/10.7202/1085079ar

Hubbard, K. and Gawthorpe, P. (2023) *Inclusive Higher Education Framework*. Available at: https://www.qaa.ac.uk/docs/qaa/members/inclusive-higher-education-framework.pdf?sfvrsn=209aaa81_6 (Accessed: 9 January 2025).

Rossi, V. (2023) *Inclusive Learning Design in Higher Education: A Practical Guide to Creating Equitable Learning Experiences*. Abingdon: Routledge.

Stripe, K. and Ntonia, I. (2023) 'Twenty-two recommendations for inclusive teaching and their implementation challenges', *Journal of Learning Development in Higher Education [Preprint]*, 28. https://doi.org/10.47408/jldhe.vi28.1034

Working in partnership

Blackwell Young, J. and Parkes, S. (2025) 'Revisiting principles of partnership working in the third space', *Journal of Learning Development in Higher Education [Preprint]*, 33. https://doi.org/10.47408/jldhe.vi33.1245

Advocating for LD

Hood, S. and Powell, E. (2024) 'Raising the profile of learning development: Thinking forwards', *Journal of Learning Development in Higher Education [Preprint]*, 32. https://doi.org/10.47408/jldhe.vi32.1416

Professional boundaries

Booth, M. (2012) 'Boundaries and student self-disclosure in authentic, integrated learning activities and assignments', *New Directions for Teaching and Learning*, 131, 5–14. https://doi.org/10.1002/tl.20023

Booth, M. and Schwartz, H. L. (2012) 'We're all adults here: Clarifying and maintaining boundaries with adult learners', *New Directions for Teaching and Learning*, 131, 43–55. https://doi.org/10.1002/tl.20026

Hilsdon, J., Bellamy, K., Hagyard, A., Hartley, P., Ridley, P. and Sinfield, S. (2012) 'Editorial: Interventions and boundaries in learning development spaces', *Journal of Learning Development in Higher Education [Preprint]*, 4. https://doi.org/10.47408/jldhe.v0i4.157

Schwartz, H. L. (2012) 'Reflection and intention: Interpersonal boundaries in teaching and learning', *New Directions for Teaching and Learning*, 131, 99–102. https://doi.org/10.1002/tl.20030

Chapter 9

Professional development

This chapter provides an overview of
- The importance of continuing professional development (CPD) and ongoing learning.
- Options for professional development in Learning Development (LD).

You will be guided on
- Informal and formal professional development activities that you might choose to access.
- How to set ongoing learning and professional development goals.

What is professional development?

A core value underpinning the practice of LD is to demonstrate 'critical self-reflection, ongoing learning, and a commitment to professional development' (ALDinHE, 2024a). Professional development, also referred to as CPD, are the activities and learning that you undertake to enhance and develop your skills as a Learning Developer (LDer) working in higher education (HE). The word 'continuing' is important. It presupposes that professional development should be regular and sustained throughout your career. Ideally, then, CPD becomes an integral and deliberate part of your practice rather than an afterthought. In reality, this ideal might not always be possible; therefore, as well as highlighting formal opportunities for CPD, this chapter also explores informal means for professional development that do not put onerous demands on your time or other resources.

As a new or early career LDer, the automatic thought that might come to mind when hearing the term CPD may be, 'Do I have to do a course?' The next thought might then be, 'I just don't have the time!' However, as mentioned earlier, there are many ways to demonstrate 'commitment to professional development' (ALDinHE, 2024a) that do not take lots of time or require you to complete a formal class or certification. For instance, although you might not view them as CPD activities, what you do on a day-to-day basis within your role provides extensive scope for 'ongoing learning' and CPD. Today, for example, you may have written some reflections on your experience of a tutorial or workshop that you held; possibly you read a blog post or followed a professional social media account by another LDer; perhaps a student asked you for advice on an unfamiliar topic and you did some research into it; or maybe you sought guidance from a colleague after teaching a challenging skills workshop. Such informal activities provide ample scope for helping to develop your practice even though they might not have been undertaken by you with this objective in mind.

There are also many formal activities that demonstrate commitment to developing your professional practice. For instance, you might attend lectures, talks, and conferences related to LD and HE; you may undertake a formal CPD or training course; you might apply for accreditation in recognition of your practice via professional bodies such as the Association for Learning Development in Higher Education (ALDinHE) or Advance HE, a membership organisation, based in the UK but with an international reach, that promotes good practice and excellence in HE (ALDinHE, 2024a; AdvanceHE, 2024a). You might get involved in writing for publication or undertaking funded research. Such activities may entail a significant amount of time and financial investment on your or your institutions' part and, in these cases, it will be necessary to have discussions with your line manager or human resources team about potential funding or relevant leave to dedicate to such activities. However, many formal CPD activities can also be accessed for free or with little time commitment involved – more on this shortly.

The prospects for professional development in LD (and HE in general) are vast, and it really will be to you – bearing in mind your workload and in negotiation and discussion with your line manager or LD colleagues – to decide the extent and time to which you choose to partake and dedicate to such opportunities. In this chapter, we consider examples of informal and formal practices that provide scope for professional development. We will also look at keeping a log or record of the activities that you undertake, both as a personal record and as evidence and an aide memoire when applying for further professional opportunities within and external to your university.

Why is CPD important?

Buckley and Frith (2024, pp. 34–42) posit that there are five stages or shifts in professional identity that LDers may encounter during their careers. This is illustrated in Figure 9.1.

The circular networking model emphasises a growing sphere of influence in LD with the inner stages at a more influential level. These five stages are summarised in Table 9.1 as follows.

Professional development   177

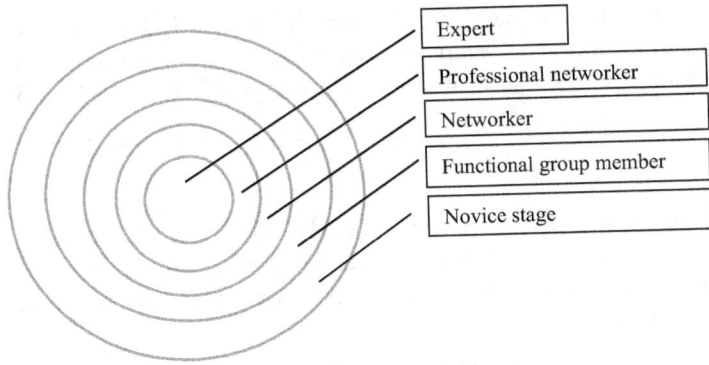

Figure 9.1 The five stages of networking capital accumulation.

Source: From Buckley and Frith, 2024, p. 36; used with permission from Taylor & Francis Informa UK Ltd. – Books.

Table 9.1 Adapted summary of Buckley and Frith's categorisation of networking capital.

Stage	Meaning	Likely Experience Level
Novice stage	At the novice stage, LDers are new to the role and likely 'occupy a marginal role' (p. 35) where they are beginning to negotiate their understandings of the role and working out how to 'be' in the field.	New/Early Career LDers.
Functional group member	At the functional group member stage, LDers are developing 'confidence' in their role and its function(s) (p. 35).	Early Career/Experienced LDers
Networker	At the networker stage, LDers are increasingly likely to engage with colleagues to 'exchange and [to] experiment with ideas' about doing LD (p. 35).	Experienced LDers
Professional networker	At the professional networker stage, LDers can make clear their stance in relation to LD and are engaged at a more strategic level in initiatives such as 'curriculum development' and developing novel methods to teaching and learning (p. 36).	Highly experienced LDers
Expert	At the expert stage, LDers have a developed and secure understanding of the aims and 'nuances' of LD practice and a 'clear professional position' (p. 36).	Expert LDers

Source: (2024, pp. 35–36) with permission from Taylor & Francis Informa UK Ltd. – Books.

These stages, they suggest, are dynamic. That is, as LDers, our professional 'selves' may transition between the stages in a non-linear way depending on the professional context and situation (Buckley and Frith, 2024, p. 36).

> **Task**
> - Where do you position yourself in relation to these five stages?
> - Do you see yourself as a novice, functional group member, networker, professional networker, expert, or somewhere in between or overlapping?

As a new or early career LDer, you will likely position yourself at the novice or functional group member stage. This is perfectly normal in the early years in your professional role. However, if we accept that these stages are dynamic, then we might begin to question how to transition from the novice stage, which is a very necessary stage of our practice, towards a more influential and experienced professional self. One answer would be to partake in and dedicate time to such activities that demonstrate commitment to CPD. This entails developing a deeper understanding of what LD is about, regular self-reflection, scholarly or practical research, and other such activities that allow you to enhance your skills and knowledge. As a new LDer, you might not perceive CPD as a priority at this stage of your practice when you are getting to grips with the day-to-day role. However, to transition beyond the novice or functional group member stage, you will need to take steps to partake in professional development that extends beyond your immediate role and institutional concerns. This chapter will provide ideas for how to do so.

Professional development is also important so that your practice does not become disconnected from external developments affecting the sector. At the time of writing, HE, and education more generally, is in a state of flux. Emerging technologies, such as generative artificial intelligence, are changing the educational landscape and disrupting the nature of 'how we teach' in universities (Bobula, 2024; Kay et al., 2024). The aftermath of the COVID-19 pandemic has altered the way in which teaching and learning in HE are delivered (García-Morales et al., 2021; Arday, 2022) and has impacted factors such as students' mental health and wellbeing (Jones and Bell, 2024). Alongside this are the regulatory and accountability pressures faced by higher education institutions (HEIs), including increasing pressures on finances, and the need to attract and retain home and international students (or from a more neoliberal slant 'customers') in an increasingly competitive market (Wareing, 2024). Within such a context, it becomes essential, not optional, to think about how your professional practices might evolve.

CPD and ongoing learning are also important if we think about it from the position of the students that we work alongside. Tikly (2025) argues that universities are 'microcosms of society' reflecting its diversity and concerns. If we are to 'embrace and respect diverse learners through critical pedagogy and practice' (ALDinHE, 2024a), then, as LDers, we need to take steps to ensure that we are aware of current research and good practice and use this to inform and improve our work. CPD looked at from this perspective is something that is mutually advantageous for the benefit of the diverse students and staff we work alongside and for our own sense of professional identity.

Where should I start with professional development?

There is no need to rush and seek out lots of professional development opportunities all at once. Part of the process of being a new or early career LDer is familiarising yourself with the practical aspects of the role, and this will be your immediate concern in your early years. Further, undertaking lots of formal CPD opportunities at once may leave you overstretched and overwhelmed. Remember that many of the informal and day-to-day activities that you undertake in the role already provide scope for learning and self-reflection and could be categorised as CPD. That is, you are already committing a significant amount of your professional working time to CPD without being aware of it. A starting point might be to document or reflect on the types of activities that you do over a period, as in Table 9.2.

Logs or records such as these do not have to be in tabular form. You could draw or generate images, doodles, and diagrams that show what you did and what you learned as a result or use tools such as Padlet to create a digital record. The point is that by documenting your activities over a period, say over the course of a week, you will start to identify and have evidence of areas where you are already investing a significant amount of time to professional learning and development. You can then start to think about how you might carve out additional or more deliberate time for similar such activities in your schedule.

Another starting point when deciding where to start with CPD could be to consider your developmental goals in relation to the ALDinHE community values. As a reminder, the values espouse:

1. Working in partnership with students and staff to make sense and get the most out of HE.
2. Embracing and respecting diverse learners through critical pedagogy and practice.
3. Adapting, sharing, and advocating effective LD practice to promote student learning.
4. Commitment to a scholarly approach and research related to LD.
5. Critical self-reflection, ongoing learning, and a commitment to professional development.

(ALDinHE, 2024a)

Table 9.2 Example of an informal CPD log.

Date	Activity	My Thoughts	Next Steps
5 March 2024	Read and liked a #Take 5 blog post about using storytelling when teaching.	Interesting ideas. I've never really thought about using storytelling as a method when teaching.	I'll try using a story (or scenario) in one of my upcoming workshops and see how it goes.
7 March 2024	Spoke to an LD colleague about an upcoming embedded skills session to ask for advice about managing student questions.	It was helpful to speak with my colleague. He suggested that I don't need to be the expert in the disciplinary content and that I can plan for questions and suggested resources. He also suggested that if I really don't know the answer to a student question, then I can say so, investigate it, and then get back to them.	I'm going to create a frequently asked question bank and some links to resources. I can have this to hand in my next embedded session.
8 March 2024	Did some research online to find practical activities for teaching critical thinking.	I found a PowerPoint resource on the ALDinHE LearnHigher site which looks helpful.	I'll use this resource in my upcoming workshop, though it may need some slight adaptations.

Each value could be taken as a basis for exploring your CPD priorities. For instance, you might consider doing a simple analysis, as in Table 9.3, to think about your developmental need, its link to the values, and the actions you might take as a result.

A further starting point might be to consider your CPD needs in relation to specific aspects of your practice. For instance, you might wish to work on conducting more effective workshops. This general goal could then be analysed by doing a strengths, weaknesses, opportunities, threats (SWOT) analysis to identify areas upon which your CPD could focus, as in Table 9.4.

The SWOT analysis could provide the basis to formulate a more specific goal. For instance, the generic goal, 'I want to ensure the online resources that I develop are inclusive and accessible to all learners' in Table 9.3 could be made more precise. For example,

> I want to ensure that I include at least two interactive activities during my next hour-long online workshop. I will use an interactive tool (Mentimeter as this is available via my institution) to incorporate interactivity and to encourage student participation and engagement. I will seek student feedback after the workshop as a basis for gathering data to evaluate the impact of incorporating such tools.

Professional development 181

Table 9.3 Identifying developmental needs in relation to the ALDinHE values.

Developmental Need	Which ALDinHE Values Does This Link to?	What Action Will I Take?	What Was the Outcome? What Did I Learn?
I want to ensure the online teaching resources that I develop are inclusive and accessible to all learners.	Working in partnership with students and staff to make sense and get the most out of HE Embracing and respecting diverse learners through critical pedagogy and practice Critical self-reflection, ongoing learning, and a commitment to professional development	I will do some research using the LearnHigher and Neurodivergence resource banks to see if I can find good models of resources that are accessible. I could then use or adapt these for my own online workshops.	I found an excellent checklist for creating accessible materials on the Neurodivergence Resource Bank. I have saved it and now use it regularly to check my own resources for inclusivity and access.

Table 9.4 Example SWOT analysis on delivering workshops.

Strengths
I have received positive student feedback (anecdotally) that they find my workshops interesting and helpful.

Opportunities
I can speak to a colleague about how to better advertise my workshops to manage student expectations about what to expect from the content.
I could also ask my colleague to observe one of my sessions, specifically focusing on ideas for improving the interactivity and structure.
I could continue to gather data more formally, in the form of a questionnaire to see if the concerns about interactivity are widely shared.

Weaknesses
Several students have fed back (again verbally) that they find the workshops could be more interactive and more clearly structured.

Threats
Sometimes it is hard to receive negative feedback, so I worry about what the survey data will say. However, I could use this feedback to improve my workshops.

Developing SMART goals

You may be familiar with the idea of specific, measurable, achievable, realistic, and timebound (SMART) goals. The concept of SMART goals has its roots in the field of business and management (Lawlor and Hornyak, 2012), but it is now a commonly used approach for creating clear and manageable goals. Table 9.5 provides an example of a SMART goal for developing accessible skills workshop materials.

Once you have SMART goals, you might then plan to set aside formal time to allocate to achieving these. For instance, if your goal is to improve the structure of your workshops, you could dedicate a weekly reading hour to read an article or opinion piece about conducting workshops from the *Journal of Learning Development in Higher Education* (*JLDHE*) or similar publication. You might then schedule in your diary a regular debrief meeting with an LD colleague after you teach an optional skills workshop. Scheduling time for such activities can be a helpful way to build in sufficient time to dedicate to your ongoing learning and professional development.

What types of informal CPD might I pursue?

There are many forms of informal CPD that you can pursue. In this section, I outline several of these, but the examples provided are not exhaustive. As such, be creative and open-minded in your approach to how you might develop your professional practice informally.

Keeping a journal or diary

Keeping a journal or diary is a simple and effective way to develop your professional practice. Journals can be used to document your experiences and to

Table 9.5 Example SMART goal.

SMART Goal: Developing Accessible Workshop Materials	
Specific	Ensure all workshop slides and handouts for my upcoming optional skills workshops for term one are accessible for students with visual impairments.
Measurable	All workshop slides and handouts should be reviewed and cleared with the 'check accessibility' tool on PowerPoint or Word.
Achievable	Set aside an hour in my weekly timetable to review and check the accessibility of slides and handouts. This seems manageable.
Relevant/Realistic	Reviewing the accessibility of my materials will help to ensure that all students can access and engage with them.
Timebound	Achieve this goal by the beginning of September in preparation for the upcoming term.

evidence critical self-reflection. A benefit of a diary or log is that no one else needs to see it and they can be in any form that best suits you; indeed, you might find yourself keeping multiple journals or reflective documents. For instance, you could keep a paper or physical journal or, if you are digitally inclined, you could experiment with different tools, from a simple Word or Excel document to online specialist diaries, apps, trackers, and journals. The journal or diary might include sections where you write comments, thoughts, doodles, or draw images related to positive and challenging aspects of your day-to-day practice. The journal entries can be completed as frequently as you like. Taking the journal idea one step further, there are also opportunities to contribute to (or read) an online collective diary written by members of the ALDinHE community on or around the fifteenth of every month. The following is an example entry:

> A reflective entry in the online collective ALDinHE diary, 15 September 2024 (ALDinHE, 2024g). Extract used with permission from Dr Zara Hooley Senior Lecturer (Centre for Learning and Study Support) De Montfort University.
>
> I started the day with a meeting about what data we need to pull together for a feedback report on student engagement with our service for our colleagues in Faculty. I am then attending a meeting with a colleague to plan for the Welcome Weekend induction day which welcomes freshers to the University. 12–1 pm I will be working in a student-facing assignment drop-in session. Tutoring students on academic writing. Quick lunch. 1–2 pm I am running a staff-facing session on AI-resilient assignment design. 3–6 pm I am taking leave to work on some of my own academic writing. This is a typical day for me, a mixture of meetings and student-facing work, and a certain amount of admin.

Networking

Networking with colleagues and staff within and external to your institution can provide an excellent means for professional growth. The term networking can strike fear into the hearts of even the most gregarious and conjures up images of standing in a busy room, holding finger food, whilst making small talk with someone who also looks like they want to escape. However, here I refer to this term to mean simply opening yourself up to having conversations and dialogue (through verbal or written means) about your practice with other professionals. For instance, your institution will have staff networks related to specific interests that you could join. You might also network with

LD colleagues to ask questions of their practice and connect with them in informal situations.

If you prefer to network online, there are many such opportunities. For example, you might look to use social media platforms like LinkedIn or BlueSky, or professional mailing lists such as those available through JiscMail.[1] Such forums provide you with the scope to converse with education and LD colleagues working worldwide. The open networking and expertise directory on ALDinHE also offers the opportunity to connect with LDers with specialism in an area of concern that you have questions about (ALDinHE, 2024b). Later in the chapter, we will look at formal opportunities for networking, including joining an ALDinHE community of practice (CoP), attending the International Consortium of Academic Language and Learning Developers (ICALLD) events, and participating in conferences and symposia.

Webinars and talks

Webinars (online seminars) and talks related to LD and HE in general provide another source of informal CPD. At the time of writing, ALDinHE provides a series of webinars titled LD@3 and occasionally LD@12. These are regular monthly talks at 3 pm or 12 pm Greenwich Mean Time covering topics related to LD. For instance, recent presentations have covered the art of storytelling for LDers (Jewitt, 2024) and the impact of one-to-one appointments on student attainment (Hawke, 2023). LD@3 (or LD@12) sessions tend to be interactive with opportunity to ask questions and partake in tasks.

You might also wish to attend talks, webinars, and seminars related to HE more generally. Working in HE provides many opportunities to attend research-based talks and lectures both online and in-person. Such talks are advertised regularly on university websites, university social media accounts, and JiscMail lists. During or after attending a talk or online seminar, aim to record the key learning points in a log or journal to document your learning.

Observations and co-teaching

Observations can be arranged informally or formally. For instance, you might organise to sit in informally on a workshop run by an experienced LD colleague to get some ideas for your teaching practice. If you do so, it is good to have a specific focus with which you go into the observation. For instance, you might wish to focus on how the LDer uses questioning in a workshop, how they manage class interactions, or how they organise different activities to promote student engagement. It can be helpful to take notes during the observation as well as to write questions that you can follow up with afterwards. If your colleague is willing, meet with them post-observation to discuss your thoughts and get your questions answered. Your next step after an observation could then be to carry out further research into the aspect of the practice you observed or to write a reflective statement about what you saw and learned. You could also seek out an LD colleague to observe you in the classroom either formally or informally, asking them to focus on a specific aspect of your teaching.

Co-teaching involves teaching alongside another LDer or relevant academic or professional services staff. Co-teaching offers scope for developing your practice in many areas including planning and development of materials, classroom management, and working collaboratively. As a new LDer, co-teaching can also provide a level of reassurance as you can work together to respond to student questions and manage the classroom environment whether online or in-person. As with observations, after a co-teaching session think about what went well and what could be improved. You could do so by having an informal discussion with your colleague and by thinking through or writing down your own reflections.

Reading

Reading academic articles, papers, or blogs on topics that pertain to LD can provide many opportunities to develop and advance your understanding of the field. Journals that cover topics specific to HE and LD include the *JLDHE*, *Teaching in Higher Education*, *Higher Education: the International Journal of Higher Education Research*, the *International Journal for Academic Development* (this focuses on educational development and support for academics and teaching staff), and the *Educational Research Review*. The *JLDHE*, for instance, contains a vast bank of articles (and a video library) stemming back to 2009 in the form of opinion pieces, papers, and other forms of written submission. It also contains special issues or editions which cover areas of specific interest such as LD as a third space. You might also read more generally about HE on sites such as WonkHE and the Times Higher Education Supplement (THES).

Whilst reading is often viewed as a solitary activity, there is also opportunity to join reading or discussion groups such as the online *JLDHE* reading club. These reading clubs are attended by LD practitioners and those in associated roles and often host the writer of the specific article to be discussed. Talking with other practitioners about what you have read can provide the space to clarify challenging concepts, debate ideas, and gain a shared understanding, as you work to construct meanings with others.

Podcasts

Podcasts provide an entertaining and engaging way to participate in professional development. There are many podcasts available, and it will be for you to research and find those that you enjoy and feel inspired to listen to. As a starting point, it might be that you listen to the LD project podcast, which was created by ALDinHE Steering Group members, Carina Buckley and Alicja Syska, in 2022. The podcast has hosted many guest speakers, including episode number one with John Hilsdon, the co-editor of the 2011 book *Learning Development in Higher Education*, and episode three with Tom Burns and Sandra Sinfield, highly influential members of the LD community.

There are also a wide variety of podcasts discussing HE more generally that you might be interested in exploring. For instance, WonkHE hosts weekly topical panel conversations on 'The WonkHE Show' related to UK and international HE education policy (WonkHE, 2025). The Teaching in Higher Ed podcast, hosted weekly by Bonni Stachowiak and with an international reach, also covers a vast range of topics including diversity and inclusive teaching practices, creative approaches to teaching, and educational technology (Stachowiak, n.d.). After listening to podcasts, aim to note down some thoughts in a reflective log, journal entry, or online tool such as Padlet as a record of your observations and what you learned.

Social media

There are many ways to use social media to aid with professional development. Social networking sites, such as the increasingly popular Bluesky or LinkedIn, act as a forum to connect with and learn from professionals in different institutions both nationally and internationally. You could, for instance, follow the social media accounts for ALDinHE, ICALLD, or similar bodies as well as your own and other HE institutions that interest you. You might follow these more passively, for instance, reading articles and posts but not engaging in comments. This is fine. Or you might be an active user, posing questions or comments to the community, and following and liking LD- and HE-related posts. It is to you to choose if and to what extent you engage with social media.

Other social networking tools such as Instagram, YouTube, TikTok, and WhatsApp, if available in your context, provide scope for learning about the work of others in the field, or connecting in a more 'personal' manner. Do take the necessary precautions when using social media such as being aware of what personal data you are sharing and with whom. If you are finding social media is doing more harm than good, perhaps in terms of overwhelm of information, or people engaging in hostile debate or making disparaging comments, then it might be worthwhile putting it on pause and thinking about how to harness other forms of activities for professional development.

Writing blogs or creating vlogs

Writing for an academic blog is a low-stakes starting point for testing out your ideas, gaining feedback from the wider community, and developing your writing skills. For instance, the ALDinHE #Take5 blog, which is international in reach, offers the opportunity to blog and contribute your thoughts, research, and comments on all things LD. If you enjoy creating and using digital media, you might also choose to create video logs (vlogs) about your practice which would be a novel approach in the LD field.

What formal methods of CPD might I pursue?

Professional development within your institution

Your institution should offer structured opportunities for professional development. This might include an annual review (often called a professional development review (PDR)) where you reflect on your achievements and set developmental goals, in the context of your professional role. For this, you should be provided with the opportunity to meet with your line manager or a member of HR to review your PDR. Your PDR goals should be specific, timely, and actionable. Other institutional CPD opportunities to consider, if available, are joining staff discussion or writing forums, internal conferences organised through your institution, joining staff networks, and seeking out supported external opportunities for professional development.

ALDinHE CPD programme

ALDinHE is currently developing a structured CPD pilot programme for new LDers. The programme aims to fill a gap after it was recognised that there was a scarcity of structured professional development activities available for new LDers. Subsequently, the CPD Working Group was created and a pilot programme developed with input from the LD community. The programme is intended to cover the practical functions of the role as well as its theoretical underpinnings and will incorporate training, seminars, and practical interaction. As a new LDer, this would be the recommended starting point for developing your professional practice. It will be of interest to see the programmes' uptake and how it evolves over time, as well as the impact on new LDers who participate.

ALDinHE Working Groups and Steering Group

ALDinHE offers many opportunities to be actively involved in the organisation. In the next few sections, I highlight some of these opportunities, though this is not an exhaustive summary, so it is recommended to look at the ALDinHE website for further information.

One option is to join an ALDinHE Working Group. These are groups of LD practitioners that meet regularly to 'work on' or discuss, develop, and agree strategies in relation to distinct areas of LD practice or issues. Current Working Groups include the Events Group, the Professional Recognition

Group, the CPD Working Group, the Equality, Diversity and Inclusion Working Group, the *JLDHE* Editorial Board Working Group, and the Peer Mentoring Working Group. Joining a Working Group requires a time commitment and may involve significant responsibilities and additional 'work' so it is important to be conscious of not taking too much on and being realistic about whether you have adequate capacity to be involved. However, it is an excellent opportunity to participate in ALDinHE and to contribute your views about key aspects of LD.

You could also consider getting involved as a member of the ALDinHE Steering Group. With input from the wider LD community, this group leads or 'steers' the direction of the association. A 'call' for new members is made via the Learning Development in Higher Education Network (LDHEN) in April each year (ALDinHE, 2024f). Becoming a member of the Steering Group involves a process of self-nomination which needs to be backed by an existing member of the group (ALDinHE, 2024f). Once you are elected and this is ratified, you would then usually take up the post for a minimum duration of two years, initially as a member without 'portfolio' (additional leadership responsibilities) before taking on a specific role (ALDinHE, 2024f). Membership of the Steering Group involves attending monthly online meetings and twice yearly in-person 'away days' for collaboration and planning. Being involved in the Steering Group can be beneficial in terms of giving you a sense of the strategic direction of ALDinHE, can be helpful when applying for accreditation and career opportunities, and is evidence of making impact outside your immediate institution.

ALDinHE formal mentorship

Mentorship is a useful way of engaging with a more experienced LD practitioner in a structured way that is tailored to your specific needs. Mentorship can arise organically and in more informal ways, for instance, if you regularly seek the advice of a trusted colleague. However, there are also formal opportunities to participate in mentoring programmes. As a mentee, you will meet with your mentor regularly over a specified period and work towards exploring issues, areas of concern, or specific goals that you may have. You might seek out opportunities for mentorship through your institution, and this might be an in-built element of your probationary period if you are required to complete one.

If formal mentorship is not available via your institution and you are a member of ALDinHE, you could apply to participate as a mentee through the ALDinHE mentoring scheme. As well as a general mentoring scheme, they provide mentoring for specific involvement such as if you wish to submit an article to the *JLDHE* or want to develop a resource for LearnHigher via ALDinHE, or for the professional recognition process. Being a mentee offers structured opportunity to reflect on your practice and to think about how the ALDinHE values are evident in your work.

The mentoring relationship is a complex one and usually involves working with a mentor that is more experienced than you in the area that you wish to develop. It is also possible to flip the relationship around such that a less experienced staff member mentors a more experienced person, a process referred to as reverse mentoring (Browne, 2021). The rationale for this approach is that it promotes communication and sharing of knowledge across experience levels as well as potentially impacting positively on wider factors such as inclusion and diversity (Browne, 2021). Whomever you decide to work with in a mentoring relationship, it is important that you feel comfortable and safe to have authentic conversations with your mentor about your professional role. It is also necessary to consider carefully what you wish to gain from being a mentee and to be clear about sharing this with your mentor so that you can manage expectations about what is and is not possible over the mentoring relationship. However, if the mentoring relationship is not working and you are not comfortable, it is okay to say so and to seek an alternative mentor. The benefits of being involved as a mentee are vast, and it is an excellent way of developing and building your confidence. With experience, you might also choose to become a mentor yourself at a later stage in your career.

Conferences and regional symposia

Attending conferences is another way to meet colleagues working in different institutions and to develop your understanding of good LD practice. HE conferences are sessions held by professional associations involving keynote (main) or mini-speeches, talks, poster presentations, and workshops on topics related to education. They can be held online or in-person and usually take place over several days. In addition to providing opportunities for learning and networking, they can also be hugely enjoyable. However, conferences can be expensive to attend. As well as the cost for the conference itself, you may need to factor in the cost of travel and accommodation. Typically, institutions have a budget to cover the expense of work-related conferences; however, if your institution does not provide this, some conferences, such as the annual ALDinHE conference (see later), offer several funded places depending on eligibility.

There are many professional HE conferences. As a starting point, ALDinHE holds an annual conference (colloquially known as ALDcon) focused specifically on LD practice, typically in June. This takes place both online and in-person and is a three-day conference involving talks, discussion, keynote speeches, and workshops. However, you are not limited to attending only the ALDinHE conference. You may find other associated bodies like the Staff Educational Development Association (SEDA) or the British Association of Lecturers in English for Academic Purposes (BALEAP) that offer conference topics that resonate with your practice or in which you are simply interested. If attending conferences appeals to you, you can sign up to a professional email list on JiscMail as this is where institutions and colleagues regularly announce conferences, current research, and professional development opportunities. As you develop confidence in your practice, you might choose to present a session at a conference. For this, you should keep a lookout for calls for proposals or papers related to specific conference themes such as on the LDHEN and SEDA JiscMail list.

Regional symposia are local-level gatherings related to a specific educational theme. These are like conferences but tend to be on a smaller scale or focus on one specific theme or topic. Regional symposia are often advertised via professional mailing lists such as the LDHEN JiscMail or in ALDinHE communications such as the Love LD Magazine (ALDinHE, 2024e). ICALLD also runs an annual online international symposium with delegates and speakers from ALDinHE, the South African Association for Academic Literacy Practitioners (SAAALP), the Learning Specialists Association of Canada (LSAC), the Scottish Higher Education Learner Developers' network (ScotHELD), and the Association of Tertiary Learning Advisors Aotearoa New Zealand. Symposia can be an excellent source of networking and idea-sharing with colleagues with similar interests. Associations such as ScotHELD and SAAALP offer similar opportunities for involvement as ALDinHE.

Communities of practice

You might also choose to join a CoP. These are informal communities of practitioners that meet regularly to share a concern, or an interest related to their roles such that they learn how to improve it (Wenger-Trayner and Wenger-Trayner, 2015). The three elements of a CoP are the domain (the area of shared interest or expertise), the community itself, and the practice (these are the ideas and resources suggested by the community to solve a problem or work on an issue (Wenger-Trayner and Wenger-Trayner, 2015)). For instance, ALDinHE hosts various CoPs including ones related to artificial intelligence, reflection, neurodiversity, and research. You might also seek out CoPs within your own institution or, with more experience, you could create your own. The benefits of joining a CoP are that it enables you to share good practice, to work out solutions to common professional problems, and to network with colleagues from different institutions with shared interests.

Academic writing

Writing enables you to give voice to your thoughts (Zinsser, 1976) on paper or a digital medium. It is a powerful method of exploring issues, concerns, and practice related to LD. Writing can also aid with clarifying and refining your own understanding of core aspects of the LD role as you work through the process of getting your message across with clarity. Writing typically involves research and can be hugely fulfilling when others read and benefit from your words. In addition, writing as a practice aligns with the LD value of, 'adapting, sharing and advocating effective learning development practice to promote student learning' (ALDinHE, 2024a). Many people find writing challenging or difficult and so tend to veer away from doing so. However, writing is an excellent way of getting your views heard, particularly if you are of a more introverted nature, and it can provide opportunity for reciprocal feedback from the LD community.

I have already highlighted opportunities for informal writing, but there are also more formal opportunities if you are a keen writer or have something that you want to communicate about the practice of LD or HE more generally. As mentioned, a starting point would be to test out your ideas via a #Take 5 blog post. However, you could also try to publish more formal writing such as a paper or article outlining research you are undertaking, or an opinion piece, by submitting to a journal such as the *JLDHE*. The submission process for the *JLDHE* is a formal but supportive one and involves peer review of your piece which is undertaken by members of the LD community. If this sounds daunting, the *JLDHE* editorial team offers guidance and mentorship during the submission process.

If you enjoy writing (and do not mind the time commitment), you might also choose to publish an academic book or book chapter based on your experiences of LD or of HE more generally. You could pursue 'traditional' methods of publishing through an academic publisher or undertake the self-publication route. LD benefits from all voices, so if you are keen on writing and publishing your work but lack confidence, seek out advice from experienced members and writers in the LD community via the ALDinHE Publishing in LD and Collaborative Writing expertise directory (ALDinHE, 2024b).

Research activity

If you have an interest in research related to LD, you might seek to get involved in small-scale independent research or to collaborate with other LDers or HE researchers (within and external to your institution) on a shared research project. LD research can be related to any aspect of your role or professional interest. Conducting formal research would follow the same protocol as research in academia more generally, that is, deciding a research question or focus, putting together a proposal for the research, designing and testing your research, conducting a review of the literature, seeking ethical approval, deciding the research methodology and methods, seeking funding for the project, conducting the research and writing up the results, and disseminating your findings. Unless you are already an experienced researcher, whether through gaining a formal research degree or via previous work experience, this might seem quite daunting. In this case, you might seek support or mentoring for your research project from the Research and Scholarship Development Working Group through ALDinHE. There are also avenues to apply for funding for specific projects through ALDinHE which currently offers research funding of £1,200 per project or up to £1,500 if the project involves student partnership (ALDinHE, 2024h).

There are many approaches you might take to LD research. As examples, you might choose to undertake an action research project where you explore and reflect on the impact of an intervention or change in relation to a specific aspect of your practice. Depending on your research aims and objectives, you might wish to undertake empirical research using a qualitative, quantitative, or mixed methods approach or you might prefer to carry out a more theoretical or desk-based project where you review and analyse the LD and educational literature that is pertinent to your area of interest. The research possibilities are endless and so, even as a new LD, if this is an area that interests you and you have no research background, do seek out support through ALDinHE or similar channels.

How can I gain recognition for my practice?

ALDinHE accreditation and awards

You can join the ALDinHE as an institutional member (i.e. paid for by your university) or as an individual member (paid for by you). Many of the ALDinHE resources and benefits can be accessed without having a paid-for subscription but to apply for professional recognition, you will need to be a member. ALDinHE offers professional accreditation at two levels: Fellow of ALDinHE (F-ALDinHE) and Senior Fellow of ALDinHE (SF-ALDinHE).[2] The scheme recognises LDers' practice and commitment to LD values (ALDinHE, 2024c). F-ALDinHE status is for LDers who can evidence involvement with ALDinHE values at the institutional level, whilst SF-ALDinHE status is relevant to those who can show participation with the ALDinHE values beyond their immediate institution (ALDinHE, 2024c).

As a new LDer, you will likely initially apply for F-ALDinHE and then SF-ALDinHE status at a later, more experienced, stage of your professional practice as the requirements for engagement are more extensive for SF-ALDinHE. An application for F-ALDinHE (and SF-ALDinHE) entails evidencing, through critical reflection, how your professional practice aligns with the five ALDinHE professional values. The process involves completing an application form, plus a supporting reflective statement illustrating how your role evidences the values, and a supporting reference from someone who is aware of your practice (ALDinHE, 2024c). ALDinHE offers support through the application process in the form of formal mentorship and structured writing retreats where you can gain feedback and guidance. Whilst there is a necessary time commitment in terms of preparing, evidencing, and writing your submission, the process itself is straightforward. On successful submission, you receive certification, a digital badge, mention on the ALDinHE website, and are permitted to use the nominal letters F-ALDinHE or SF-ALDinHE (ALDinHE, 2024c).

ALDinHE also offers regular awards including the annual LD Team award for exceptional LD practice by a team and the recently established Tom Burns Memorial Award. Tom Burns was an Associate Teaching Professor and pioneer in the field of LD (ALDinHE, 2024d), and this annual award recognises LD practice that 'encourages the practices of eliciting, representing, promoting, and/or publishing work focusing on students' interpretations of aspects of their learning experiences' (ALDinHE, 2024d).

Advance HE accreditation

Another way to gain professional accreditation is through Fellowship of Advance HE. Advance HE is a membership body, 'promoting excellence in HE teaching and learning' (AdvanceHE, 2024a). Fellowship standards progress from Associate Fellowship, Fellowship, Senior Fellowship to Principal Fellowship. As an early career LDer, it is likely that you would begin by applying for Associate or Fellowship which is commensurate with ALDinHE F-ALDinHE status. The process for applying for Associate or Fellowship status with Advance HE involves completing an application form, including a detailed reflective statement evidencing how your practice aligns with Advance HE's Professional Standards Framework, plus supporting references (AdvanceHE, 2024b). There is a cost to the application, and this can be funded by your institution or paid for by you independently. A successful application for Fellowship can be used to support an F-ALDinHE or SF-ALDinHE application and vice versa. Your institution may provide training and guidance on completing an application for Fellowship status, and Advance HE also provides training opportunities as the process can be quite demanding. Fellowship demonstrates your professionalism which can be helpful when seeking future professional opportunities. It is also a useful exercise in allowing you to reflect deeply on your practice. As you progress through your career and develop considerable experience, there are also opportunities to apply for the AdvanceHE National Teaching Fellowship scheme which recognises outstanding contributions to the sector (AdvanceHE, 2024c).

Formal study

You could also choose to undertake formal study in the form of a Postgraduate Certificate in Academic Practice (PGCAP) which is available in the UK and internationally or a Postgraduate Certificate in Higher Education (PGCHE). Both the PGCAP and PGCHE are designed to focus on developing the teaching skills and practice you will need for working in HE. They are not geared specifically towards LD and require a time commitment of between 12 and 24 months. However, they offer a structured approach to learning about effective pedagogical practice in HE and could be a worthwhile investment of your time. Successful completion of the PGCAP or

PGCHE can also often lead to an award of Fellowship of Advance HE which circumvents the need to make a separate application for Fellowship. You could also choose to pursue a master's or doctoral-level degree if you do not have one or wish to gain additional qualifications. For instance, a master's degree in Higher Education Teaching and Learning is offered at many universities. Your institution may offer partial or full funding for you to undertake such studies so do seek out guidance from your line manager if you are interested in pursuing this.

Reflecting on next steps

> ### Task
>
> We are nearing the end of this book. As a final task in this chapter, reflect on your next steps in relation to your professional development.
>
> - What is your current priority for CPD?
> - Set yourself a SMART goal in relation to this priority.

Professional development is an essential element of your practice as an LDer. Ideally, it should be ongoing and regular, helping you to develop and grow in your professional role as well as impacting upon the work you do with students and staff. This chapter has outlined some examples of professional development activities that you might choose to undertake, but it is not an exhaustive list. There are many other opportunities, and it will be for you to decide how much time you wish to commit to professional development. Hopefully, this chapter has shown the potential benefits to your confidence and growth as an LDer from being deliberate about your approach to CPD and ongoing learning.

> ### Summary
>
> - In this chapter, we looked at what CPD is and why it is important for developing your professional practice and understanding of LD.
> - We considered several types of CPD that might be undertaken including both formal and informal CPD opportunities.
> - You had the opportunity to reflect on your next steps in terms of developing your CPD goals.

Notes

1 JiscMail lists can be accessed at https://www.jiscmail.ac.uk/. These are professional email discussion lists for practitioners in the education and research community. It is a UK-based site but has many subscribers worldwide. The lists cover a range of professional interests including the Learning Development in Higher Education Network (LDHEN). You can sign up to as many JiscMail email lists as you wish.
2 F-ALDinHE was previously referred to as Certified Practitioner (CeP), and SF-ALDinHE was previously referred to as Certified Leading Practitioner (CeLP).

References

AdvanceHE (2024a) *Home*. Available at: https://www.advance-he.ac.uk/ (Accessed: 23 December 2024).

AdvanceHE (2024b) *Fellowship*. Available at: https://www.advance-he.ac.uk/fellowship (Accessed: 23 December 2024).

AdvanceHE (2024c) *National Teaching Fellowship*. Available at: https://www.advance-he.ac.uk/awards/teaching-excellence-awards/national-teaching-fellowship (Accessed: 23 December 2024).

ALDinHE (2024a) *About ALDinHE*. Available at: https://aldinhe.ac.uk/about-aldinhe/ (Accessed: 23 December 2024).

ALDinHE (2024b) *Networking & Expertise Directory*. Available at: https://aldinhe.ac.uk/support/expertise-directory/ (Accessed: 23 December 2024).

ALDinHE (2024c) *Professional Recognition Scheme*. Available at: https://aldinhe.ac.uk/accreditation/recognition/professional-recognition-scheme/ (Accessed: 23 December 2024).

ALDinHE (2024d) *ALDinHE Awards*. Available at: https://aldinhe.ac.uk/accreditation/aldinhe-awards/ (Accessed: 23 June 2025).

ALDinHE (2024e) *Love LD Magazine*. Available at: https://aldinhe.ac.uk/news/loveld-magazine/ (Accessed: 23 June 2025).

ALDinHE (2024f) *Steering Group*. Available at: https://aldinhe.ac.uk/about-aldinhe/meet-the-working-group-members/steering-group/ (Accessed: 23 June 2025).

ALDinHE (2024g) *Collective Diary 15 September 2024*. Available at: https://aldinhe.ac.uk/collective-diary-15-september-2024/ (Accessed: 23 July 2025).

ALDinHE (2024h) *Research Funding*. Available at: https://aldinhe.ac.uk/research/scholarship-funding/ (Accessed: 23 July 2025).

Arday, J. (2022) 'Covid-19 and higher education: The times they are a' changin'', *Educational Review*, 74(3), 365–377. https://doi.org/10.1080/00131911.2022.2076462

Bobula, M. (2024) 'Generative artificial intelligence (AI) in higher education: A comprehensive review of challenges, opportunities, and implications', *Journal of Learning Development in Higher Education [Preprint]*, 30. https://doi.org/10.47408/jldhe.vi30.1137

Browne, I. (2021) 'Exploring reverse mentoring; "win-win" relationships in the multi-generational workplace', *International Journal of Evidence Based Coaching and Mentoring*, S15, 246–259. https://doi.org/10.24384/jkc9-2r51

Buckley, C. and Frith, L. (2024) 'The development of expertise and identity within a community of practice: A networking model', in A. Syska and C. Buckley (eds) *How to be a Learning Developer in Higher Education: Critical Perspectives, Community and Practice*. Abingdon: Routledge, 34–42.

García-Morales, V. J., Garrido-Moreno, A. and Martín-Rojas, R. (2021) 'The transformation of higher education after the COVID disruption: Emerging challenges in an online learning scenario', *Frontiers in Psychology*, 12. https://doi.org/10.3389/fpsyg.2021.616059

Hawke, S. (2023, 20 July) *LD@3: Impact of 1:1 Appointments on Student Attainment* [Webinar]. ALDinHE [Online].

Jewitt, K. (2024, 27 June) *LD@3: The Art of Storytelling for Learning Developers: How to Transform Complex Ideas into Compelling Narratives* [Webinar]. ALDinHE [Online].

Jones, C. and Bell, H. (2024, 6 March) 'The increasing pressure on students after Covid-19', *SRHE Blog*. Available at: https://srheblog.com/2024/03/06/the-increasing-pressure-on-students-after-covid-19/ (Accessed: 27 December 2024).

Kay, J., Husbands, C. and Tangen, J. (2024, 11 March) *The Continued Success of Universities Hinges on the Response to the Generative AI Reckoning*. WonkHE. Available at: https://wonkhe.com/blogs/the-continued-success-of-universities-hinges-on-the-response-to-the-generative-ai-reckoning/ (Accessed: 23 December 2024).

Lawlor, K. B. and Hornyak, M. J. (2012) 'Smart goals: How the application of SMART goals can contribute to achievement of student learning outcomes', *Developments in Business Simulation and Experiential Learning*, 39, 259–267.

Stachowiak, B. (n.d.) *Teaching in Higher Ed podcast*. Available at: https://teachinginhighered.com/episodes/ (Accessed: 12 January 2025).

Tikly, L. (2025, 16 January) *Supporting Learning in a Multicultural Environment: The Richness and Challenge of Diverse Universities* [Lecture] Inspiring Learning New Year Lecture. Heriot Watt University [Online].

Wareing, S. (2024, 21 January) *Policymakers Need to Realise that Financial Turbulence in Higher Education will Hurt the Whole Nation*. WonkHE. Available at: https://wonkhe.com/blogs/policymakers-need-to-realise-that-financial-turbulence-in-higher-education-will-hurt-the-whole-nation/ (Accessed: 23 December 2024).

Wenger-Trayner, E. and Wenger-Trayner, B. (2015) *Introduction to Communities of Practice: A Brief Overview of the Concept and Its Uses*. Available at: https://www.wenger-trayner.com/introduction-to-communities-of-practice (Accessed: 9 April 2025).

WonkHE (2025) *The WonkHE Show – the Higher Education Podcast*. Available at: https://wonkhe.com/podcast/ (Accessed: 18 May 2025).

Zinsser, W. (1976) *On Writing Well*, 30th anniversary edn. New York: HarperCollins Publishers, 2006.

Ideas for further reading

Professional development opportunities

Briggs, S. (2024) 'Professional development and recognition in LD', in A. Syska and C. Buckley (eds) *How to be a Learning Developer in Higher Education: Critical Perspectives, Community and Practice*. Abingdon: Routledge, 220–229.

Moriau, L., Matolay, R., McKenna, E., Toarniczky, A., Gáspár, J., Frigyik, M. and Bates, C. (2025) 'Enhancing professional development for third space roles: Reflections on the added value of learning circles', *Journal of Learning Development in Higher Education [Preprint]*, 33. https://doi.org/10.47408/jldhe.vi32.1228

Chapter 10

Final thoughts and further inspiration

> **This chapter provides**
> - A summary of the preceding chapters.
> - Ideas for continuing to develop in your role as a Learning Developer (LDer).
> - Concluding thoughts around adding your voice to the field and the joy of making mistakes.
>
> **You will have the opportunity to reflect on**
> - Your key learning points.
> - Your next steps in development of your practice.

Summary

The aim of this book was to provide guidance for new and early career LDers and those in related roles working in higher education (HE) contexts. Following the introduction, Chapter 2 began by considering what Learning Development (LD) is and what it means to 'do' LD. It situated LD as an emerging, exciting field in which to work but one with its own unique challenges. We learned about the five guiding community values as espoused by the Association for Learning Development in Higher Education (ALDinHE) and how these can underpin effective LD practice. As challenging and disorienting as it can be for new students to acclimatise to being part of the academy, so too can it be for new LDers. As such, in Chapter 3, we explored the functions and purposes of a university and considered some of the wider contextual issues impacting HE.

We then moved on to look at the practical aspects of the job. Chapters 4 and 5 considered two of the primary student-facing aspects of the role – tutorials and workshops – and outlined ways for preparing for, conducting, and

DOI: 10.4324/9781003604266-10

evaluating these. Chapter 6 explored the significance of embedded provision in LD practice. We saw that through embedded work, LDers have the scope to work in partnership with staff and students to integrate skills and academic literacies development into disciplinary teaching. Chapter 7 provided ideas for developing teaching and learning materials, including a discussion on the ethical use of generative artificial intelligence (GenAI) technologies for doing so. In Chapter 8, we turned to consider the importance of working effectively with students and staff and looked at pragmatic tips for doing so emphasising the need to have regard for equality, diversity, and inclusion in LD practice. We noted that LD does not exist in a bubble and that LDers need to be aware of the statutory and regulatory framework as pertinent to their role. In Chapter 9, the focus was on continuing professional development (CPD), and we examined options for informal and formal CPD. We considered how CPD should be an ongoing and essential element of an LDer's work, aiding us to better fulfil our responsibilities as well as providing the means to progress further in our individual careers.

In this chapter, we will consider further ideas for continuing to develop in your role as an LD and you will have the opportunity to reflect on your key learning points from the book. Finally, the chapter outlines some of the inspirational practice and research taking place in the field of LD and ends with concluding thoughts about adding your voice to the LD community.

How else might I continue to develop in my role?

This book has hopefully aided you with feeling more anchored as you embark on your career in LD. Here, I outline a few more ideas for where you might seek guidance in relation to your role as an LDer.

In the day-to-day 'doing' of LD, we often have little time for conversations about what LD 'is' and why we do things in the way we do. However, making yourself available to speak and reflect with others who are LDers can provide a fruitful source of support, inspiration, and insight for your own practice. Start with your immediate institution. Are there colleagues there who might be able to advise you on an aspect of LD that you find challenging? Is there anyone who can offer opportunities for shadowing or mentorship? Is there a trusted colleague that you feel able to talk with informally when you are finding the workload overwhelming? Seeking out such opportunities can provide you the space to ask questions about all the practical elements of the role like conducting workshops, running tutorials, and finding resources. Conversations with more experienced LD colleagues can also aid as a springboard for ideas and signal to you that you are taking the right approach. However, guidance does not necessarily need to come from colleagues with more experience. You might also seek tips or advice from those working at a similar stage of their career to you. Such relationships can provide a space to share relatable challenges and teaching ideas. If this is not possible, or if you are the sole LDer in your institution, remember that you are also part of a wider LD network of professionals and can access guidance from colleagues working across the world through forums like the LDHEN JiscMail, online communities of practice, social media, and networking expert directories, such as those available on the ALDinHE website.

If you have not yet joined a professional LD association as a member, then it is a good idea to do so. As we have seen, ALDinHE is a UK-based professional association for LDers. Although situated in the UK, it has an international reach with colleagues across the world participating in its events, networking opportunities, and using its resources. Organisations such as the Scottish Higher Education Learner Developers (ScotHELD) network, the South African Association for Academic Literacy Practitioners (SAAALP), and the Association of Tertiary Learning Advisors of Aotearoa New Zealand (ATLAANZ) offer similar offerings to their members and are affiliated with ALDinHE. Together with the Learning Specialists Association of Canada (LSAC) and the Association for Academic Language and Learning (AALL), they form part of a larger consortium known as the International Consortium of Academic Language and Learning Developers (ICALLD). This means that you have access to a global community of LD professionals and scope to learn about how LD practice is carried out outside your immediate country and cultural context.

To be a member of ALDinHE, your university or college may subscribe (known as an institutional membership) or, if they do not subscribe, you can choose to pay yourself for an individual membership. Although there are many free resources on ALDinHE and ways you can interact without a subscription, membership opens many other opportunities. This includes, for instance, the scope to apply for professional recognition (see Chapter 9) and access to the formal mentoring programme. It is possible to become very actively involved in ALDinHE, including becoming a Steering Group member or Chair of a Working Group. However, if this is not for you, ALDinHE and the associations that make up ICALLD also offer many developmental opportunities which do not entail being at the forefront such as participating in conferences and symposiums, researching and writing, joining communities of practice, and developing and reviewing teaching and learning resources, such as that available on the LearnHigher directory.

There is a huge amount of inspirational work happening in the field of LD. For instance, LD colleagues are currently involved in innovative research and practice around GenAI and its implications for teaching and learning in HE, colleagues in the field are working on issues related to equality, diversity, and equality, and there is novel research being carried out into creative LD practices. Such innovative work can seem daunting as a new LDer. You may question how to add your voice to what may feel like a saturated field.

One suggestion is to try to engage with the wider LD community beyond your immediate institution as this will help to build your confidence in relation to what LD 'is', what its values are, and how colleagues across different institutions are doing the job. Through this, you will meet colleagues who are pioneering and who might challenge your practice in some way. This is a good thing. Chapter 9 on *Professional Development* outlined practical approaches for engaging with the LD community and developing in your professional role. However, getting involved in the wider LD community does not necessarily require 'networking' or doing lots of self-promotion. It could be as simple as investigating what other LDers place on their student-facing websites or conducting some informal online research to see the range of LD workshops typically offered by other institutions. Participating in the wider LD community can promote confidence as you will be interacting with like-minded professionals who share common values in relation to teaching and learning. You may even find that you surprise yourself that you are already doing a lot of things 'right'. The following box provides a few final words of encouragement and advice from experienced colleagues in the field.

> **Guidance from experienced colleagues**
>
> You're not alone. There's a raft of resources to help. Get involved in ALDinHE. Ask for help and guidance. Never stop learning and stay research active. Ask your students for feedback on what you do well and what they think you could do better. You're not expected to know everything or have all the answers. Ask students how they'd like to be supported. Use who, what, where, and how questions to encourage dialogue. Be open and seek constructive feedback on your own performance.
>
> Dr Katharine Jewitt, Associate Lecturer,
The Open University
>
> At first, being an LDer can feel like being an outsider. That's a status we can feel OK with embracing and challenging equally at different times. Don't worry if it feels confusing for a while – keep faith and keep learning. Network straight away – around your institution and with your country's Professional Association (ALDinHE and ScotHELD in the UK). Together they can help you learn how to 'do' Learning Development faster.
>
> Dr Ian Johnson, Teaching Fellow in Learning
Development at the University of Portsmouth

Key learning points

We have nearly reached the end of this book. Did you dip in and out to find a section relevant to a specific need such as how to develop teaching and learning resources or did you read the book through in its entirety? Spend a few moments jotting down some thoughts on what you will take away from your reading. Were there any specific learning points that stood out for you? Is there a particular resource or idea you would like to try? Do you want to do more reading on the theoretical and scholarly basis of LD? Is there an area of professional development that you would like to start working on? What other questions do you have about LD and where might you find the answers? What will you do differently now that you have read this book or a section of this book?

For this, you might wish to complete a simple what I know, what I want to know, and what I have learned (KWL) chart as in Table 10.1:

Table 10.1 KWL chart.

K	W	L
What I *know* already I have a basic understanding of the five ALDinHE values.	What I *want* to know How do I go about getting support to further develop my understanding of how to demonstrate these values in my practice?	What I have *learned* I can get support from ALDinHE, for instance, via the mentoring scheme or in the expertise directory.

Concluding thoughts

This book stemmed from the idea that a 'manual' might be useful to those new to LD. Whilst there existed seminal works on LD from Syska and Buckley (2024a) and Hartley et al. (2011), it offered a different slant in that it focused on the practicalities of doing the job rather than critical or theoretical perspectives on the nature of LD. However, the practice of LD can never be disassociated from its underlying values and its theoretical and philosophical basis about the nature of teaching and learning. Therefore, throughout this book, I drew heavily on the five community-driven values espoused by ALDinHE (2024) as a way of anchoring and structuring the guidance around how to do the job. The book recognised that LD takes place in a range of contexts and as such there were activities included throughout to aid with applying the guidance to your specific situation. Whilst it acknowledged that our work environments are distinct, the premise throughout was that LD is about relationships and is driven by the underlying aim to 'work in partnership with students and staff to make sense of and get the most out of HE' (ALDinHE, 2024). This invisible thread ties us together in spirit regardless of our individual institutional differences and situations.

In the closing chapter (paradoxically titled 'Opening') to their edited collection, Syska and Buckley (2024b, p. 248) state that 'LDers have unique insights to offer. We cannot wait for permission to contribute. . . . What [LD] could become depends on us. This is your invitation to join and grow that conversation'. Their statement surely does stand as an 'opening' or provocation for members of the community to add their voice to the debate about what LD is and what it could be. This includes you. As a new LDer, sitting there on my first day having heart palpitations and feeling like an imposter, I could not have conceived that I would be involved in the community in the way I have been through my involvement with ALDinHE and contributions to the *Journal of Learning Development in Higher Education (JLDHE)*, let alone write a book about LD. However, the more I learned about LD and got involved, the more a spark grew, and I realised that I was good at my role and could make meaningful contribution. I would not have written this book if I had waited for someone to give me permission to do so. The same goes for you. As a new or early career LDer, you are well placed to bring unique and fresh insights to the field. Your skills, initiative, and creativity are valued and welcome regardless of whether you are an extrovert, introvert, or something in between. Whatever form it takes, whether book, blog, conference poster, or presentation, through joining a community of practice, through participation in a working group, by posting comments on professional social media accounts, through the LDHEN JiscMail, or any other means, the community wants to hear your voice. Do not wait for permission to come.

Throughout I emphasised that although this book might aid as a starting point for those new to LD, it is not intended as prescriptive. We work in a complex sector and our institutions reflect this complexity. Moreover, our role hinges on building positive relationships with students and staff. Given the demands of working in a student-facing role, and the varied contexts in which we find ourselves, the process of growing and developing as an LDer will entail learning on-the-job and adapting to new challenges. This means that making mistakes will be an inescapable part of the learning process. However, do not be afraid of making errors or of experiencing the dreaded 'failure' as this is where growth happens. Like we saw in Chapter 8, rather than running from mistakes, you can think of such experiences as a professional learning tool that enables you to consider and reflect on what you might do differently next time.

Being courageous and unafraid to fail can be hard. However, we work with students with a developmental ethos – that is, we continually emphasise the evolving and fluid nature of learning. The same can be said for you as a new or early career LDer. It is okay to learn, make blunders, and develop rather than feeling that you must be a finished and 'perfect' version of an LDer. There is, indeed, no perfect LDer, though maybe the next 'breed' of AI will eventually create one? Until then, know that you are 'doing' good enough and that whenever you need a guiding friend you can return to this book. Know too that you do not have to be brave in isolation. You are joining an incredible international community of collaborative professionals who are always willing to assist when needed. We look forward to seeing your impact on the field of LD. Welcome and I wish you all the best.

Summary

- This chapter summarised the key points from the preceding chapters. It explained how the book offered practical guidance on the primary functions of LD including provision of tutorials, workshops, embedded provision, the development of teaching and learning materials, working with students and colleagues, and professional development.
- The chapter considered ideas for how to continue to develop in your role as a new LDer, including seeking guidance from the wider LD community.
- It also considered the importance of and opportunity to add your voice to the field of LD.
- Finally, the chapter highlighted the normalcy of making mistakes and experiencing failure as being a positive learning tool to continue developing and growing in your role as an LDer.

References

ALDinHE (2024) *About ALDinHE*. Available at: https://aldinhe.ac.uk/about-aldinhe/ (Accessed: 9 April 2024).

Hartley, P., Hilsdon, J., Keenan, C., Sinfield, S. and Verity, M. (eds) (2011) *Learning Development in Higher Education*. Basingstoke: Palgrave Macmillan.

Syska, A. and Buckley, C. (eds) (2024a) *How to be a Learning Developer in Higher Education: Critical Perspectives, Community and Practice*. Abingdon: Routledge.

Syska, A. and Buckley, C. (2024b) 'Opening', in A. Syska and C. Buckley (eds) *How to be a Learning Developer in Higher Education: Critical Perspectives, Community and Practice*. Abingdon: Routledge, 247–248.

Ideas for further reading

Abegglen, S., Kamal, S., Burns, T., Akhbari, M. and Sinfield, S. (2023) '(Re)imagining higher education: An inspirational guide for academics', *Journal of Learning Development in Higher Education*, 29. https://doi.org/10.47408/jldhe.vi29.1099

ALDinHE (2024) *Accreditation*. Available at: https://aldinhe.ac.uk/accreditation/ (Accessed: 9 April 2024).

Bickle, E., Allen, S. and Mayer, M. (2022) 'Learning development 2030', *Journal of Learning Development in Higher Education [Preprint]*, 25. https://doi.org/10.47408/jldhe.vi25.972

Kukhareva, M. and Buckley, C. (2023) 'Why and how you matter: Learning development as everyday leadership', *Journal of Learning Development in Higher Education [Preprint]*, 29. https://doi.org/10.47408/jldhe.vi29.1079

Appendices

Appendices

Appendix 1: ALDinHE collective diary entries

Ursula Canton – Glasgow Caledonian University

A long Friday! 4 hours with dissertation students – 3 groups and each class consists of a mixture of feedback on work in progress (intro/lit rev) I've read, and advice on methodology adapted to each programme of study. It's interesting and challenging and enjoyable, but intense to switch from one to another. One group is very talkative and happy to discuss; another prefers to listen in silence, but they did that last time and various of those silent listeners later sent me work to review for this class, commenting on how useful it had been to hear the earlier analysis of typical problems with research questions (too vague, too big . . .).

I also need to prepare a feedback class for a level 1 computing module. After a short introduction, they had to complete a worksheet that scaffolded the steps towards writing a section for their assignment: identifying 2 additional sources, extracting information related to the task from each, synthesising this to see what they now know about the topic and finally relating it to their practical task. It's a huge module (almost 200 students), so just above 50 submissions is not a great percentage, but still a good bit of work for a Friday afternoon. The resulting feedback lecture has really good examples of good and not so good practice with sources; however, so it feels very worthwhile and I'm looking forward to delivering it next week. It was also useful to identify some common misinterpretations of the task, so I can adapt the worksheet for next year.

ALDinHE (2024, 15 March) 'Ursula Canton – Glasgow Caledonian University', *Collective Diary*. Available at: https://aldinhe.ac.uk/collective-diary-15-march-2024/ (Accessed: 17 July 2025).

Zara Hooley – De Montfort University

I started the day with a meeting about what data we need to pull together for a feedback report on student engagement with our service for our colleagues in Faculty. I am then attending a meeting with a colleague to plan for the Welcome Weekend induction day which welcomes freshers to the University. 12–1 pm I will be working in a student-facing assignment drop-in session. Tutoring students on academic writing. Quick lunch. 1–2 pm I am running a staff-facing session on AI-resilient assignment design. 3–6 pm I am taking leave to work on some of my own academic writing.

This is a typical day for me, a mixture of meetings and student-facing work, and a certain amount of admin.

ALDinHE (2024, 15 September) 'Zara Hooley – De Montfort University', *Collective Diary*. Available at: https://aldinhe.ac.uk/collective-diary-15-september-2024/ (Accessed: 17 July 2025).

Claire Olson – Edge Hill University

It's been a bit of a mixed bag today, basically me trying to catch up on lots of different things before it gets crazy busy during Semester 1! I can feel the clock ticking for the new term, and my diary is filling up rapidly. I've had an interesting week, with two full days away from my desk. One day spent with my team on a planning day for the year ahead, and another spent at an ALDinHE regional event in Leeds. Both days proved to be a good opportunity to reflect and also plan ahead. But whilst it's been great to have these days, it's meant I've been playing catch up since – with lots of emails, prep work, etc. still to be done. Overall, I've managed to complete quite a few tasks today, so it's been a good day. I've finished editing and launching surveys for our workshop offer and created the QR codes needed to prompt students to complete the survey. This was one task I definitely wanted finished before the end of the week. I spent time tweaking slides for future sessions (which always takes longer than I think it will) and completed a couple of training feedback requests that I also needed to do. I've finished with a bit of reading around AI, as I'll be delivering Academic Integrity sessions soon and I could do with feeling a bit more confident about what I want to say. I'll be logging off for the weekend with a slightly shorter to-do list than I started with, despite adding to it as the day went on.

ALDinHE (2023, 15 September) 'Claire Olson – Edge Hill University', *Collective Diary*. Available at: https://aldinhe.ac.uk/collective-diary-15-september-2023/ (Accessed: 17 July 2025).

Robert Ping-Nan Chang – University of the Arts London

It has been hectic since coming back from the summer holiday, with two members of the team leaving, the welcome week to start on Monday, the arrangement of embedded LD sessions to resume, and lots of teaching in the pipeline to prepare. In this entry, I would, however, like to share the afternoon session in a staff development event I joined this Wednesday. It's a very hands-on and interactive workshop about 'positionality'. There was no PPT to go through or a lecture to listen to. Rather, we actively engaged in the workshops through painting, talking, walking, cutting, and writing. Two activities I found especially interesting are 'painting to music' and 'making a positionality wheel'. We spent five minutes doing watercolour painting in response to the music played by the facilitator and another five minutes doing the second painting to another piece of music. While the instructor did not ask us to 'rationalise' or 'analyse' what we painted, I found the activity allowed me to explore myself through a means (art/painting) that I am familiar with. In one, I painted a wall of red bricks. This reflected not only my interpretation of the rhythm but also my liking of patterns, geometrical shapes and lines, and routines. As for the last task of the workshop, we used paper, scissors, pens, push pins, and disposable paper trays to create our own positionality wheels. The inner circle is about myself, the middle circle about me in the institution (UAL), and the outer layer is about how the society sees me. While this was a really interesting activity to explore myself, I can see the potential to adopt it as a fun tool to kick off reflection.

ALDinHE (2023, 15 September) 'Robert Ping-Nan Chang – University Arts London', *Collective Diary*. Available at: https://aldinhe.ac.uk/collective-diary-15-september-2023/ (Accessed: 17 July 2025).

Barry Poulter – University of Bedfordshire

The morning starts with emails as usual. A new lecturer has been introduced to me, and with it a new opportunity to embed support for our second and third years. While I'm glad to have made a new in-road, it can feel a little disappointing knowing that there are still areas of the university that we have been unable to reach even with our renewed push for integration. The feelings of disappointment are then balanced out over the course of my day by several chats with colleagues, some Learning Developers, and others from adjacent teams, reminding me how connected we actually are.

This integration is immediately highlighted by the community of practice (CoP) meeting: a monthly meetup of many of our university third space teams, and one of the most valuable meetings for my understanding of how these other teams work. Of course I'm aware from other, more formal, meetings what each team does, but these CoPs have really highlighted our different perspectives and approaches to questions that overlap each of our areas of expertise – this time on the topic of independent learning and how to foster it in our students. We also received an extra helping of good news in the CoP today hearing that resit rates were down across the university, and so too was the proportion of students having at least one resit. Though it is hard to attribute such a broad success to any specific initiatives, it's motivation enough to keep pushing forward with the sometimes difficult conversations we have to have.

ALDinHE (2025, 15 May) 'Barry Poulter – University of Bedfordshire', *Collective Diary*. Available at: https://aldinhe.ac.uk/collective-diary-15-may-2025/ (Accessed: 17 July 2025).

Tim Worth – University of Bristol

After a brisk bike ride across North Bristol, my Thursday began with the Study Skills team meeting. At this time of year, we're very much in looking-ahead mode. Undergraduate teaching and assessments are mostly over, while PGT students aren't quite ready for support with their dissertations, so it's the perfect opportunity for us to discuss summer projects and start thinking of plans for the next academic year – ways to improve training for our team of student advocates, plans for a new online resource on literature reviews, upcoming conferences, etc.

With no students to see today, I then took the opportunity to go through some much-neglected JISC mailing list emails, trimming the number of unread messages in that folder down to a paltry 791, and frantically signed up for 6 or 7 webinars I should have registered for much earlier. Various ad hoc tasks ensued – clearing out boxes from a downstairs store cupboard to make way for renovations, chatting with a colleague about online archives of historical newspapers, and filling out a survey on AI in HE.

I do appreciate the quietness of this time of year. It gives me time to catch up on the things I've mentally classified as un-urgent, of secondary importance, things which no one is going to notice if I don't do them but which of course have value. Without that quietness, I wouldn't have registered for those webinars or found that survey, and I certainly wouldn't have discovered ALDinHE's collective diary!

ALDinHE (2025, 15 May) 'Tim Worth – University of Bristol', *Collective Diary*. Available at: https://aldinhe.ac.uk/collective-diary-15-may-2025/ (Accessed: 17 July 2025).

Appendix 2: Example workshop plan

Workshop aim: The aim of this online introductory-level hour workshop is for students to be able to identify the key features of critical essay writing.

Stage aim (state the aim of the stage focusing on the learning rather than the activity, e.g. To evaluate . . . To identify . . .)	Timing (state estimated time for the activity, e.g. 5–10 min)	Interaction (state who is interacting with who, e.g. students–tutor student–student)	Procedure (describe what you are you doing/what the students are doing)	Material/Resources (describe what you will use)	Evaluation/Tutor's Comments (after the workshop write your thoughts on what worked well/did not go so well at each stage)
1. To gauge students' starting points/previous understanding in relation to the workshop aim	2 minutes	Whole class Tutor–students	Display the following question on an interactive slide: what is your current confidence level in relation to critical essay writing? Students to select from unconfident to extremely confident. Tutor to comment on students' responses.	Interactive slide with poll	This activity worked well overall. It took longer than two minutes as some students didn't know how to use the interactive poll, so next time I need to factor in more time for explaining how to use the tool. Some students chose to contribute to the chat instead.

(Continued)

(Continued)

Stage aim (state the aim of the stage focusing on the learning rather than the activity, e.g. To evaluate ... To identify ...)	Timing (state estimated time for the activity, e.g. 5–10 min)	Interaction (state who is interacting with who, e.g. students–tutor student–student)	Procedure (describe what you are you doing/what the students are doing)	Material/Resources (describe what you will use)	Evaluation/Tutor's Comments (after the workshop write your thoughts on what worked well/did not go so well at each stage)
2. To introduce students to the learning objective	1 minute	Tutor–students	Display the LO on a slide and talk through. Tutor to say that whatever their starting point, by the end of the workshop they should hopefully feel more confident in understanding the key features of critical essay writing.	Slide with LO/ intended aims	All fine
3. To understand what is meant by critical thinking	2 min 5 min 3 min	Tutor–students Student–student Whole class	Display a concept cartoon with four different stances in relation to critical thinking, e.g. 'critical thinking means being negative' 'critical thinking involves reaching a reasoned judgement'	Slide with concept cartoon Slide with concept cartoon Slide with a definition of critical thinking	The concept cartoon activity worked well. I might try this as a whole class activity next time as some of the participants dropped out of the call when I mentioned breakout rooms. Assigning students roles also worked well as all groups were able to contribute their ideas.

(Continued)

Appendices 213

(Continued)

Stage aim (state the aim of the stage focusing on the learning rather than the activity, e.g. To evaluate . . . To identify . . .)	Timing (state estimated time for the activity, e.g. 5–10 min)	Interaction (state who is interacting with who, e.g. students–tutor student–student)	Procedure (describe what you are you doing/what the students are doing)	Material/Resources (describe what you will use)	Evaluation/Tutor's Comments (after the workshop write your thoughts on what worked well/did not go so well at each stage)
			Ask students to discuss the four stances and which they agree/disagree with. Put students in small breakout groups to do this. Assign roles, e.g. notetaker, person to feedback. Take whole class feedback and clarify any misconceptions, e.g. critical thinking does not necessarily mean you have to be negative. Explain that critical thinking is the basis for critical essay writing and provide a written definition.		

(Continued)

(Continued)

Stage aim (state the aim of the stage focusing on the learning rather than the activity, e.g. To evaluate ... To identify ...)	Timing (state estimated time for the activity, e.g. 5–10 min)	Interaction (state who is interacting with who, e.g. students–tutor student–student)	Procedure (describe what you are you doing/what the students are doing)	Material/Resources (describe what you will use)	Evaluation/Tutor's Comments (after the workshop write your thoughts on what worked well/did not go so well at each stage)
4. To understand why demonstrating criticality in essay writing is important	5 min 5 min	Tutor-students Tutor-students	Display Bloom's Taxonomy on a slide. Ask if students are familiar with the taxonomy. Explain how it progresses from lower-order to higher-order skills. Explain that whilst there are criticisms of the taxonomy, it demonstrates what skills lecturers are aiming to develop. Discuss how criticality is a higher-order skill and more complex to demonstrate – therefore, it can lead to higher marks in assignments. Take any questions.	Slide with a visual showing Bloom's Taxonomy.	This stage felt a bit too lecture heavy. Next time, I might get the students to piece together a cut up version of Bloom's Taxonomy to identify lower/higher-order skills themselves.

(Continued)

(Continued)

Stage aim (state the aim of the stage focusing on the learning rather than the activity, e.g. To evaluate . . . To identify . . .)	Timing (state estimated time for the activity, e.g. 5–10 min)	Interaction (state who is interacting with who, e.g. students–tutor student–student)	Procedure (describe what you are you doing/what the students are doing)	Material/Resources (describe what you will use)	Evaluation/Tutor's Comments (after the workshop write your thoughts on what worked well/did not go so well at each stage)
5. To be able to identify features of critical essay writing	5 min 10 min 5 min	Tutor–students Student–student Whole class	Display an essay extract/share it in the chat. Model annotating key features that demonstrate criticality. Provide students with a different essay extract and a checklist of features. Students work in pairs (in breakout rooms) to annotate features in the extract that make it critical. They tick these features off on the checklist. Whole class feedback. Encourage students to share their ideas as to what makes the piece critical in the chat, on the microphone or on the interactive slides.	One essay extract displayed on slide and shared in the chat. One essay extract per student	Students found it helpful to see a 'real' essay extract and the checklist criteria helped to provide a scaffold for identifying the features themselves. Next time, I will send out the essay extract in advance to students who have booked or give this activity more time.

(Continued)

(Continued)

Stage aim (state the aim of the stage focusing on the learning rather than the activity, e.g. To evaluate ... To identify ...)	Timing (state estimated time for the activity, e.g. 5–10 min)	Interaction (state who is interacting with who, e.g. students–tutor student–student)	Procedure (describe what you are you doing/what the students are doing)	Material/Resources (describe what you will use)	Evaluation/Tutor's Comments (after the workshop write your thoughts on what worked well/did not go so well at each stage)
6. To apply understanding of the key features of critical essay writing	10 min	Student–student	Give students another short essay extract that does not include critical features. Working independently and using the checklist, they identify three ways to improve the piece. Take whole class feedback.	One essay extract per student	This activity needed more time. Would have worked better as a whole class annotation activity on an interactive whiteboard.
7. To gauge whether students feel they have met the LO and their confidence levels now	5 min	Whole class	Display slide from stage 1, and check whether there has been a shift in students' confidence levels by asking students to respond to the poll. Review LO and check via a poll whether the students feel this has been met.	Interactive slide with poll Interactive slide with poll	Good to see students' perceptions about the change in their confidence levels. There was a clear improvement. I need to remember to emphasise that these are skills that can be improved.
8. To signpost to further support/ resources	2 min	Tutor–students	Share final slide with resources for critical essay writing and signpost to further support. Share link to feedback form. Take any final questions.	Slide with resources listed	I forgot to mention the survey link so must do this next time.

Appendix 3: ChatGPT response to prompt generated on 27 March 2025

'Write five multiple choice quiz questions about structuring an argumentative essay. The questions should be targeted at first year undergraduate students who are new to essay writing. Include answers'.

Note that ChatGPT uses mainly American English spellings.

Question 1:

Which of the following is the primary purpose of an introduction in an essay?

A) To summarize the entire essay
B) To present the thesis statement and set up the structure of the essay
C) To provide detailed analysis and evidence for your argument
D) To restate the conclusion

Answer: B) To present the thesis statement and set up the structure of the essay

Question 2:

In an essay, what is typically included in the body paragraphs?

A) A summary of the conclusion
B) The main arguments or points supporting the thesis, with evidence and analysis
C) The introduction to the topic
D) An overview of the research methods used

Answer: B) The main arguments or points supporting the thesis, with evidence and analysis

Question 3:

Which of the following is NOT a characteristic of a well-structured essay conclusion?

A) It restates the thesis in a new way
B) It introduces new, unrelated arguments
C) It summarizes the main points discussed in the essay
D) It provides a final thought or calls for further research

Answer: B) It introduces new, unrelated arguments

Question 4:

What is the purpose of transitions between paragraphs in an essay?

A) To introduce a new topic completely unrelated to the previous one
B) To link ideas and ensure a smooth flow of thought from one paragraph to the next
C) To provide personal anecdotes
D) To restate the thesis

Answer: B) To link ideas and ensure a smooth flow of thought from one paragraph to the next

Question 5:

Which of the following best describes a clear thesis statement in an essay?

A) A broad statement that introduces the topic
B) A detailed summary of the introduction
C) A specific claim or argument that can be supported with evidence
D) A question the essay will attempt to answer

Answer: C) A specific claim or argument that can be supported with evidence

Index

Note: page numbers in *italics* indicate figures; page numbers in **bold** indicate tables on the corresponding page.

academic integrity 208
academic literacies theory, Learning Development (LD) and 17–18
academic writing, professional development 190–191
accessibility, checking for 163
accessible 8, 9, 14, 21; design 146; learners 78, 87, 94, 97, 116, 135, 159, 180; materials 8, 97, 112, 125–126, 163, **182**; QR code 77; space 22; student-friendly language 49; tutorials 47
accreditation, ALDinHE 192–193
adapting, sharing and advocating, Learning Development (LD) 21–22
AdvanceHE 176; accreditation 193
AdvanceHE National Teaching Fellowship scheme 193
Advisory Committee on Degree Awarding Powers 30
advocating, LD working with colleagues 166–168
agency: self- 13, 14, 105; student 9, 20, 151, 164
ALDinHE (*see*) Association for Learning Development in Higher Education (ALDinHE)
American Psychological Association (APA) 108
annual review, professional development 187
artificial intelligence (AI) 126
assignments, 'proof' or 'resilient' 37
Assignment Survival Kit, University of Kent 144

assignment writing skills, resource 142–143
Association for Learning Development in Higher Education (ALDinHE) 3, 6, 7–9, 24, 36, 176, 197; academic writing 190–191; accreditation and awards 192–193; Advance HE accreditation 193; ALDcon 189; collective diary entries 207–210; communities of practice (CoP) 190; conferences and regional symposia 189–190; CPD programme 187; embedded LD provision 106; expertise directory 115, 121; formal mentorship 188–189; formation 16–17; identifying developmental needs **181**; key learning points 201, **201**; LearnHigher resource bank 97; Learning Development Scholarship Library 25n3; Steering Group 188; website 20, 151; Working Groups 187–188
Association for Academic Language and Learning (AALL) 3, 199
Association of Tertiary Learning Advisors Aotearoa New Zealand (ATLAANZ) 3, 190, 199
audio, use in workshops 94
Australia, Tertiary Education Quality and Standards Agency 31
awards, ALDinHE 192–193

Black, Asian and minority ethnic (BAME) backgrounds, students 156
Blackboard Learn, digital materials 132

Blair, T. 17
blogs, informal professional development 186–187
Bloom, B. 81
Bloom's Taxonomy, learning 81, *82*, 83, **214**
BlueSky 184
British Association of Lecturers in English for Academic Purposes (BALEAP) 189
Buckley, C. 186
Burns, T. 186, 193

Canada, regulation of universities 31
Canton, U. 207
Canva, GenAI tool 136
Canvas, digital materials 132
case studies: embedded session 113–114; school staff meeting 167; teaching and learning materials 140–142; use in workshops 94–95
Centre for Applied Special Technology (CAST) 135
Centre for Excellence in Teaching and Learning, LearnHigher 16
Chang, R. P.-N. 208–209
Charity Commission 29
ChatGPT 36; creating materials with 133–135; ethics of using 109, 111; GenAI tool 141; generating ideas for teaching 126; generating quiz questions 134; response to prompt questions 217–218
Children and Families Act (2014) **158**
circular networking model, continuing professional development (CPD) 176, *177*
citing, resources 145
class management, workshops 98–100
classroom management, embedded sessions 116–117
Claude 36; GenAI tool 141
collaboration/collaborative work 4, 15, 21–22, 90, 106, 115, 121, 151, 171, 185, 191
colleagues: guidance from experienced 200; Learning Developer (LDer) working with 166–168
community of practice (CoP) 184, 209; professional development 190
Completing Your PhD (book series) 145
concept cartoons *140*; teaching and learning 139–140
conferences, formal professional development 189–190

confidence 2, 64, 194, **211**, 216; building 168, 170, **177**, 189–190, 200; concept 68; developing 9, 21, 62, 67, 98, 121, 131, 146, 164; essay writing 141; lack of 46, 52, 99, 116, 152, 191; professional 153–154; students growing 46, 70, 85–86, 99, 101, 167
constructive alignment, session outcome 114
continuing professional development (CPD) 7, 9, 22, 37, 161, 198; academic writing 190–191; Advance HE accreditation 193; ALDinHE CPD programme 187; ALDinHE formal mentorship 188–189; ALDinHE Working Groups and Steering Group 187–188; annual review 187; communities of practice 190; conferences and regional symposia 189–190; description of 175–176; formal methods 187–192; formal study 193–194; gaining recognition 192–194; informal CPD log **180**; Learning Developer (LDer) 170; research activity 191–192 (*see also*) professional development
Cornell University 143
co-teaching, informal professional development 184–185
Cottrell, S. 52, 141, 143
Council on Higher Education, South Africa 31
counselling mode, students 62–63
COVID-19 pandemic 35; aftermath of 178; workshops 78
CPD (*see*) continuing professional development (CPD)
creating vlogs, informal professional development 186–187
Creative Commons (CC) license 125, 126, 136
critical essay writing, workshop plan **211–216**
critical pedagogy: Learning Developers (LDers) 160–161; professional development 179
critical self-reflection, Learning Development (LD) 22
critical thinking, reading, and writing skills 143
Critical Thinking Skills (Cottrell) 143
critical writing online guide, University of York 143

De Montfort University 183; diary entry 207–208
Department for the Economy, Northern Ireland 33
dialogic approach, tutorials 56, 69
dialogue, workshops 92
diary, informal professional development 182–183
digital: interactive tools in workshops 91–92; literacy resources 145; teaching and learning in creating materials 131–133
Digital Learning Advisers 163
Digital Learning Developers 163
disability 22, 96, 132, 135, 154 digital teaching and learning, creating materials 131–133, 156, 170; services 33, 65, 162; students 54, **59**, 97; tutorials 45
Disability Discrimination Act (1995) **157**
dissertation skills 145–146
diverse learners, LDers working with respect for 161–163
diversity: definition 156; recognising and respecting 161–162; workshop design for 96–97
dyslexia 53, 54
Dyslexia Association 54

Edge Hill University, diary entry 208
Educational/Academic Developers 3
Educational or Academic Developer 150, 167
Educational Research Review 185
emancipatory, practice 16
embedded provision 104; common in LD practice 105–107; getting buy-in for sessions 107–108; proponents of 106; success of 107–108
embedded sessions: addressing problems in 115–117; case study 113–114; creating materials for 128, **128**; evaluating and showing impact of 118–120; getting buy-in for 107–108; planning and structuring 108–109, 111; planning template for embedded teaching **110**; pre- and post-session tasks **110**, 111–112; resource for materials for **110**, 114–115; roadmap for overview 109; support for 112; understanding 120–121
embracing, Learning Development (LD) 21

England, UK qualifications frameworks **30**
English for Academic Purposes (EAP) Foundation 144
English for Academic Purposes (EAP) teaching 18
equality: definition 156; promoting 161
equality, diversity, and inclusion (EDI) 161, 163
Equality Act (2010) 96, **157**, **158**, 171
equity, definition 156
essay writing: resource skills 142–143; slides for teaching 129, **130**; workshop plan **211–216**
ethos 6, 8, 12, 20; developmental 14, 24, 202
European Association for the Teaching of Academic Writing (EATAW) 3
European General Data Protection Regulation (GDPR) 69
exams, revising and taking 144
expert 15, 37, 58, 93, *93*, 121, 164, 165, *177*, **177**, 178, **180**, 199
expertise directory 115, 121, 170, 184, 191, **201**

F-ALDinHE/SF-ALDinHE 192, 195n2
fellowship 193, 194
flexibility, tutorials 67
formal study, professional development 193–194
formulation model: structuring tutorials 58, **59–60**; summary of 5Ps **59–60**; tutorials 58, **59–60**, 69
Framework for Higher Education Qualifications of UK Degree-Awarding Bodies (FHEQ) 30
Freire, P. 39
frequently asked questions (FAQs) 65

generative artificial intelligence (GenAI) 8, 29, 127, 133, 198; creating materials with 133–135; debate on 36–38; student learning 86
Gibbs' reflective cycle: embedded session 114; tutorials 63, 63–65, 70
Glasgow Caledonian University, diary entry 207
Google Classroom 124
Google Images 136
grammar, teaching and learning 144–145
Grammar-Monster.com 144

group work: jigsaw approach to *93*; workshops 92–94
guidance, tutorials 65

Harvard Graduate School of Education 135
higher education (HE) sector 8, 24, 40; LDers working with students and staff 150–151; new to Learning Development in 28–29; study skills remedial model 106; topical issues impacting 34–36
Higher Education and Research Act (2017) 40n5; Office for Students (OfS) 31
Higher Education Funding Council for England (HEFCE) 16, 25n4
Higher Education Funding Council for Wales (HEFCW) 31, 33
higher education institutions (HEIs) 3, 7, 45; professional development 178; professionalizing tutor role 45; workload allocation model 107
Higher Education Statistics Agency (HESA), institution data 153–154, 155
Higher Education Teaching and Learning, master's degree 194
Hilsdon, J. 3–4, 10n1, 13, 186
hooks, b. 39
Hooley, Z. 183, 207–208
How to be a Learning Developer in Higher Education (Syska and Buckley) 7, 8, 24
hub and spoke model 5
human side, tutorials 65–66

images: teaching and learning materials 136–139; use in workshops 94
impact of LD: embedded provision 118–120; evaluating tutorials 68–69; evaluating workshops 100–101
imposter syndrome, Learning Developers (LDers) 152–154
inclusion 97, 156, 159, 160, 161, 198
inclusivity: enabling 162–163; Learning Developers (LDers) 159–160; teaching and learning materials 135–136; workshop design for 96–97
independent work, workshops 92–94
influence 4, 14, 24, 120, 151, 161, 176
information technology skills, resource 145

in-person teaching, creating slides for *129*, 129–131, **130**
Instagram 186
integrating LD provision 105
intended learning outcomes (ILOs) 82; teaching and learning materials 128, **128**
International Consortium of Academic Language and Learning Developers (ICALLD) 184, 186, 199
International Journal of Academic Development 185

Jewitt, K. 19, 153, 200
jigsaw approach, group work 93, *93*
JISC, mailing list 210
JiscMail 23, 25n6, 37, 40n7, 48, 70n2, 121, 125, 147n1, 170, 184, 189, 190, 195n1, 199, 202
JLDHE (see) Journal of Learning Development in Higher Education (JLDHE)
job title, Learning Developer (LDer) 5–6
Johnson, I. 20, 153, 200
journal, informal professional development 182–183
Journal of Learning Development in Higher Education (JLDHE) 17, 22, 127, 168, 182, 185, 188, 191, 202

Kahoot, workshops 91

language, teaching and learning 144–145
LDHEN (see) Learning Development in Higher Education Network (LDHEN)
leadership roles, universities **34**
LearnHigher 23; Centre for Excellence in Teaching and Learning 16; resource bank 132; resource website 114–115, 125; website 136
LearnHigher resource bank 8
learning: acquisition of skills 14 (*see also*) teaching and learning materials
Learning Corner, website 144
Learning Developers (LDers) 1, 3; articulating need for LD 168–169; caring for self in professional role 169–171; case study of staff meeting 167; critical pedagogy and practice 160–161; day-to-day tasks 19–20; equality, equity, and diversity 156,

157–158, 159; imposter syndrome 152–154; inclusive teaching and learning practices 159–160; job title 5–6; new to LD in higher education 28–29; people becoming 18; professional development 175–176; respecting equality, diversity, and inclusivity 161–163; responsibilities when working with students and staff 155–156; thoughts from experienced 153; tutorials 45; types of staff to be working with 165–166; types of students to be working with 154–155; working effectively with colleagues 166–168; working in partnership with students 163–164; working with students and staff 150–152, 171; working with students as outsider to their specialty 164–165; workshops 73 (*see also*) continuing professional development (CPD); professional development

Learning Development (LD) 1, 201–203; academic literacies theory and 17–18; articulating the need for 168–169; best way to 'do' 23; continuing to develop role in 198–200; defining 15–16; description of 3–5, 12; on doing 13–16; embedded provision 104; embedded provision in LD practice 105–107; emerging in higher education 16–17; guiding values of 20–22; learning about context of 23–24; mindset 6, 23; promoting LD workshops 76–77; as 'third space' 15, 24; tutorials 44–46; tutorials commonplace in 46–47; in universities 39; workshops 74–75; workshops commonplace in 75–76

Learning Development in Higher Education (Hartley et al) 7, 23–24

Learning Development in Higher Education (Hilsdon) 186

Learning Development in Higher Education Network (LDHEN) 16, 23, 25n6, 37, 40n7, 48, 101, 121, 125, 170, 188, 195n1, 199

learning objectives, workshops 81–83

learning points, KWL chart 201, **201**

Learning Scientists, website 144

Learning Specialists Association of Canada (LSAC) 3, 190, 199

legacies of institutional harms 16
LGBTQIA+ students 156, 159
libguides, teaching and learning materials 126
LinkedIn 184
LinkedIn Learning 133
literacy practices, understanding 17–18
Love LD Magazine 190

Manchester Academic Phrasebank 144
materials (*see*) teaching and learning materials
Mentimeter: interactive learning 138; interactive slides 132; slide creation 130; workshops 79, *85*, *86*, 91–92, 99
mentoring 45, 188–189, 191–192, 199, 201; reverse 189
mentorship, formal professional development 188–189
Microsoft, AI image generator 135
Microsoft Access, embedded provision 120
Microsoft Bookings 50
Microsoft Designer, GenAI tool 136
Microsoft Excel 68; embedded provision 120; workshops 101
Microsoft Learn Educator Centre 133
Microsoft PowerPoint, accessibility 163; images 136; slide creation 130, 131; workshops 79
Microsoft Sway, slide creation 130
Microsoft Word 68; accessibility 163; images 136
Midjourney, GenAI tool 136
mindset, Learning Development (LD) 6, 23
Miro, workshops 79
Moodle 124; digital materials 132

national student survey (NSS) 33
neoliberal education system 35
neoliberalism, term 35
networking, informal professional development 183–184
networking capital accumulation, five stages 176, *177*, **177**
Neurodivergence Resource Bank 125
neurodiversity 190
Northern Ireland: Higher Education Division of the Department for the Economy 31, 33, UK qualifications frameworks **30**

observations, informal professional development 184–185
Office for Students (OfS) 3, 28, 156; conditions of registration **32**; Higher Education and Research Act 2017 31–33; Teaching Excellence Framework (TEF) 32–33; Transforming Access and Student Outcomes in Higher Education (TASO) 40n6
Olson, C. 208
one-to-ones 13, 14, 19, 44–46, 49, 53, 167, 184
on-going learning, Learning Development (LD) 22
online booking form, tutorials 50
online learning, creating slides for *129*, 129–131, **130**
online teaching: breakout room or not for workshops 90–91; cameras on or off 91
Open University 19, 145
Oregon State University, Learning Corner 144
organisation skills 144
OSCOLA (*see*) Oxford Standard for the Citation of Legal Authorities (OSCOLA)
Oxford Standard for the Citation of Legal Authorities (OSCOLA) 108, 145

Padlet: online visual organiser 146; workshops 79, 99
Panopto, interactive study skills tutorial 132
paragraph structure, PEEL (point, evidence, explain/evaluate, link) 138, *138*, *139*
partnership: LDers working with colleagues 166–168; LDers working with students 163–164; professional development 179
Pauk, W. 143
pedagogy: Learning Developers (LDers) 160–161; of kindness 65; workshops 96–97
PEEL (point, evidence, explain/evaluate, link) paragraph structure 138, *138*, *139*
Peer Mentoring Working Group 188
performance management, culture 39
performativity 39
personalised toolkit, resource 142
Pinterest, online visual organiser 146
Pixabay 136, *137*, *138*
plagiarism, avoiding 145
Planning Your PhD (book series) 145
podcasts, informal professional development 185–186
policy 47; education 186; making 4, 13; retention 68; university 38, 52, 76, 79
Post-graduate Certificate in Academic Practice (PGCAP) 192–194
Postgraduate Certificate in Higher Education (PGCHE) 193–194
Poulton, B. 209–210
PowerPoint (*see*) Microsoft PowerPoint
practice 4; embedded 105; LD 16; Learning Developers (LDers) 160–161; Learning Development (LD) 14, 20, 21, 22, 23; professional development 179; workshops 96–97
praxis 4; Learning Development (LD) 4, 23
Prezi: slide creation 130; workshops 79
Privy Council 30
professional confidence 153–154 (*see also*) confidence
professional development: circular networking model 176, *177*, **177**; COVID-19 pandemic 178; description of 175–176; developing SMART goals 182, **182**; five stages of networking capital accumulation *177*, **177**; identifying developmental needs related to ALDinHE values **181**; importance of 176, 178–179; informal 182–187; informal CPD log **180**; keeping a journal or diary 182–183; Learning Development (LD) 22; networking 183–184; next steps in 194; observations and co-teaching 184–185; podcasts 185–186; reading 185; social media 186; starting with 179–180; SWOT analysis in delivering workshops 180, **181**; webinars and talks 184; writing blogs or creating vlogs 186–187 (*see also*) continuing professional development (CPD)
professional identity 12, 152, 177, 179
professional recognition 188, 199
professional role, Learning Developer (LDer) 169–171
public good 35, 38

Quality and Assurance Agency for Higher Education (QAA) 28, 30
questions: ChatGPT response 217–218; tutorial approach 56; workshops 92, 95
Quill Bot 36

race/racism 160
reading: informal professional development 185; note-making and, skills 143
referencing, resources 145
reflective cycle, Gibbs' *63*, 63–65, 70
regional symposia, formal professional development 189–190
relationships 2, 10, 108, 159, 171, 199, 202; authentic and respectful 69, 152, 166; professional 9, 52, 151, 152, 166, 168; working 106
reparative perspective, LD 16
research 38
research activity, formal professional development 191–192
Research and Scholarship Development Working Group 191
Research Excellence Framework (REF) 33
research project skills 145–146
resources 6, 13; creating a 'toolkit' of 140–146; critical thinking, reading, and writing skills 143; digital literacy and information technology skills 145; dissertation and research project skills 145–146; essay and assignment writing skills 142–143; language and grammar 144–145; LearnHigher resource bank 97; materials for embedded LD sessions 110, 114–115; personalised toolkit 142; reading and note-making skills 143; referencing, citing, and avoiding plagiarism 145; revising and taking exams 144; time management and organisation skills 144; toolkit of 'go-to' 8; tutorial follow-up with students 57–58; tutorials 65
respecting diverse learners, Learning Development (LD) 21

scenarios: teaching and learning materials 140–142; use in workshops 94–95
scholarship 38
Scotland, UK qualifications frameworks **30**
Scottish Funding Council (SFC) 31, 33
Scottish Higher Education Learner Developers' network (ScotHELD) 190, 199
self-disclosure, tutorials 66
self-reflection 9, 20, 22, 63, 151, 160, 171, 175, 178–179, 180, **181**, 183
Senior Fellow of ALDinHE (SF-ALDinHE) 192, 195n2
Shutterstock, images 136
Sinfield, S. 186
slides: creating, for online and in-person teaching *129*, 129–131, **130**; fonts 131; presentation tools 130–131
SMART goals: concept of 182; professional development **182**; workshops 101
Social Educational Needs and Disability Act (SENDA) (2001) **158**
social media, informal professional development 186
Socrates 56
South Africa 31
South African Association for Academic Literacy Practitioners (SAAALP) 3, 190, 199
South African Qualifications Authority 31
Special Educational Needs and Disabilities (SEND) Code of Practice (2014) **158**
specific learning differences (SpLDs) 36, 54, 97; embedded sessions 117; students 156
SQ3R method, note-making and reading skills 143
Stachowiak, B. 186
staff, LDers working with 150–152, 165–166
Staff Educational and Development Association (SEDA) 37, 189, 190
storytelling, tutorials 66–67
student(s): assessing learning in workshops 89, *89*; attending tutorials 49–51; encouraging engagement during workshops 91–95; essay writing workshop plan **211–216**; LDers working in 'partnership' with 163–164; LDers working outside of students' specialty 164–165; LDers working with 150–152, 155–156;

responding to questions in workshops 95; types working with LDers 154–155; voice 90
student engagement 28, 91–95, 183, 207
student experience 4, 16–17, 34, 85, 119
student learning: developmental model 105–106; professional development 179
study skills: remedial model 106; resource categorisation 115
Study Skills Handbook, The (Cottrell) 52, 141
SWOT (strengths, weaknesses, opportunities, threats) analysis, delivering workshops 180, **181**
Syska, A. 186

talks, informal professional development 184
tasks, Learning Developers (LDers) 19–20
teaching 24, 93
Teaching and Learning, inclusive practices 159–160
teaching and learning materials 124–125, 146–147; creating, for workshops and embedded teaching 128, **128**; creating a 'toolkit' of resources 142–146; creating digital 131–133; creating slides for online and in-person *129*, 129–131, **130**; critical thinking, reading and writing skills 143; digital literacy and information technology skills 145; dissertation and research project skills 145–146; essay and assignment writing skills 142–143; examples of 136–142; future 146; inclusivity of 135–136; language and grammar 144–145; libguides 126; personalized toolkit 142; reading and note-making skills 143; referencing, citing, and avoiding plagiarism 145; revising and taking exams 144; sources of 125–128; time management and organisation skills 144; using case studies and scenarios 140–142; using concept cartoons 139–140, *140*; using GenAI for creating 133–135; using images and visuals 136–139, *137*, *138*, *139*

Teaching Excellence Framework (TEF), Office for Students (OfS) 32–33
Teaching in Higher Ed podcast, Stachowiak 186
Teams: embedded sessions 116; slide presentation 131; tutorials 47; workshops 78, 79, 83, 90, 99
theory, word 4
third space: Learning Development (LD) as 15, 24; staff identifying as, practitioners 165–166
TikTok 186
time management 144
Times Higher Education (THE) 34
Times Higher Education Supplement (THES) 185
Tom Burns Memorial Award 193
toolkit of resources 142–146 (*see also*) resources
transformative 20, 68
Transforming Access and Student Outcomes in Higher Education (TASO) 40n6, 70n5
tutorials: challenges in 61–63; description of 44–46; evaluating impact of 68–69; flexibility 67; follow-up after the session 57–58; formulation model for structuring 58, **59–60**; Gibbs' reflective cycle *63*, 63–65, 70; how to end 57; how to start 55; ideal length of time for 48–49; locations for 47–48; log sheet **52**; online booking form 50; preparation for 51–52; preparing beforehand 53–55; pre-tutorial email 51; resources 65; resources and guidance 65; self-disclosure 66; showing your human side 65–66; structuring 53–58; students attending 49–51; term 49; thoughts on effective 52–53; tips for conducting 65–67; use of storytelling 66–67; what to do during 55–57

UDL (*see*) Universal Design for Learning (UDL)
United Kingdom (UK), degrees by level and powers to award them **30**
Universal Design for Learning (UDL) 97, 112; teaching and learning materials 135–136, 146, 147
universities: common leadership roles and function in **34**; definition

38; function of 29–30; Learning Development (LD) in 39; purpose of 38–39; regulation of 31; UK degrees by level and powers to award them **30**
Universities and Colleges Admissions Service (UCAS) 155
University of Bedfordshire, diary entry 209–210
University of Bristol, diary entry 210
University of Exeter 163
University of Kent, Assignment Survival Kit 144
University of North Carolina at Chapel Hill, Writing Center 126, 143
University of Portsmouth 20
University of the Arts London, diary entry 208–209
University of York 126; academic writing 142–143; critical writing online guide 143
University World News 34
Unsplash, images 136

values 2, 47, 106, 160–161; ALDinHE 7, 21, 22, 46, 70, 135, 151, 179, **181**, 188, 192, **201**; community 12, 20, 23, 24, 25, 39, 151, 197, 201; LD 12, 16, 20–23, 25, 58, 96, 169
video, use in workshops 94
virtual learning environment (VLE): embedded or integrated provision 105; referencing skills 109; tutorials 49–50; workshops 76–77
visuals, teaching and learning materials 136–139
vlogs, informal professional development 186–187

Wales: Higher Education Funding Council for Wales (HEFCW) 31; UK qualifications frameworks 30
walk in students' shoes 4
webinars, informal professional development 184
WhatsApp 186
whiteness, LD field 160
widening participation 24; agenda in higher education (HE) 17, 24

WonkHE 34, 185
'WonkHE Show, The' 186
workload allocation model, higher education institutions (HEIs) 107
workshops 73–74, 101–102; asking questions 92; assessing students' learning 89, *89*; beginning of 83–87; Bloom's taxonomy of learning 81, *82*; challenges with class management 98–100; clear objectives and outcomes 81–83, *84*; commonplace in Learning Development (LD) 75–76; creating materials for 128, **128**; creating slides for *129*, 129–131, **130**; description of 74–75; digital interactive tools 91–92; duration of 79–80; encouraging student engagement during 91–95; example of plan **211–216**; gauging students' stances *86*; how to design for diversity and inclusivity 96–97; how to end 96; incorporating group, pair and independent work 92–94; jigsaw approach to group work *93*; locations for 78–79; main part of 87–91; measuring and evaluating impact of 100–101; multimodal tasks in 87, *88*, 89; online teaching 90–91; promoting LD 76–77; responding to student questions 95; SMART goals 101; starter activity *85*; structure of 80–87, *84*; SWOT analysis in delivering 180, **181**; using images, video, and audio 94; using scenarios and case studies 94–95
Worth, T. 210
writing, academic, in professional development 190–191
writing blogs, informal professional development 186–187
Writing Center, University of North Carolina at Chapel Hill 126, 143

YouTube 133, 143, 145, 186

Zoom: embedded sessions 116; slide presentation 131; tutorials 47; workshops 78, 79, 83, 90, 99

For Product Safety Concerns and Information please contact our EU
representative GPSR@taylorandfrancis.com
Taylor & Francis Verlag GmbH, Kaufingerstraße 24, 80331 München, Germany

www.ingramcontent.com/pod-product-compliance
Lightning Source LLC
Chambersburg PA
CBHW071407300426
44114CB00016B/2215

9 781032 991726